THE BROAD FORK

RECIPES FOR THE WIDE WORLD
OF VEGETABLES AND FRUITS

o o o o o o o o o o o o o o o o o o o o o o o o o

HUGH ACHESON

PHOTOGRAPHS BY RINNE ALLEN

CLARKSON POTTER/PUBLISHERS
NEW YORK

Published in the United States by Clarkson Potter/
Publishers, an imprint of the Crown Publishing Group,
a division of Random House LLC, a Penguin Random House
Company, New York.
www.crownpublishing.com
www.clarksonpotter.com

CLARKSON POTTER is a trademark and POTTER with colophon is a
registered trademark of Random House, Inc.

Library of Congress Cataloging-in-Publication Data
Acheson, Hugh.
   Broadfork: recipes for the wide world of vegetables and
fruits / Hugh Acheson; photographs by Rinne
Allen.–First edition.
      pages   cm
   Includes index.
   1. Cooking, American–Southern style.   2. Seasonal
cooking.   3. Farm produce.   I. Title.
   TX715.2.S68A249   2015
   641.5975–dc23   2014023531

ISBN 978-0-385-34502-6
eBook ISBN 978-0-385-34503-3

Printed in China

Design by Rae Ann Spitzenberger
Cover photographs by Rinne Allen

10 9 8 7 6 5 4 3 2 1

First Edition

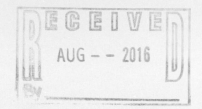

CONTENTS

INTRODUCTION

"WHAT THE HELL DO I DO WITH KOHLRABI?" MY NEIGHBOR ASKED ME.

I had some answers deep down in my culinary repertoire, but his forwardness came at me like a cannonball. The odd-looking vegetable had hit the height of its season, it was all over the farmers' markets and taking over our CSA boxes, and my fellow community-supporter-of-agriculture resorted to the last possible hope: ask that chef guy who lives down the street. I blurted out, "Slaw?"

But he wanted more from me. I mulled over this . . . maybe he was looking for something more highbrow. "Roasted kohlrabi with lobster, scallion, garlic, fennel, and curry butter?" He nodded. "A shaved kohlrabi salad with arugula, pecans, lime, paprika, and marjoram?" I was rolling now.

"Pickles?" he asked.

"Yes, pickles are great, too. Just make sure the pickling liquid isn't too acidic and shave them thin. Put it on a hot dog." (This is a great culinary response because darn near everything tastes good on a hot dog.) He went on his way, satisfied, surely to pickle up some kohlrabi and to find a lobster. I meandered home, thinking through my endless fascination with the links between food and community.

I am keen on becoming a better member of my food community. So I walk. My walk takes me out my front door, usually accompanied by my daughters, and we meander down the street. We turn left at the house owned by the dear old woman who always says hello, walk down the street with no sidewalk, two blocks to the end, and hobble up the dangerously steep stairs to our friend Alex's house. On the porch are about a hundred boxes of vegetables, arranged for

pickup by many of our neighbors. The boxes come from a farm, Woodland Gardens, five miles away, nestled behind the tiny airport in our town, Athens, Georgia. Woodland is an awe-inspiring organic farm that grows a beautiful array of vegetables for many of the high-end joints in the big city to the west, Atlanta. But to me, Woodland is about my friends Celia and John, farmers who work very hard to grow goodness every day. This realization—that someone took the time and effort to put a seed in the ground, toiled in the fields nurturing a young plant, harvested the offering, washed it tenderly, packed it into a simple box, and brought it to my neighborhood—is a moment everyone in our world needs to have. It's a connecting of the dots after many years of disconnection.

By cooking and enjoying as many vegetables as Celia and John and other farmers nearby grow, I'm taking a step in the direction of supporting people I admire, of eating more healthfully, and of eating deliciously. But, as my neighbor made me realize, many people might not know what to do with the bounty of produce as it comes into season. So this book is part of my small-steps plan to becoming a better food citizen.

The recipes here are all about vegetables— what to do with them, ideas to get you excited to cook and eat them. It's not a manual to a vegetarian lifestyle, but rather a compendium of seasonal recipes to help you bring vegetables to the center of your plate—from quick things you can do right away with what you just picked up to longer, more involved dinners.

I am not perfect. If you come into my kitchen you will find many things that you might not expect: Jif peanut butter, mass-production bread, sliced American cheese, pancake mix, forgotten cheap condiments, juice boxes, and store-bought mayo. My last name is definitely not Kingsolver. I can make an excuse for each one: The peanut butter is for the basic PB&J sandwiches that my kids love. The bread is part of that relationship. The American cheese is an abhorrence when eaten on its own, coaxed with difficulty from its plastic sheathing, but to us it is the only cheese for a true American cheeseburger. The pancake mix is all about the lazy Sunday, a sequence of hours when my family mimics the movements of slothlike creatures (this is often accompanied by Dunkin' Donuts). Juice boxes, the bane of landfills, provide a sadly quick and easy resource to make sure my kids don't become dehydrated scurvy sufferers, a worry that sometimes does keep me up at night. Store-bought mayo is the angel and devil on my shoulder: it reminds me of the self-sufficiency I had in sandwich-making as a child, and it pokes me in the eye with the reminder that we are way too busy in our lives to even make homemade mayo, something I am remarkably good at. Again, I am not perfect. But to me, it's all about taking small steps.

Mostly I shop at our local farmers' market. We eat a lot of vegetables. We're members of a CSA. Being a member of a CSA, or community supported agriculture, is like buying a subscription to vegetables, paying it forward for a bounty to come later from a local and sustainable farm, a farm where you know the names of the people who till and seed and harvest, a place that seeks to ensure that the land is in as good or better shape when they leave it as when they first dug in. It's a support system for those farms you respect and admire, a destination for their hard work and beautiful results. It is a way to eat with the seasons and a gateway to enjoying the bounty of your community.

In the CSA box we pick up on our walk are tender arugula, early lettuces still dewy from a morning picking, crisp tatsoi, baby ginger that Celia is experimenting with, a mix of late-season string beans, bunches of icicle radishes, tiny young mustard greens, perfectly round small turnips, and a lone butternut squash that signals the oncoming cold that our farmers will experience as winter swoops in. In my mind I am going through the dishes I will make. I will roast the turnips, sauté the greens, and pickle the stems. I will cook the tatsoi at high heat and finish it with some very finely chopped ginger and toss it with roasted chicken to be served over sushi rice. I will make a salad with finely cut beans to pair with a simple tuna sandwich. I will roast the butternut squash, scoop out the amazingly flavorful flesh, and

make tender little gnocchi to serve with crisp sage and brown butter. The radishes will be a snack and the arugula will garnish most meals in some way. It's a good plan.

We make a lot of plans at my house and we are pretty good at pushing through most of the agenda, but the juggling of school, work, afternoon activities, sports, dance, violin, more work, trips to the vet, taking the car in for a tune-up, or just falling prey to laziness makes cooking great food at home a struggle against time. We must make time. The most memorable markers in my life with my family have centered around food at home. I can still pinpoint the smell of homemade waffles wafting through our cottage when I was very young, the bubbling of strawberry jam as it gets to the perfect consistency on the stove in June, the pop of the pickle jar telling you that successful canning has occurred, the gentle clamor of a six-year-old Beatrice making scrambled eggs and toast to treat Mary and me to breakfast in bed. Instilled in my mind are food markers like making pepper jelly from habanero peppers with my grandmother Freda, of making cookies with my cousins, of roasting beef on Christmas Day in Toronto. Suffice it to say: you will never have beautiful family memories of heating a frozen entrée.

Feeding yourself and your family should not be as difficult as we are made to believe. Cooking has been made to seem like a sport of the Jedi, a pursuit that takes training and time and very specialized equipment. This is what the makers of ready-to-eat foods want you to believe, as they have an interest to protect. We have let large companies do our prep work, plan our meals, and map our life with food. I want to show you that it's easy to engage in your community of food, to make the relationships with what you eat and how it got to your plate. It's a beautiful experience that nurtures not only your belly, but also your larger community along the way.

Ease into the idea of good food. Stop by your weekend farmers' market and meet someone who farms for a living. Open an old cookbook that your grandmother used on a regular basis and reconnect with the cadence of the kitchen before Lean Cuisine

took over an aisle at the grocery store. Take care to make some things from scratch and you'll see that you fully understand the complexity of cooking. I have found that cooking food with my kids has made them better eaters, just by seeing food in its most basic and natural forms and then turned into meals. They grew up eating okra, turnips, and Brussels sprouts, and I don't think they'll ever turn back. I have a firm belief that if we can get all our kids to eat, and enjoy eating, their vegetables, then we'll have a better future for all.

So my suggestions are pretty basic: Get excited about food. Get excited about your community. Get excited by taking a slightly less convenient route to food on your plate. Sadly, in the last sixty years, good food has been harder and harder to come by. This only changes if you want it to. It is just silly that in October, my neighbors have a more difficult time getting apples from Northeast Georgia than ones from Chile. We have to change that.

I also feel that good-quality local foodstuffs should never be a privilege available only to those on the higher rungs of the economic ladder. If we are going to improve the whole nation, we all have to eat better and to support our local farmers, so that they in turn can produce more and sell more affordably. You eat better, then your kids eat better, then your neighbors eat better, then your schools eat better, and then pretty soon we have healthier towns, lower rates of diabetes and obesity, a direct nourishment of our economy through local spending on local products, better employment figures from farms expanding and employing more people, and a tighter-knit community. All this through understanding our most important common thread: that we all eat.

So it starts with you. Go and eat your vegetables.

THE SOUL OF MY SOUTHERN FOOD

Southern food champions its local larder. It always has. True Southern food is not an unhealthy lament; rather it is the hardwood of food histories in the United States.

Southern food didn't give us Type 2 diabetes and obesity rates like we've never seen before; the age of convenience did. The frozen entrées, the plethora of fast-food options, the instant grits and powdered mashed potatoes: those are the real causes of the American health ruin. A loss of culinary skills made food a commodity rather than an agrarian response to the seasons. Many think the perfect Southern meal is a bucket of fast-food fried chicken, but to me it is a spread of fried thighs with succotash, tomato salad, rice purloo, squash casserole, dressed dandelion greens, crisped okra, and baked grits. It is a vegetable-driven experience that we need to get back to.

I know what happened. The spiral-bound cookbooks of churches, community centers, and Junior Leagues went from being bastions of skills and smarts to time-saving tools. In the early 1950s, cream of mushroom soup and Jell-O began appearing on ingredients lists, and within forty years, we had pretty much skipped teaching a generation how to cook and started in on the convenience food that was designed to make us eat every day the stuff we used to eat in moderation—the barbecue, the fried chicken, the pies and cakes. (Of course, that wasn't just in the South; that was everywhere in North America.)

So Southern food, misinterpreted as the food that ails us, has become the fall guy of the American dietary malaise. The truth is just the opposite. I strive to preserve this true definition of Southern food, even as it shifts across time and place. It is a self-imposed duty, a duty based solely on where I live. If I lived in Oregon, I would be fully immersed in the food of that community, reacting to the farmers there and what the seasons would bring. But I am in the South, and this culinary richness is what I am happy to immerse myself in. Wherever I am, I aim to preserve the good intentions of the food community, because cooking from scratch, using the seasonal bounty and the historical foodways of a splendiferously abundant region, will always be my foundation.

HOW THIS BOOK WORKS

This is a vegetable-centric guide to seasonal offerings. Not all vegetables are touched on, but many are. Seasons vary for vegetables in North America, but I wrote it from Athens, Georgia, and focused on what's in season from that vantage point. So put on a B-52s album and get in the Athens mind-set—you won't regret it. Typically, four recipes—three quick or straightforward ones and one more in-depth—accompany each vegetable. It is a book that I hope will live in your kitchen rather than on your coffee table, because not one of us cooks at our coffee table. This book should encourage you to find great local foods, to feel confident that you'll know what to do with them, to discover and make new dishes, and to feed your family well.

FALL

THE HARVEST MOON FESTIVAL

Like every other chef in the world, I get asked to do fund-raisers and to donate gift certificates, signed books, cooking lessons, private dinners, and wine events for various causes. Restaurants, contrary to popular belief, are a very low margin business: My nest egg is a change jar in my bedroom, and I am quietly hoping my daughters get scholarships for college and elope for their marriages (definitely in that order). But we do try to help out often, and I like to make sure the impact is felt in my backyard.

There is a wonderful community organization in our town that I like a lot. The Athens Land Trust is dedicated to land preservation, improving urban neighborhoods, increasing energy efficiency in low-income housing, and expanding urban farming. Every year they hold a Harvest Moon Dinner to raise money for their initiatives, and it's something that I happily get behind. It's a hoot of a time, showcasing what's special about fall in Georgia. It's about squashes and apples, mushrooms and figs, persimmons and sunchokes, lettuces and pecans. We highlight these things in their full glory to remind people that there is a season for such things, that they are cyclical and do not have the drab constancy that supermarkets often make them out to have. The Land Trust dinner is a wonderful spread of tables outdoors and about 120 diners, most all of them friends and neighbors. Oh, and sometimes there's kohlrabi.

APPLES

There is no greater letdown in food than biting into a mushy, cold-stored, months-old apple, and the way we counter this is to find out when our local apple season is and relish that abundance. During the season we use apples in so many ways: to add crunch to salads, baked to sweetness in pies, slowly cooked into butters and jams, or as a match with pork or duck.

APPLE OF MY EYE

Apples are a touchstone, a harbinger, a symbol of something better. Or they are the canary in the coal mine, the epitome of an overlooked local crop.

"The apple of my eye" means something that you are enamored with and in awe of, something worthy of your love. And indeed, for me, apples from Northeast Georgia fit that bill. My heart is aflutter for the apples whose names have not been copyrighted. Arkansas Black, Winesap, Rome Beauty, Roxbury Russet, and Esopus Spitzenburg are all illustrious varietals that will join the long roster of extinct Southern apples unless we do one simple thing: buy them. Sadly, we have convinced a generation that love is cheap and always available on the supermarket shelf, with its little affixed stickers and small-print labels that whisper of faraway origins. These are commodities that have slowly pushed the local harvest to obscurity. I want to rekindle a romance.

SLOW COOKER APPLE BUTTER

This apple butter is a solid start to breakfast, or a versatile condiment at dinner, or a great component in an apple pie. It is a slow-cooked smooth, spice-laden treat and a great answer to the conundrum of what to do when faced with a bushel of apples. Get some beautiful bread, toast it deeply, spread some really good butter on it, and then add a big slather of this apple butter.

Find a farm stand that sells local apples and buy a bushel. I love Arkansas Blacks, but you can use any good firm apple that you find. Our family makes this every year to give to our kids' teachers. It's always a hit. *Makes 9 pints*

1 teaspoon ascorbic or citric acid powder, or 2 teaspoons freshly squeezed lemon juice

9 pounds local apples

2½ cups sugar

¼ teaspoon ground cloves

½ teaspoon ground nutmeg

½ tablespoon ground cinnamon

½ teaspoon ground allspice

½ teaspoon kosher salt

1 teaspoon pure vanilla extract

1 cup nonalcoholic apple cider

1 Fill a large bowl with cold water, and stir in the ascorbic acid powder. Peel and core the apples and cut them into eighths. As you work, drop the apple pieces into the acidulated water. When all the apples are peeled and cut, drain them and discard the water.

2 Place the apples in a slow cooker (a.k.a. Crock-Pot). Add the sugar, cloves, nutmeg, cinnamon, allspice, salt, vanilla, and cider and toss well. Turn your slow cooker to high and cook for 1 hour. Then turn it down to low and cook for about 8 hours, or until the apple butter is "jammy" in consistency. Stir regularly throughout the cooking process but be careful of splatters, as nothing smarts quite like a hot jam.

3 Transfer the apple butter to clean canning jars of your choice—just make sure they are not chipped or cracked. Fill the jars to 1 inch from the top and seal with the lids and bands. Let cool for 2 hours. Hot-process according to the jar manufacturer's directions to keep on the shelf for up to 10 months, or store in the refrigerator for up to 3 weeks. This is one of those jars that love to be given away as a host gift to a neighbor.

APPLE-CABBAGE SLAW

Quick, classic, crunchy, and good for you. The yogurt takes the place of more than half of the usual mayonnaise, and the mint, parsley, and spices add nuance not normally seen in a simple slaw.
Makes 1½ quarts, about 6 servings as a side

2 cups lightly packed sliced cabbage

Kosher salt

½ cup low-fat plain yogurt

¼ cup mayonnaise

3 tablespoons cider vinegar

1 teaspoon freshly ground cumin seeds

¼ teaspoon freshly ground black pepper

2 large apples (Arkansas Blacks or any firm apple)

1 tablespoon freshly squeezed lime juice

½ cup finely sliced scallions

½ cup peeled and minced celery

¼ cup chopped fresh flat-leaf parsley leaves

¼ cup chopped fresh mint leaves

1 Place the cabbage in a large bowl and toss with ½ teaspoon salt. Set aside.

2 Make the dressing by combining the yogurt, mayonnaise, vinegar, cumin, and pepper in a small bowl. Season the dressing with salt to taste. Mix well and set aside.

3 Core and julienne the apples. Add them to the cabbage, sprinkle with the lime juice, and toss well. Then add the scallions, celery, parsley, and mint. Add the dressing, toss to coat, adjust the seasoning with more salt, if desired, and put it on the table.

PAN-ROASTED PORK TENDERLOIN WITH SORGHUM AND ROASTED APPLES

SNAPPER CEVICHE WITH APPLE AND LIME

ROASTED APPLES

PAN-ROASTED PORK TENDERLOIN WITH SORGHUM AND ROASTED APPLES

This is a straightforward dinner that I would pair with some braised cabbage—though it's a pretty basic idea, it's a stunning ode to late fall. The sauce is based on a *gastrique*, a sweetened reduction of vinegar, a classic way of balancing sweet and sour in a dish. Making a gastrique for the first time will open up a lot of ideas for you in cooking, so think of other ways of using acid and sweetness to anchor a dish.

Serves 4

1 pound trimmed pork tenderloin (such as Berkshire or another heritage breed)

Kosher salt

½ teaspoon extra-virgin olive oil

1 shallot, minced

¼ cup minced celery

1 small carrot, minced

1 sprig fresh thyme

1 bay leaf

2 tablespoons cider vinegar

1½ tablespoons sorghum molasses

1½ cups chicken stock (see page 22)

1 tablespoon canola oil

2 apples, cored and cut into ½-inch-thick rings

1 tablespoon sugar

2 tablespoons unsalted butter

Raisins (optional)

1 Preheat the oven to 400°F.

2 Cut the pork into 2 to 3 pieces, each about 5 inches long. (Tenderloins vary in size, especially in heritage breeds, because, well, pigs are not all the same size.) Season the pork evenly with salt and set it aside while you prepare everything else.

3 Prepare the sauce: Warm a small saucepan over medium heat and add the olive oil, shallot, celery, and carrot. Sauté for 2 minutes. Then add the thyme sprig, bay leaf, vinegar, and sorghum. Cook until reduced by half, about 3 minutes; then add the chicken stock and reduce by half again, about 9 minutes. Season with salt to taste. You will have just about 1 cup of sauce. Remove the thyme sprig and bay leaf and put the sauce aside in a warm spot.

4 Place a large cast-iron skillet over medium-high heat and add the canola oil. Pat the pork dry with paper towels. When the oil is just about smoking, add the pork and sear it off for about 1 minute on the first side (yes, I know that a cylinder doesn't have sides). Then roll the pork and sear off another "side." Continue doing this until the meat is evenly seared and you have cooked it for about 4 minutes on top of the stove.

5 Place the skillet in the oven and roast the pork for about 5 minutes, or until the interior of the pork reads 130° to 135°F on an instant-read thermometer. Remove the skillet from the oven, and transfer the pork to a cooling rack. The pork will rise in temperature to 135° to 140°F outside the oven, for medium. Just let it mellow and rest while you cook the apples. Leave the oven on.

6 Take the skillet you just used, lightly wipe it out with a paper towel, and place it over medium heat on the stovetop. Spread the apples on a cutting board and sprinkle with the sugar. Melt the butter in the skillet, add the apple slices, and cook for 2 minutes on each side. Then finish them in the oven for 5 minutes until well roasted.

7 Slice the pork, arrange it on a platter, and pour the sauce around and on top. Garnish with the apples and raisins, if using.

SNAPPER CEVICHE WITH APPLE AND LIME

Crisp apple and tender ceviche: contrasting textures can really mean a lot on the plate. Ceviche is one of those things that is exponentially better when you find great fish and when you feel confident in your knife skills. Take time to make the cuts pretty in all of your prep—it will pay off in the beauty of the finished dish. Serve this with crisp tortillas, and if you fry them yourself, they'll taste all the better.

Serves 2 to 4 as a light appetizer

½ pound red snapper fillet, skin off

Fine sea salt, to taste

⅓ cup freshly squeezed lime juice

¼ Granny Smith or Northern Spy apple

½ Fresno chile, seeded and thinly sliced

1 tablespoon finely chopped scallions

1 tablespoon chopped fresh cilantro leaves

1 tablespoon finely chopped fresh parsley stems

1 tablespoon extra-virgin olive oil

2 tablespoons roasted, unsalted almonds, chopped

1 Cut the snapper into ¼-inch dice and toss it with fine sea salt and lime juice in a medium bowl. Set in the fridge to chill for 10 minutes.

2 Thinly slice or dice the apple. Remove the snapper from the fridge and add the apple, chile, scallions, cilantro, parsley stems, olive oil, and almonds. Toss well to mix, and serve immediately.

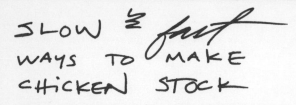

SLOW & fast WAYS TO MAKE CHICKEN STOCK

You know homemade chicken stock is liquid gold, so you plan to make some and freeze it or use it for supper the next day. Hopefully you have a slow cooker.

But sometimes you need chicken stock "on the fly" as we cheffy-types say, and you would love for it still to be of liquid gold quality. In that case, hopefully you have a pressure cooker.

The following two recipes are for chicken stock for either scenario, and I hope you'll be able to make use of them as they fit into the pace of your life. (And I'll still be okay if, in a pinch, you use the boxed stuff.)

PRESSURE COOKER CHICKEN STOCK

You know that pressure cooker you bought but never really used? Pull it out, wash it off, check the seal, and let's make great chicken stock in under an hour. I love the slow-cooker method, but this is wonderful in a time pinch—it's ready in about an hour from start to finish. The vegetables in this stock are cut bigger so the stock does not taste like overcooked carrots.

Makes 3 quarts

1 chicken, head gone but feet are good if still intact	**2 celery stalks, cut into 2-inch lengths**
2 garlic cloves, peeled	**2 bay leaves**
1 sprig fresh oregano	**1 teaspoon coriander seeds**
2 sprigs fresh thyme	**6 black peppercorns**
1 yellow onion, quartered	**1 teaspoon kosher salt**
1 large carrot, scrubbed and cut into 2-inch lengths	

1 Take the chicken and place it on a clean cutting board. Have a clean, damp towel nearby for poultry runoff. If you have the innards, keep the gizzards, heart, and neck for the stock, but set the liver aside for another day. Livers are great to accumulate in the freezer for a pâté or to finish sauces.

2 Cut up the chicken: Remove the wings and set aside. Remove the legs, separating the thighs and the drumsticks. Remove the breasts to make boneless breasts, the meat America was built on. Cut the breastbone away from the backbone and then chop those into 2 pieces each. Save the thighs and breasts

for other uses. Put the wings, drumsticks, backbone, breastbone, gizzards, heart, and neck into a clean pressure-cooker pot.

3 Fill the pot with water to reach 4 inches above the chicken pieces. Add the garlic, oregano sprig, thyme sprigs, onion, carrot, celery, bay leaves, coriander seeds, peppercorns, and salt. Cover and seal the pot, and bring it to pressure over high heat. When the pot is pressurized, reduce the heat to low and cook for 45 minutes.

4 Carefully run the pot under cold water to reduce the heat and the pressure. When the indicator shows no pressure, open the pot and strain the stock, discarding the solids.

5 Cool the stock to room temperature, and then divide it among clean pint or quart containers. Freeze some and put the rest in the fridge for use within 5 days. Before use, skim the fat from the surface and discard.

SLOW COOKER CHICKEN STOCK

Same adage as for the pressure cooker chicken stock: You have a device you never use, let's use it! Do the math: four quarts of chicken stock at the store will cost you about $14. This way, you take a $10 chicken, get all that stock, and use the breasts for another whole meal. And it's homemade chicken stock, which is better than anything in a box from the superdupermarket.

Makes about 4 quarts

1 chicken, head gone but feet are good if still intact

1 teaspoon olive oil

½ teaspoon kosher salt

2 garlic cloves, peeled

1 sprig fresh thyme

2 sprigs fresh parsley

2 bay leaves

2 medium white onions, peeled and quartered

3 large carrots, scrubbed and cut into 2-inch lengths

3 celery stalks with leaves, cut into 2-inch lengths

1 teaspoon coriander seeds

6 black peppercorns

1 Clean and cut up the chicken as on page 22. Save the breasts for another use, but reserve the thighs, wings, drumsticks, backbone, breastbone, gizzards, heart, and neck for the stock.

2 Place the largest frying pan you have on medium heat and add the olive oil to the pan. Season the chicken pieces with the salt and then place them skin side down in the pan and slowly crisp them up for 15 minutes, then turn them and cook them for 10 minutes more. Remove the chicken pieces from the pot and place in the slow cooker's porcelain pot. Discard the rendered fat from the pan, then add a cup of water and place it back over medium heat, scraping up the goodness that is stuck to the bottom of the pan. Pour the water with the pan drippings into the slow cooker pot. Add the garlic, thyme, parsley, bay leaves, onions, carrots, celery, coriander seeds, and peppercorns to the slow cooker and add enough cold water to cover by 2 inches. Turn the cooker on low and walk away for 8 hours—some people call that going to work. After 8 hours strain the stock and you'll have about 4 quarts of stock. Let it cool to room temperature in plastic pint or quart containers. Freeze what you don't think you will use within 5 days.

CELERY & CELERY ROOT

The celery we get in our CSA box is not like the celery you get in the supermarket. It is like celery on flavor steroids. Its leaves are pungent, the stalks thinner and a far cry from the watery limbs of basic celery. The variety is called Tango. It is a treat to eat. Now, the regular celery in the supermarket is no lost cause; it's just more, well, ordinary. Its leaves are aromatic and herbal, its stalk is crisp and savory, and when fully cooked, it softens to a comforting tenderness.

Its sibling celery root, or celeriac, is raised for the beautiful root bulb. Okay, so beauty is in the eye of the beholder, because the hairy bulb looks a little alien to us humans. But celery root's beauty is on the inside. Pare away and you'll find it.

CELERY ROOT PUREE

Celery root, or celeriac, is that gnarly bulb of goodness that we often overlook at the grocer or in our CSA box when it arrives in late fall. A relative of regular celery, it's the keeper of flavor for the family. Buy some and get into the bulb. *Be* the bulb. Making great creamy vegetable purees is a skill that all the cool kids are using. To me it's kind of like going full circle from baby food, but in a good way. And celery root is perfect for pureeing; it's a little like a sweet, slightly herbal mashed potato. ***Serves 4 to 6 as a side***

1 pound celery root, peeled and cut into 1-inch dice

1 cup heavy cream

2 cups chicken stock (see page 22) or water

1 bay leaf

1 sprig fresh thyme

Kosher salt

3 tablespoons cold unsalted butter, cubed

Freshly ground black pepper

1 Combine the celery root, cream, chicken stock, bay leaf, thyme sprig, and a few pinches of salt in a large saucepan. If you have it, cut a circle of parchment paper about the size of your pot to set on the liquid, kind of an inner lid. Bring to a boil over medium-high heat; then lower the heat and simmer until the celery root is tender, 15 to 20 minutes. Strain the celery root, reserving the cooking liquid. Discard the thyme sprig and the bay leaf. Work quickly because you want to blend the celery root and cooking liquid while it's warm.

2 Put the celery root in a blender and add about half the liquid. Puree on high speed, slowly adding the cold butter bit by bit until it's all incorporated. Add salt to taste, and adjust the texture with more cooking liquid if you want. I like it to have a thicker texture than a pureed soup but thinner than, say, a hummus. Finish with ground black pepper to taste, and serve warm.

3 You can make this a day before if you want and reheat it with a touch more of the cooking liquid in a small pot over gentle heat.

BRAISED CELERY HEARTS WITH GRATED EGG AND SIMPLE VINAIGRETTE

This recipe screams "thrifty Paris," even if those two words are rarely strung together. To me it exemplifies bistro simplicity. Celery hearts, literally the center of the inexpensive and unheralded bunch, have the flavor of pure celery that we search for.

So go ahead, pour a glass of Chablis and put on a beret (if you must). You'll be speaking French in no time: *céleri*. ***Serves 4 as a side or an appetizer***

1 large bunch celery

¼ cup extra-virgin olive oil

1 tablespoon red wine vinegar

1 teaspoon Dijon mustard

1 tablespoon chopped fresh flat-leaf parsley leaves

Kosher salt

1 tablespoon unsalted butter

½ cup chicken stock (see page 22)

1 hard-boiled egg, peeled and finely grated

1 Remove the first layer of celery stalks from around the bunch, leaving the heart and root intact. Quarter the heart lengthwise and set the pieces aside.

2 Make the vinaigrette by combining the olive oil, vinegar, mustard, parsley, and ¼ teaspoon salt in a mason jar. Cap the jar securely and shake vigorously. Set it aside.

3 Heat a large pan with a tight-fitting lid over medium-high heat. Add the butter. When it has melted, add the celery and cook for 3 minutes on the flat side and then 3 more minutes on the other side, developing a nice golden hue on the pale green of the celery. Season with salt to taste and add the stock. When the stock boils, cover the pan, reduce the heat to medium-low, and simmer for 10 minutes.

4 Remove the pan from the heat and add the vinaigrette, dousing the celery with it liberally. Transfer the celery hearts and the liquids to a platter, and scatter the grated egg over the hearts.

CELERY ROOT SALAD WITH BUTTERMILK DRESSING

Simple salads. That's the secret to a long life and a happy existence.

P.S. You can use the buttermilk dressing in a hundred ways, so make some extra. *Serves 4 as a side*

1 celery root (about ¾ pound)

¾ cup Buttermilk Dressing (recipe follows)

1 cup pomegranate seeds

1 cup fresh flat-leaf parsley leaves

1 cup peeled and shaved celery

1 tablespoon extra-virgin olive oil

1 teaspoon freshly squeezed lemon juice

Kosher salt

1 Use a vegetable peeler to peel the celery root, and then finely julienne it. In a bowl, dress the celery root with ½ cup of the buttermilk dressing.

2 In a small bowl, combine the pomegranate seeds, parsley, celery, olive oil, and lemon juice. Season to taste with salt, and toss well.

3 Spoon 1 tablespoon of the remaining buttermilk dressing on each plate, and spread it out with the back of your spoon. Divide the dressed celery root among the plates, and then spoon the pomegranate, parsley, and celery salad evenly over the top.

BUTTERMILK DRESSING

Makes 1 cup

½ cup buttermilk

1 tablespoon Dijon mustard

1 tablespoon freshly squeezed lemon juice

¼ cup mayonnaise

2 tablespoons crème fraîche

½ teaspoon kosher salt

Freshly ground black pepper, to taste

Combine the buttermilk, mustard, lemon juice, mayonnaise, crème fraîche, salt, and pepper in a small bowl. Whisk to combine, and serve. The dressing will keep in the refrigerator for 5 days.

REAL BUTTERMILK

When we look at artisan products popping up in the market, to me none is more important than simple buttermilk. The insipid ultraprocessed stuff that had become our only choice now has some competition.

This new stuff is cut from the oldest fabric of Southern staples: real buttermilk from real cows. Buttermilk from Cruze Farm, near Knoxville, Tennessee, is the one we often use at our restaurants and it's a far cry from that weird gummy stuff the big companies call buttermilk. Cruze's buttermilk is alive with lactobacilli, giving it that sour tang only real buttermilk has. It just tastes vivid and luscious.

So what do we do with it, you ask? We can use it in the way that the centuries have taught us, from cornbread to salad dressings to custard pies. Or we can venture off into new spheres and pay homage to other cultures with pork braised in buttermilk, a currant-buttermilk panna cotta, a corn-and-buttermilk popover. Really it just gives you a resource of endless possibilities. I so love it when we begin to reclaim goodness again.

ROASTED LAMB LOIN WITH CELERY ROOT PUREE, POMEGRANATE, AND CELERY VINAIGRETTE

If I were single and running a personal ad, it would read: "Likes quiet walks on the beach, drinking hot coffee on Sunday morning, eating lamb loin with celery root puree." This is a great dish to serve on a cold evening. Lamb loin is lauded in my house, but if you want to pair this up with some veal strip loin or pork, go right ahead—but I do think that lamb needs to be popularized in American home kitchens to keep the amazing shepherds we have here in business; it's delicious, has character, and is way too good to be eaten just as a special occasion thing. *Serves 4*

1 pound boneless American lamb loin, silver skin removed

Kosher salt

Freshly ground black pepper

2 tablespoons extra-virgin olive oil

Celery Root Puree (page 25)

¼ cup pomegranate seeds

½ cup fresh pea shoots or frisée

½ cup peeled and shaved celery

About ½ cup Celery Vinaigrette (recipe follows)

1 Preheat a large cast-iron sauté pan over medium-high heat. Dab the lamb well with paper towels to dry it, and season it with salt and pepper to taste. Add the olive oil to the pan, and when it shimmers—just beginning to get really hot but before it actually smokes—add the lamb. For rare, cook for 3 minutes on each side, and baste it with the oil for a minute at the end; if you like your meat more cooked, increase the time, using a thermometer in the center of the loin to guide you, but I don't recommend cooking it past medium rare (130°F). Remove the lamb from the pan and let it rest for 10 minutes on a cooling rack.

2 Heat the celery root puree in a small saucepan over medium heat, stirring often, for about 5 minutes or until hot. Set it aside.

3 Combine the pomegranate seeds, pea shoots, and shaved celery in a small bowl, and after shaking the jar of vinaigrette vigorously, dress the salad with 1 tablespoon of the vinaigrette.

4 Slice the lamb loin very thinly against the grain. To plate, dollop a spoonful of celery root puree on each plate. Next to that, arrange the sliced lamb and some of the salad. Spoon some more of the celery vinaigrette around each plate to finish.

CELERY VINAIGRETTE
Makes 1 cup

2 celery stalks, peeled and diced

1 teaspoon Dijon mustard

¼ teaspoon celery seeds

1 tablespoon chopped fresh flat-leaf parsley leaves

¼ teaspoon kosher salt

2 tablespoons cider vinegar

1 tablespoon freshly squeezed lemon juice

½ cup extra-virgin olive oil

Combine the diced celery, mustard, celery seeds, parsley, salt, vinegar, and lemon juice in a blender and puree until smooth. With the blender running, slowly pour in the olive oil to emulsify. Place in a jar and seal tightly. The dressing will keep for 1 week in the fridge.

CHANTERELLES & FALL MUSHROOMS

I love chanterelles. They are my favorite, like, favorite of everything. Luckily we have many avid foragers on staff and some wonderfully wayward hippies in the community who like searching through dense woods for the little golden bugles. Store them with a damp paper towel in a resealable plastic bag in the fridge; this gives you a good three to four days of freshness. When you clean them, use a dry brush or a clean toothbrush rather than water, because like most mushrooms, they just soak up the water like a sponge.

YELLOWFOOT CHANTERELLE AND GOAT CHEESE TARTS

There once was a grumpy but immensely talented chef who taught me a lot about cooking and living—mostly how to be his polar opposite if I wanted to enjoy life. But a tiny mushroom canapé was one little morsel he made so darned well, and that's what this tart is based on. I add pine nuts and fresh thyme, which make a pretty wonderful quartet when they play with goat cheese and chanterelles. You can serve these warm or at room temperature for a nice fall lunch, with a simple salad and some crisp pear. You can most certainly use any great mushroom you find at the market if chanterelles are hard to come by. *Makes four 4-inch tarts*

Savory Tart Dough (recipe follows)

All-purpose flour, for dusting

2 tablespoons unsalted butter

1 shallot, minced

2 cups brushed clean, trimmed, and quartered yellowfoot chanterelles

1 sprig fresh thyme

Kosher salt

¼ pound fresh goat cheese

2 large eggs

¼ cup heavy cream

⅛ teaspoon freshly grated nutmeg

1 tablespoon chopped fresh flat-leaf parsley leaves

1 tablespoon pine nuts, toasted and finely chopped

1 Preheat the oven to 400°F.

2 Remove the dough from the fridge and place it on a smooth floured surface. Roll it out with a rolling pin, pressing firmly in the center and rolling outwards, going from the middle of a clock to 12, middle to 3, middle to 6, and so on. The end result should be a ⅛- to ¼-inch-thick round about 13 inches in diameter. Cut four 5-inch-diameter rounds out of the dough with a circle cutter, and poke each one in a number of places with a fork to create tiny holes so it won't puff up too much during baking. Place the dough in four 4-inch tart pans, pressing it against the bottom and sides. Fill each tart with dried beans to weigh down the dough, place them all on one baking sheet, and bake for 15 minutes. Remove from the oven, let cool, and discard the beans.

3 Melt the butter in a large sauté pan over medium-high heat. When the butter bubbles and froths, add the shallot and cook for 2 minutes. Reduce the heat to medium, add the chanterelles and thyme sprig, and cook for 10 minutes, until the mushrooms are golden brown, glistening from the butter, and wilting a bit. Season the mushrooms with salt to taste. Pour the mushrooms onto a plate and let them cool while you build your tarts.

4 Crumble the goat cheese evenly into the cooled tart shells. Evenly disperse the mushrooms on top, discarding the thyme sprig. In a small bowl, combine the eggs, cream, nutmeg, ¼ teaspoon salt, the parsley, and the pine nuts. Whisk well to combine. Pour the egg mixture evenly over the mushrooms.

5 Place the tart pans back on the baking sheet and bake them for 15 to 20 minutes, or until the egg has set and the crust is cooked through. Let cool for a couple of minutes before removing from the tart pans. Serve warm or at room temperature.

SAVORY TART DOUGH
Makes dough for one 9-inch tart or four 4-inch tartlets

1 cup plus 2 tablespoons all-purpose flour

¼ teaspoon kosher salt

¼ pound (1 stick) cold unsalted butter, cut into ¼-inch cubes

3 tablespoons ice water

1 Combine the flour and salt in a food processor. Pulse a couple of times to blend. Add the butter and ice water, and blend for 10 to 12 seconds. The result should look like clumpy sand.

2 Pour the contents of the food processor into a medium mixing bowl and form it into a ball. Add a little water if you need to, but it should feel just moist enough to hold the ball shape. Wrap your dough ball tightly in plastic wrap and let it rest in the fridge for 2 hours.

ROASTED CHANTERELLE BUNDLES WITH SHALLOT, THYME, AND SHERRY BUTTER

This is a quick and easy way to prepare a mushroom side dish. If you feel like camping in style, these little packs can be thrown right into a campfire to cook. Not your average camping meal! This recipe calls for fino sherry, a very dry but assertive sherry. Do not use that cream sherry that Granny left in the cupboard. If you can't find a good fino, then go for a good dry white vermouth. *Serves 4 as a side*

¼ pound (1 stick) unsalted butter, at room temperature

½ teaspoon kosher salt, or to taste

2 tablespoons fino sherry

1 pound chanterelles, brushed or rubbed clean

1 large shallot, minced

1 sprig fresh thyme

1 Preheat the oven to 400°F.

2 In a food processor, combine the butter, salt, and sherry. Blend until smooth.

3 Take a 2-foot-long piece of foil and lay it flat on the counter. Smear half the sherry butter on the foil, leaving an unsmeared 2-inch border all around. Pile up the chanterelles on the left side of the foil, on the buttered part, and then top with the remaining sherry butter and the minced shallot. Place the thyme sprig on the mushrooms, and then fold the right side of the foil over the top, crimping the edges all the way around to seal them.

4 Place the foil pack on a baking sheet and roast in the preheated oven for 30 minutes. Remove from the oven, open the foil carefully, and serve.

ENOKI CUSTARD

Chawanmushi is a delicate Japanese custard. It's a great way to show off the beauty of local farm eggs and mushrooms—in this case the Japanese enoki, a mushroom that just loves being in custards and soups. Enoki are very thin, long-stalked mushrooms with tiny white or brown caps. If you have trouble finding them, you could use oyster mushrooms, thinly sliced. *Serves 4 as an appetizer*

3 ounces enoki (usually sold in packages that size)

1 tablespoon unsalted butter

Kosher salt

2 cups dashi (recipe follows) or chicken stock (see page 22)

2 large eggs (fresh farm eggs are preferable)

½ tablespoon maple syrup

½ tablespoon light soy sauce

2 tablespoons finely minced scallions

1 teaspoon seasoned rice vinegar

½ tablespoon olive oil

1 Preheat the oven to 300°F.

2 Remove and discard the root ends of the mushrooms and finely chop the lower 2 inches, leaving the top 2 inches in uncut lengths. Warm a small saucepan over medium heat, and add the finely chopped enoki and the butter. Cook for 4 minutes, or until the mushrooms are wilted down, and then season with a pinch of salt.

3 Add ¾ cup of the dashi and cook down until it has almost completely evaporated, about 15 minutes. Remove from the heat and spoon the cooked mushrooms evenly over the bottoms of four 6-ounce ramekins or custard cups.

4 Prepare the custard by beating the eggs in a small bowl until smooth. In a separate bowl, whisk together ¼ teaspoon salt, the remaining 1¼ cups dashi, the maple syrup, and the soy sauce. Mix the eggs with the maple/soy base, but don't whisk so much as to create bubbles. Strain the mixture through a fine-mesh sieve into another bowl to remove any remaining bubbles, and let it sit for a moment to relax.

5 Pour the custard base evenly over the cooked mushrooms in the ramekins. Cover each ramekin tightly with plastic wrap and place them in a baking dish. Add warm water to reach halfway to two-thirds of the way up the sides of the ramekins, to insulate them from direct heat during cooking. Bake in the oven for 20 to 25 minutes, or until a toothpick or cake tester comes out clean when you poke the custard. It should still be slightly

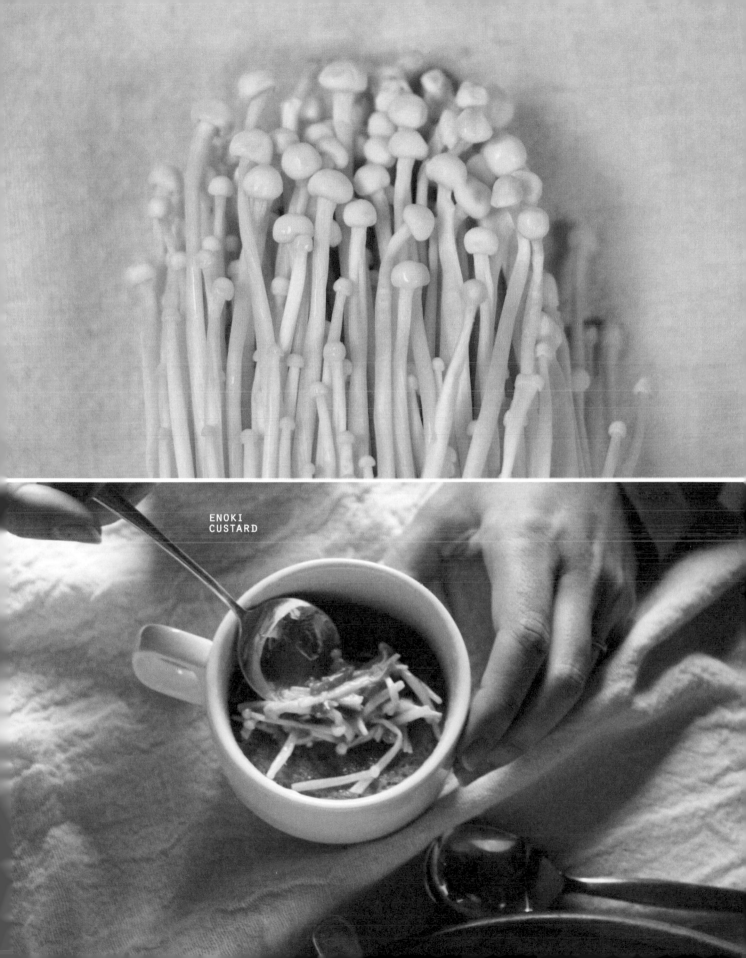

ENOKI
CUSTARD

jiggly. Remove the ramekins from the oven and cool in the fridge until ready to serve.

6 To serve, place the reserved enoki tops in a small bowl and add a pinch of salt, the scallions, rice vinegar, and olive oil. Toss to dress, and perch the raw enoki on top of each custard. Serve.

DASHI

Dashi is the mother stock of Japanese cuisine and is worth getting schooled in. It provides an inexpensive and very flavorful base for soups, stews, vegetables, and simple sauces. Instead of water you could make a more pronounced dashi with chicken stock (see page 22). *Makes 1 quart*

4 cups cold water
1 ounce kombu

1 ounce bonito flakes

Place the water and kombu in a pot and bring to just below the boiling point. Simmer for about 10 minutes, until the seaweed is soft; then remove the kombu. Bring the stock to a full boil. Lower the heat to a simmer again and add the bonito flakes. Bring that to a boil and remove from the heat. Let the dashi cool for 10 minutes. Skim off any foam that has risen to the top of the stock, and then strain, discarding the bonito and reserving the dashi. It will keep for 1 week in the fridge.

MUSSELS WITH PORCINI, MUSTARD, AND CREAM

Prince Edward Island is the smallest province in Canada. I have been there once. I remember a three-legged cat at the Anne of Green Gables house. I was six years old. Thus I am an expert on all things related to PEI. Oh, and their mussels are awesome. Porcini and other boletus varieties will run you a third mortgage, but a life in good food is worth every penny. (Though they are not as special as porcini, you could substitute shiitakes here.) This is best served with toasted bread, the lifelong partner of all steamed mussel dishes. *Serves 4*

2 pounds mussels (from Prince Edward Island if possible!)
1 tablespoon unsalted butter
1 shallot, minced
1 tablespoon extra-virgin olive oil
½ pound fresh porcini or shiitake mushrooms, brushed clean
Fine sea salt

½ cup dry vermouth
½ cup chicken stock (see page 22)
1 tablespoon whole-grain mustard
¼ cup heavy cream
¼ cup chopped fresh flat-leaf parsley leaves
Half a baguette or crusty bread loaf, sliced into large pieces and toasted

1 Immerse the mussels in a pot of very cold water and discard any that are broken or are visibly open and do not close when prodded. With your fingers, pinch any "beards" that extend from the mussel shells and pull them off. Remove the mussels from the water and set aside.

2 Place a very large skillet (one with a lid) over medium-high heat and add the butter. When the butter bubbles and froths, add the shallot and cook for 2 minutes. Then add the olive oil and the mushrooms and cook, stirring occasionally, for 5 minutes; season with sea salt to taste. Add the mussels. Pour the vermouth over the mussels and add the chicken stock, mustard, and cream. Cover and steam for 5 minutes, or until the mussels are open and just cooked. Finish with the parsley, and serve immediately with the bread.

CHICKEN OF THE WOODS MEETS CHICKEN OF THE SEA: TUNA AND MUSHROOMS

"Chicken of the woods" is another name for the sulfur shelf mushroom. It is an odd-looking beast but is meaty and beautiful when cooked correctly. You could use whole shiitakes, chanterelles, or even portabellos in this recipe and still have a winner. A "two-pan pickup" is kitchen talk for a dish where all the elements are cooked in just two pans. This is one of those. Just trying to keep you up to speed with the lingo. *Serves 4*

¾ pound sushi-grade tuna

Kosher salt

2 teaspoons unsalted butter

1 tablespoon plus 1 teaspoon peanut oil

½ pound chicken of the woods or other mushrooms, brushed clean and sliced into thin strips

1 tablespoon cider vinegar

½ cup chicken stock (see page 22)

¼ cup whole fresh flat-leaf parsley leaves

1 tablespoon toasted sesame seeds

2 sheets toasted nori, torn into small pieces

1 Season the tuna on both sides with kosher salt and set it aside.

2 Place a large sauté pan over medium-high heat and melt 1 teaspoon of the butter in it. Add the 1 teaspoon peanut oil and the mushrooms. Cook for 10 minutes, stirring frequently, until the mushrooms are lightly browned and softened. Deglaze the pan with the vinegar, scraping at the bottom of the pan with a wooden spoon to release all of the tasty bits. Add the chicken stock and cook the stock down by half, about 3 minutes. Season to taste with salt. Finish by stirring in the remaining 1 teaspoon butter, just until it forms a glaze. Take the mushrooms off the heat and let them rest while you cook the tuna.

3 Heat another heavy sauté pan over high heat and add the remaining 1 tablespoon peanut oil. Pat the tuna very dry with paper towels. When the oil is smoking hot, sear the tuna for about 1 minute per side, just enough to brown the outside. I suggest a very rare tuna. That's why you bought really good stuff, right? Remove the tuna from the heat and slice it very thin with a sharp knife. Arrange the slices on a platter and top with the warm mushrooms. Garnish with the parsley leaves, sesame seeds, and nori.

Tuna is a contentious topic these days, but there are still some species that are sustainable to eat. Eating has responsibilities and we have to pay attention to this stuff because life would suck without tuna. Bigeye tuna is my favorite right now in the "good choices" list. It has a beautiful color and full flavor. Avoid bluefin. They used to abound, but they need some time to come back to a steady population. Realize your power as a consumer. It's like voting: never think your choice doesn't matter. It does, so choose with a well-informed mind. There was a time when swordfish was whittled down to one lonesome fish in the pond, but through better fisheries management and chef leadership, we brought it back from the brink. We can do this.

EGGPLANT

Globe, Fairy Tale, Galine, Mangan, and Beatrice are all varieties of eggplant. Sometimes they appear in our CSA box, and figuring out which eggplant is which usually means a call to the farmers. It is an easily answered query, but I wish my mind would retain all of the beautiful images matched with the beautiful names, because at the end of the day I just want to get to know my eggplants better. The wonderful thing is that regardless of variety, they all cook up about the same, depending on size, so rock out these recipes with the best ones you can find.

ROASTED EGGPLANT WITH BOILED PEANUT SAUCE

The Lebanese know their way around an eggplant, so when you are looking for more eggplant ideas, think about cookbooks showcasing the Middle East. Here, the sauce is kind of like the tahini sauce for a falafel, but Southern in its roots. This would make a great side next to lamb or roasted fish. Some hot sauce, some cold beers . . . those would be nice, too. *Serves 4 as a side*

1 medium globe eggplant (about 1 pound)

⅓ cup extra-virgin olive oil

Kosher salt and freshly ground black pepper

2 tablespoons minced fresh flat-leaf parsley leaves

2 tablespoons minced fresh oregano leaves

2 tablespoons minced fresh mint leaves

2 tablespoons minced fresh hot chile (such as red jalapeño)

½ teaspoon crushed red pepper flakes

2 garlic cloves, minced

2 tablespoons freshly squeezed lemon juice

1 cup Boiled Peanut Sauce (recipe follows)

1 Preheat the oven to 425°F.

2 Cut the eggplant in half along the length, removing the calyx (the leafy green part where the eggplant was attached to the plant). Cut ½-inch-thick slices from each half, resulting in about 24 half-moon shapes.

3 Pour half the olive oil into a big roasting pan. Arrange the eggplant slices in a single layer in the pan and drizzle with a tablespoon of the remaining olive oil. Season the eggplant with kosher salt and pepper to taste. Roast in the oven for 15 minutes, until the eggplant is soft in the center but not hammered (restaurant-speak for really overcooked). Remove the eggplant from the oven but keep it in the roasting pan.

4 In a small bowl, combine the remaining olive oil with the parsley, oregano, mint, hot chile, red pepper flakes, garlic, lemon juice, kosher salt to taste, and a couple of grinds from the pepper mill. Stir to combine, and then spoon evenly over all of the eggplant.

5 Transfer the eggplant to a serving platter, and drizzle with the peanut sauce.

6 Serve.

BOILED PEANUT SAUCE
Makes 1 cup

½ cup shelled boiled peanuts (canned will work if need be)

4 garlic cloves, minced

2 tablespoons freshly squeezed lemon juice

2 tablespoons olive oil

2 tablespoons chopped fresh flat-leaf parsley leaves

1 teaspoon smoked paprika (pimentón)

Kosher salt

Combine the boiled peanuts, garlic, ½ cup of water, and the lemon juice in a blender and puree until smooth. With the motor running, slowly pour in the olive oil. Then turn off the blender and add the parsley and smoked paprika. Season with kosher salt to taste. Stir to combine and set aside. This sauce will keep in the fridge for 2 to 3 days.

SMOKY EGGPLANT PUREE

When I saw people cooking eggplant in the Middle East, it was a revelation: cook the eggplant, whole, over an open flame until it is wonderfully smoky and tender on the inside. It's so utterly simple and wonderful with toasted pita as a snack, as a sauce for roasted lamb, or as a layer for a simple turkey sandwich. If you have a gas stove, it's the easiest eggplant recipe ever. You can also fire up the grill to the same effect, or just roast them whole in the oven. *Serves 4 as a side or a good snack*

1 medium round or cylindrical eggplant, or 2 small baseball-size ones (about 1 pound)

2 tablespoons extra-virgin olive oil

1 tablespoon freshly squeezed lemon juice

1 tablespoon red wine vinegar

1 garlic clove, minced

1 teaspoon Aleppo chile flakes

Kosher salt

1 Pierce the eggplant all over with a fork. If you have a gas stove, turn a burner to medium heat and place the eggplant directly over the flame. Roast, turning the eggplant occasionally so that it blackens all around, until it is very soft, about 15 minutes. Remove from the heat and set aside to cool. (You can also roast the eggplant in a preheated 450°F oven for about 40 minutes, or until very tender.)

2 When the eggplant is cool enough to handle, peel away the charred skin and lightly chop the eggplant flesh. Place it in a food processor and add the olive oil, lemon juice, vinegar, garlic, chile flakes, and kosher salt to taste. Puree until smooth and serve whenever. Yummy.

CRISP EGGPLANT WITH YOGURT, TOMATOES, AND BASIL

NAZARETH, GEORGIA, EGGPLANT WITH TAHINI AND YOGURT

INDIAN EGGPLANT PICKLE (PAGE 47)

NAZARETH, GEORGIA, EGGPLANT WITH TAHINI AND YOGURT

Okay, so there is no town called Nazareth, Georgia. Rather, this is an ode to a trip I took to Israel, where I ate a beautiful meal in the house of a Muslim woman. Her "kitchen" in the small third-story walk-up apartment stretched from the thin galley in her home to the landing outside her door, where there was a little gas oven for baking bread and an open burner for frying. The three generations of family who traipsed around being wonderful hosts just exuded a loving bond with their food. It was a stunning meal, one I will never forget. One dish, baked eggplant with tahini and yogurt, was so unctuous and fresh that I set off to make my own version of it. *Serves 6 to 8*

2 medium globe eggplants (about 2 pounds total)

2 cups torn French bread (½-inch pieces)

1 tablespoon extra-virgin olive oil

Kosher salt

1 large red bell pepper, roasted, peeled, seeded, and cut into strips

¼ cup fresh mint leaves, chopped, plus whole leaves for garnish

2 garlic cloves, minced

⅓ cup tahini

1½ cups whole plain yogurt

1 Place the eggplants on a metal rack set over a gas burner or directly on the burner. Turn the flame to medium and cook, rotating them every minute or so, until they are evenly charred and the flesh feels tender when poked, about 15 minutes. Transfer the eggplants to a cutting board and let them cool for 10 minutes.

2 Meanwhile, preheat the oven to 375°F.

3 Cut the cooled eggplants in half lengthwise and scoop out the flesh, discarding the skins. Chop the flesh roughly, ending up with a pulpy mixture. Place the eggplant in a medium bowl and add the torn bread, olive oil, and kosher salt to taste. Toss well and spread the eggplant mixture out in a 10 × 8-inch baking dish.

4 Toss the bell pepper strips and the chopped mint together. Layer most of the peppers over the eggplant in the baking dish, reserving just a bit for garnish.

5 Mix the garlic, tahini, and yogurt together in a medium bowl and pour the sauce over the peppers. Finish with the reserved peppers and bake for 45 minutes.

6 Garnish with more mint and serve immediately.

CRISP EGGPLANT WITH YOGURT, TOMATOES, AND BASIL

You're going to read the ingredient list and ask, "What is Crisp Film?" It's a refined cornstarch that keeps fried food really crisp. We buy it through Terra Spice in Chicago, but you can also just use regular cornstarch. This salad looks awesome and tastes even better 'cause what's better than tomatoes with crisp eggplant on top? *Serves 4*

1 cup whole plain Greek yogurt

1 teaspoon freshly squeezed lemon juice

Kosher salt

2 pounds mixed heirloom tomatoes

½ teaspoon freshly ground black pepper

2 tablespoons extra-virgin olive oil

1 tablespoon red wine vinegar

¼ cup fresh basil leaves

2 cups peanut oil

1 medium globe eggplant (about 1 pound)

1 cup all-purpose flour

1 cup Crisp Film or cornstarch

1 In a small bowl, combine the yogurt with the lemon juice, and season with a generous pinch of kosher salt. Set aside.

2 Cut the tomatoes into various shapes and sizes (hopefully you have found pretty tomatoes that don't look like they were developed in a lab to fit into a shipping box). Place the tomatoes in a bowl and season with kosher salt and the black pepper. Add the olive oil, vinegar, and basil leaves. Toss to combine and set aside.

3 Heat the peanut oil to 350°F in a large, deep cast-iron sauté pan. Slice the eggplant very thin (⅛ inch) on a mandoline. You will have about 32 slices. Combine the flour, the Crisp Film, and a pinch of kosher salt in a shallow bowl, and dredge the eggplant slices, one at a time, in the flour mix. Fry the eggplant slices, in batches, for 30 to 45 seconds, or until golden brown and crisp. As they finish frying, transfer the slices to a cooling rack perched over paper towels. Season with a pinch of kosher salt, as you would potato chips.

4 Spoon the yogurt onto individual plates, then pile on some tomatoes. Arrange the fried eggplant on top. Eat.

DUCK BREAST WITH INDIAN EGGPLANT PICKLE

Perfect duck breast matched with complex Indian spices and smoky eggplant . . . this entrée just feels right on a cool fall evening. The pickle is richly flavored and versatile and can be a staple condiment in your larder. I love this dish with cooked farro alongside. *Serves 4*

2 large Moulard duck breasts (about 1½ pounds total)

Kosher salt

1 tablespoon canola oil

1 tablespoon unsalted butter

1 cup Indian Eggplant Pickle (recipe follows)

1 tablespoon extra-virgin olive oil

1 Preheat the oven to 400°F.

2 Score the fat side of the each duck breast with a sharp paring knife, cutting about ¼ inch deep but cutting only into the fat, not the actual meat of the breast. Season the breasts all over with kosher salt, and set aside.

3 Set a large, heavy, ovenproof sauté pan over medium-low heat. Add the canola oil, and then place the breasts in the pan, skin side down. Cook about 15 minutes to render off the fat and crisp the skin, occasionally spooning out the fat if it starts to really pool up. Low and slow wins this race.

4 When the skin is crispy, raise the heat to medium-high, turn the breasts over, and cook on the meat side for 2 minutes. Add the butter to the pan and baste the breasts with the melted butter. Place the pan in the oven and roast for 2 minutes, or until the breasts are on the rare side of medium-rare. Transfer the duck breasts to a cutting board and let them rest for 5 minutes.

5 Slice the duck against the grain, and fan the slices out on a platter. Top with copious amounts of the eggplant pickle. Drizzle with the olive oil and make people happy.

INDIAN EGGPLANT PICKLE
Makes 1 quart

1 pound Japanese eggplants

2 tablespoons extra-virgin olive oil

½ teaspoon fine sea salt

¼ cup vegetable oil

1 tablespoon minced fresh ginger

1 teaspoon ground turmeric

1 teaspoon mustard powder

1 tablespoon toasted and ground cumin seeds

2 garlic cloves, minced

2 tablespoons minced pickled hot chiles

½ cup sliced yellow bell pepper

2 tablespoons sorghum molasses

1 tablespoon tamarind paste

¼ cup chopped fresh cilantro stems and leaves

½ cup rice vinegar

½ teaspoon kosher salt

¼ cup fresh basil leaves

1 Preheat the oven to 400°F. Line a baking sheet with parchment paper.

2 Cut the eggplants into ½-inch-thick rounds and place them in a medium bowl. Add the olive oil and sea salt, and toss to coat. Arrange the slices on the prepared baking sheet, and roast the eggplant in the oven for 10 minutes. Remove from the oven and let cool.

3 Let's make a pretty highly spiced pickle base: Heat the vegetable oil in a large, shallow pot over medium-high heat. When the oil is hot, add the ginger and cook for 1 minute. Then add the turmeric, mustard powder, and ground cumin. Cook, stirring often, until very fragrant. Add the garlic, the pickled chiles, and the bell pepper, and cook for another 2 minutes. Then add the sorghum, tamarind paste, cilantro, and vinegar. Dilute with ½ cup of water, and then season with the kosher salt. Add the eggplant and cook for 10 minutes, stirring well. Remove from the heat and finish with the basil leaves. Store the eggplant pickle in the refrigerator for up to 10 days, or pack it into clean jars and process according to the jar manufacturer's directions to store it for up to 6 months.

FIGS

Figs are seasonally elusive. Sometimes they start dropping, heavy with their sugars and moisture, in August, but sometimes it doesn't happen until September. I got a bit flummoxed on where to set them in a seasonal context. To confuse matters even more, sometimes we even get a little teaser crop in late spring. So I put them in fall, because to me, the figs get plump and then the leaves start falling off the trees. My logic is Vulcan-like.

I am blessed to have amazing people who choose to work in the restaurants I own. One such person is Paul, a waiter who has worked for me for more than fifteen years at 5&10 in Athens. Paul lives on a stunning piece of land outside of town, a piece of land with a lot of fig trees. Paul brings bags and bags of the small Celeste variety to me in the early fall, and wants a pittance in return, because it is a gesture more than a transaction. In our neck of the woods there is a constant, and beautiful, currency in our yearly fruit.

FIG JAM

When you bite into a perfectly ripe fig, it is so naturally sweet and luscious that the world just makes sense. What I have never understood is why people make the jam with pounds and pounds of sugar and hide that natural sweetness of the fig.

My friend Brendan gifted us a fig tree after our daughter Beatrice was born. We planted it and it grew and grew and grew. Within three years it was about twenty feet high and weighted with fruit. If I don't make jam, the figs will fall to the ground, and then they'll ferment and rot, giving some poor squirrel the hangover of his life. So we make jam and slather it on toasted bagels, serve it with roasted chicken or pork loin, and add dollops to cups of Greek yogurt. *Makes about 3 pints*

2 pounds fresh, ripe figs	1 tablespoon powdered pectin
1 teaspoon grated orange zest	1 cinnamon stick
1 tablespoon freshly squeezed lemon juice	1 bay leaf
1 tablespoon cider vinegar	1¼ cups sugar

❚ Remove the stems and then quarter the figs. Place the cut fruit in a heavy pot and add the orange zest, lemon juice, vinegar, and pectin. Place the pot over medium heat and cook for 15 minutes. Then add the cinnamon stick, bay leaf, sugar, and 1¼ cups of water. Raise the heat to high and bring to a boil, stirring constantly, and cook at a boil for 3 minutes. Be careful, as getting hit with hot jam is never fun. Remove from the heat.

❚ Remove and discard the bay leaf and cinnamon stick. Transfer the hot fig jam to clean jars and process according to the jar manufacturer's directions to store for up to 1 year on the shelf. Unprocessed jam can be kept in the refrigerator for up to 6 weeks.

ROASTED FIGS WITH PECORINO ROMANO AND FRISÉE

Pecorino Romano is an interesting cheese. For a dry cheese, it's moist and barnyard-rich in taste. You might think, is that a good thing? Well, it is in moderation. Here, with plump figs and the crisp apple, it becomes a meal of a salad. *Serves 4 as an appetizer*

1 tablespoon whole-grain mustard	Freshly ground black pepper, to taste
1 teaspoon chopped fresh tarragon leaves	16 fresh, ripe figs
2 tablespoons fig vinegar (see page 52)	1 apple
¼ cup plus 1 tablespoon extra-virgin olive oil	4 cups torn and loosely packed frisée lettuce
Kosher salt, to taste	2 ounces Pecorino Romano, thinly shaved with a vegetable peeler

❚ Preheat the oven to 400°F.

❚ Make the vinaigrette: Put the mustard in a small bowl and whisk in the tarragon and the fig vinegar. Slowly whisk in the ¼ cup olive oil until emulsified, and then finish with a few pinches of kosher salt and some pepper. Set aside.

❚ Trim the stems off the figs. Toss the figs with the remaining 1 tablespoon olive oil, and place them in a large cast-iron pan. Roast in the oven for 10 minutes.

❚ Core and thinly slice the apple. In a large bowl toss the frisée, apple, and Pecorino Romano with 2 tablespoons of the vinaigrette. Add half the figs and gently toss again.

❚ Spoon some more vinaigrette on a platter and arrange the salad on top of the vinaigrette. Finish by arranging the remaining figs around the salad. Eat.

ROASTED FIGS WITH
PECORINO ROMANO
AND FRISÉE

FIG VINEGAR

When it's fig season, I make vinegar. Acetobacter (vinegar culture) wants to thrive on sugar and booze, like many citizens of the U.S. If you give it an environment that promotes that, you will make vinegar. So I create the environment by putting together sugar, fresh figs, grain alcohol, water, and Bragg live-culture cider vinegar. Then I cap the mixture with an airlock to keep mold growth to a minimum and put it in the cupboard for 4 to 6 weeks. Using this same method, I have made celery vinegar, pepper vinegar, even orange vinegar. It's just a matter of adding sugar and alcohol when needed to create that happy acetobacter environment.

Making things like vinegar means that then you have to come up with ways to use the newfound condiment. That's where your Spidey sense has to come into play. A fig and peach salad with shaved aged goat cheese, doused with fig vinegar and torn basil? How about a pork chop nicely browned in a cast-iron skillet and then the pan juices deglazed with fig vinegar and fresh figs? Duck breast slowly cooked and then finished with a fig agrodolce, the vinegar cutting through the richness of the meat and sweetness of the figs? These all work for my culinary logic. And that's how you get better in the kitchen: you adapt to a product in the fridge, at the market, or in your pantry. But first, make some vinegar.

Makes 1 quart

YOU WILL NEED

A netted suit to keep the mosquitoes away (optional)

A ladder

A basket

An 11-year-old helper named Beatrice (age and name can vary)

Using the netted suit, ladder, basket, and Beatrice, pick 1 pound of fresh, ripe figs.

THEN YOU WILL NEED

¼ cup sugar

1 tablespoon pickling salt

½ cup live-culture cider vinegar (I like Bragg)

A sterilized quart-size mason jar

¼ cup grain alcohol (such as Everclear)

1½ months of patience

Combine 1 cup of water, the sugar, and the pickling salt in a small pot and bring to a boil. Let the mixture cool to room temperature, and then add the cider vinegar. Cut the figs in half, and place them in the quart jar. Pour the cooled liquid over the figs. Top with the grain alcohol. Fit with an airlock, or if you don't have one, cover the jar with a piece of paper towel and an elastic band to secure it in place. This will allow the liquid to breathe and encourage the vinegar to do its thing. Place the jar in your cupboard and leave it for 6 weeks, skimming once in a while if you see any white silty mold gathering on top of the vinegar. It's done when it tastes like fig vinegar. Strain and use.

FIGS, HONEY, CRISP FARRO, AND YOGURT

The figs are plump, the honey is sweet, the farro adds crunch, and the yogurt adds savory acidity and creaminess. Together it is a simple starter that looks stunning and will get rave reviews. The best time to make it is when you cooked farro for a dish the night before and set some aside for this dish. This recipe starts it all from scratch, though, so don't you worry auybout a thing. *Serves 4 as an appetizer*

½ cup farro

Kosher salt

8 large fresh, ripe figs, stems removed

2 tablespoons wildflower honey

1 tablespoon champagne vinegar

¼ cup fresh mint leaves

½ cup chopped arugula leaves

Olive oil

¾ cup whole plain Greek yogurt

1 In a small saucepan, cover the farro with 2 cups of water and bring to a boil. Then lower the heat to a simmer, add ½ teaspoon kosher salt, cover, and cook for 20 to 25 minutes, until the farro is tender. Drain well, and then pour the farro onto a dry kitchen towel to get as much moisture off of it as you can.

2 Cut the figs into quarters and lay them in a heatproof bowl. Combine the honey and the vinegar in a small pot and bring to a boil; then pour it over the figs. Add the mint and arugula, sprinkle with a pinch of kosher salt, toss lightly, and set aside.

3 Generously slick a nonstick skillet with olive oil and set over medium-high heat until it shimmers. Add the drained farro in a single layer (work in batches if necessary) and cook for about 5 minutes, stirring often to get it evenly crispy. Pour the farro onto paper towels to drain.

4 Take 4 plates and spoon a generous dollop of the yogurt on each one. Arrange the figs, mint, and arugula on the yogurt and finish with the crisp farro. Serve.

DUCK PROSCIUTTO WITH POACHED FIGS AND CIPOLLINI RISOTTO

Figs, duck, caramelized onions, rice: there is nothing wrong with a quartet like that. When you are working with cipollinis, soak them in cold water for about an hour before peeling them—it will make the job a lot easier. As for the figs, I suggest using whatever variety you can find that's in season, ripe, and stunning.

You will need to begin this dish one week ahead of time. Do the duck prosciutto recipe first, wait out the week, then make the risotto to finish. *Serves 4*

2 cups dry red wine

¼ cup maple syrup

1 cinnamon stick

8 fresh figs, stems removed

4 cups chicken stock (see page 22)

2 tablespoons unsalted butter

8 cipollini onions, peeled and quartered

Kosher salt

1 cup short-grain risotto-style rice (Carnaroli, Arborio, or Vialone Nano)

¼ cup finely grated Parmigiano-Reggiano cheese

½ pound Duck Prosciutto (page 54), thinly sliced

1 In a medium saucepan, combine the red wine with the maple syrup and cinnamon stick and bring to a boil over medium-high heat. When it boils, reduce the heat to very low and add the figs. Poach the figs for 30 minutes. Then strain the figs, reserving the poaching liquid. Return the poaching liquid to the pot and reduce over high heat until just ¼ cup remains. Pour the reduced liquid into a bowl and set it aside.

2 Pour the stock into a saucepan and place it on a back burner on low heat. Place a larger pot on a front burner on medium heat, and add 1 tablespoon of the butter to the pot. Add the onions and cook for 15 minutes, or until nicely caramelized. Add a few pinches of kosher salt and the rice. Toast the rice for 1 minute and then gradually add the warm stock, about 1 cup every 5 minutes or so, stirring and cooking after each addition until the stock is absorbed. The rice is just about done when it has a trace of crispness to the core of each kernel and the overall consistency is wet but creamy. Add the remaining tablespoon of butter, the Parmigiano-Reggiano, the figs, and the reduced poaching liquid. Add salt to taste, remembering that the duck prosciutto is salty. Stir well, and then immediately spoon onto 4 plates.

3 Arrange the duck prosciutto with the risotto, and eat.

DUCK PROSCIUTTO

I use Quebec duck in this because it's my homeland and they produce beautiful Moulard ducks, primarily raised for foie gras, but also as eating birds. Recently laws enacted in California have displaced a number of duck farmers and the result is a label that says Sonoma but the product is actually from Quebec. Strange. *Makes ¾ pound*

1 duck breast (about 1 pound)	¼ teaspoon ground cloves
3 cups kosher salt	¼ teaspoon freshly ground black pepper
1 tablespoon light brown sugar	
½ teaspoon toasted and ground allspice berries	1 tablespoon chopped fresh thyme leaves

1 Rinse the duck breast under cold water and pat it dry. In a deep nonreactive container, combine the salt, brown sugar, allspice, cloves, pepper, and thyme. Mix well, and then immerse the duck breast in the mixture, scooping it over the breast to cover it well. Cover the container and place it in the fridge to cure for 24 hours.

2 Remove the cured duck breast from the fridge and rinse it under cold water. Pat it dry and wrap it tightly in a couple of layers of cheesecloth, twisting the ends of the cheesecloth to torque the duck breast into an even cylinder. Tie the cheesecloth tightly on each end, and make room in your fridge to place it where it doesn't come into contact with anything else. If you have a second fridge this will be easy. If you don't, you'll just have to figure it out; MacGyver-style, hang it up from your refrigerator shelving using kitchen twine to air-dry, ensuring it gets airflow all around it. Let it dry for 1 week.

3 Remove the cheesecloth, wrap the duck prosciutto tightly in plastic wrap, and store it in the fridge. The duck breast will stay good, if tightly wrapped, for up to 10 days.

4 To serve, slice the duck breast very thinly against the grain.

DUCK PROSCIUTTO

KOHLRABI

Ye olde cabbage turnip. That's literally what the word *kohlrabi* means, and it kind of tastes like a cross between the two. It is the vegetable that started this whole book for me, since the questions about the alien-looking cabbage would line up in September. It's not actually the root that you eat—though it looks a lot like a round root—but rather it's a swollen stem. The leaves are delectable as well, so don't just hack off all of them. Think about pickling, braising, or slawing them.

KOHLRABI SALAD
WITH PECANS, LIME,
PAPRIKA, AND MARJORAM

STEAMED KOHLRABI
WITH SHALLOT AND
CELERY LEAVES

KOHLRABI
PUREE

KOHLRABI PUREE

Vegetable purees are versatile bases for good meals. Kohlrabi is a perfect candidate and the results are luscious and delicious. I use a Vitamix blender and the results are very, very smooth, but any blender or food processor will make a creamy puree. Add a chiffonade of the greens and this can be your study in kohlrabi.
Serves 4 to 6

2 tablespoons unsalted butter

½ yellow onion, diced

1 pound kohlrabi, peeled and chopped, greens and stems reserved for garnish

1½ cups chicken stock (see page 22)

1 sprig fresh thyme

Kosher salt

1 In a medium saucepan over low heat, melt 1 tablespoon of the butter. Add the onion and then the kohlrabi. Cook for 2 minutes, stirring the vegetables to coat them in the butter. Then add the chicken stock and the thyme sprig. Bring to a boil over medium-high heat, then turn back down to a simmer. Place a round of parchment paper on top of the mixture, and simmer until the kohlrabi is tender, about 15 minutes. Remove from the heat and let cool slightly.

2 Transfer the mixture to a blender, add the remaining tablespoon of butter, and puree until smooth. Season with kosher salt to taste. Serve alongside finely sliced reserved kohlrabi stems and greens.

KOHLRABI SALAD WITH PECANS, LIME, PAPRIKA, AND MARJORAM

I once worked with a wonderful pastry chef who had also been a savory chef for a very long time. I will always remember her describing marjoram as the sweet, good-natured daughter of thyme and oregano. I fell for the description then and still fall for the versatility and delicacy of marjoram today. *Serves 4*

¼ cup extra-virgin olive oil

1 teaspoon hot smoked paprika (pimentón)

2 tablespoons freshly squeezed lime juice

1 teaspoon finely chopped fresh marjoram leaves

1 shallot, minced

Kosher salt

Freshly ground black pepper, to taste

1 bulb kohlrabi, peeled, halved, and sliced into thin half-moons

½ cup pecan halves, toasted

4 cups arugula leaves

1 Combine the olive oil, paprika, lime juice, marjoram, and shallot in a mason jar. Add a couple pinches of kosher salt and some black pepper. Seal the jar and shake it up.

2 Put the kohlrabi in a large bowl and add half the vinaigrette. Let it sit for about 1 hour to soak up the flavors and soften.

3 Add the pecans and arugula to the kohlrabi, season with kosher salt to taste, and toss well. Place the salad on a large platter and circle it with a little more vinaigrette. Eat.

STEAMED KOHLRABI WITH SHALLOT AND CELERY LEAVES

This is a minimalist recipe that really shines. Shallot, kohlrabi, celery leaves, and benne, a.k.a. sesame seeds, come together in a celebration of fall.
Serves 4 as a side

2 bulbs kohlrabi

2 tablespoons unsalted butter

1 shallot, cut into thin rings

¼ cup fresh celery leaves

2 sprigs fresh thyme

Kosher salt

1 tablespoon toasted benne or sesame seeds

1 Peel the kohlrabi and cut it into ½-inch dice.

2 In a heavy-bottomed saucepan, melt the butter over medium-high heat. When the butter has bubbled and frothed, add the kohlrabi cubes. Stir well, and then add the shallot, celery leaves, and thyme. Reduce the heat to medium, add ¼ cup water, and cover the pan. Cook for 6 minutes, or until the kohlrabi is just tender; remove the lid to evaporate the remaining water if necessary. Season with kosher salt to taste, and finish with the benne seeds. Serve immediately.

SKILLET KOHLRABI, LOBSTER, FENNEL, AND CURRY BUTTER

Make sure you buy lobsters alive and kicking, and buy them when they are in season. They really don't take that long to cook. I usually figure about 5 minutes per pound in boiling water, and onto the table. In this recipe, we cook it a little further in the pan, so I shorten the boiling time, to 4½ minutes per pound.

Serves 2 as an appetizer or a light main course

3 tablespoons Curry Butter (recipe follows)	1 live lobster (1¼ to 1½ pounds), boiled for 4½ minutes per pound, cleaned, and cut into pieces (see sidebar)
½ bulb kohlrabi, peeled, halved and sliced into ¼-inch-thick half-moons	Kosher salt
½ fennel bulb, cored and thinly sliced	2 scallions, thinly sliced on the bias
2 garlic cloves, thinly sliced	1 teaspoon freshly squeezed lime juice

1 In a large sauté pan, melt half of the curry butter over medium heat. When it begins to bubble and froth, add the kohlrabi and the fennel. Cook for 5 minutes to soften the vegetables. Then add the garlic and the lobster pieces. Season with kosher salt to taste.

2 Cook for 3 minutes, to warm through and finish cooking the lobster pieces. Then add the scallions, lime juice, and the remaining curry butter, stirring well to fully incorporate the butter, beautifully glazing the vegetables and the lobster.

3 Spoon the contents of the pan onto a platter, and serve. Maybe a chilled white Burgundy will appear if you think nice thoughts.

CURRY BUTTER

Makes 1 cup

¼ pound (1 stick) plus 1 tablespoon unsalted butter, at room temperature	1 teaspoon ground ginger
	1 teaspoon curry powder
1 tablespoon minced shallot	1 teaspoon freshly squeezed lime juice

1 Melt the 1 tablespoon of butter in a small saucepan over medium heat. When it bubbles and froths, add the shallot and cook for 2 minutes. Add the ginger and curry powder and cook for 1 minute more. Then add the lime juice, stir to combine, and remove from the heat. Set the mixture aside to cool to room temperature.

2 In a small bowl, mix the remaining stick of butter with the sautéed shallot, ginger, and curry. Mix well, then place the mixture in a jar and refrigerate.

HOW TO COOK A LOBSTER

I remember my family committing culinary atrocities with the classic Canadian lobster. Boiling it for too long in insipid water made for a less than regal end for the poor little crustacean. To me, lobster is an attainable luxury, so one should know how to turn it into an impressive meal. *Makes 1 lobster*

2 tablespoons Old Bay Seasoning	4 bay leaves
1 lemon, thinly sliced	Sea salt
3 sprigs fresh thyme	1 live East Coast lobster

1 Pour 2 gallons of water into a large stockpot set over high heat. Add the Old Bay, lemon slices, thyme sprigs, bay leaves, and enough sea salt so that the water tastes pleasantly like the ocean. Bring to a boil and then add the lobster. Cook for 5 minutes per pound—so a 1¼-pounder will take 6 minutes—and then transfer it to a platter (if you are going to eat it then) or to an ice water bath. If it's the former, get a bib, some claw crackers and picks, and go to town. If the latter, then let's clean it up.

2 Place the lobster on a couple of paper towels on top of a cutting board, and twist off the tail. Using poultry shears, cut off the outer side of the tail's shell, being careful not to actually cut into the flesh. Twist off the claws and knuckles, and cut the shells on those too and remove the meat. (Sometimes it is safer to use a claw cracker than shears. I leave this to you.) Inside each claw is a sheer piece of shell that runs inside the meat. Pull this out from the back of the claw meat. It will look like a little translucent boomerang. Take all the meat you have freed from the shells and rinse it quickly under cold water to remove the white stuff that accumulates on the cooked meat. This is hemolymph, which is kind of what the lobster has instead of blood. Chop the shells and carcass up for a bisque or stock, and chop the reserved meat into pieces or prepare as your recipe indicates.

LETTUCES

I think I would be fine with returning as a rabbit in a second life, since I could live happily eating lettuces. These days it's easy because the ubiquitous romaine, iceberg, and Bibb have moved aside and made room for Lolla Rossa, Cherokee, Crispino, Reine des Glaces, Little Gem, Truchas, and Salvius, too. Revel in lettuce.

SEARED LETTUCE WITH PINE NUTS, BUTTER, AND LEMON

I have a soft spot for cooked lettuce—how tender and flavorful it is—and this dish is a beauty. It is so simple and so good. By the way, I don't want to be the harbinger of bad news, but throw away those pine nuts you bought two years ago and get some fresh ones from a store that moves a lot of pine nuts. When you toast them, pay attention, as burning nuts is a very common mistake, even among professional chefs. *Serves 4*

1 large head romaine lettuce, outer leaves discarded

2 tablespoons unsalted butter

Kosher salt

2 tablespoons chicken stock (see page 22)

1 teaspoon freshly squeezed lemon juice

2 tablespoons fresh pine nuts, toasted

1 Place a large, heavy sauté pan over medium-high heat. While it heats up, cut the romaine head in quarters lengthwise, leaving the root intact. Put 1 tablespoon of the butter in the pan, and when it's done foaming, put the romaine in the pan and cook for 3 minutes, until nicely browned. Season with a few pinches of kosher salt, and then add the chicken stock and lemon juice. When the stock hits the hot pan it will start reducing, and when it has reduced by about half, add the remaining tablespoon of butter and stir well to create an emulsion between the butter and the stock. Add the pine nuts to the pan.

2 Arrange the cooked lettuce on a platter, spooning the stock and the pine nuts over the top. Deliver to the table and make people happy.

LETTUCE WITH POMEGRANATE, TANGERINE, AND CIDER VINAIGRETTE

There is that time of year when our CSA box seems like a cloning device for lettuces. I hear the lament all the time: "It was just hard to use up all of those lettuces." Maybe I actually *am* part rabbit because I do love the leafy greens, and they are quickly made into a meal with a great vinaigrette and some other core ingredients to show off. In this case, that's two cool-weather treasures—Satsuma tangerines and plump pomegranates.

The best way to free pomegranate seeds from the white pith is to cut the pomegranate in half and then, holding the cut side gently against your palm with your hand held over a large bowl, whack the skin side with a wooden spoon. The seeds will fall right out pretty readily. And it's a great way to get out any anger you have. *Serves 4 as an appetizer*

½ pound green leafy lettuce, such as Bibb, chopped

¼ cup fresh mint leaves

½ cup fresh pomegranate seeds

2 Satsuma tangerines, peeled and sectioned

2 tablespoons Cider Vinaigrette (page 64)

Kosher salt

In a large bowl, combine the lettuce, mint leaves, pomegranate seeds, and tangerine segments. Add the vinaigrette and some salt, and gently toss. Add more vinaigrette or salt if you like. Serve on a platter.

BUTTER LETTUCE WITH ROASTED CAULIFLOWER AND BRUSSELS SPROUTS

I think the world needs to embrace the salad bowl, give it a high five, and show it some respect. How about we change the way kids eat by showing them the bounty of vegetables early in life, by making them aware of the beauty of the radish when they are two years old, not twelve? By then it's too late and they have shaped their likes and dislikes. You may get them back onto the vegetable trail later in life, maybe after college when they dine with a date or a boss and have to eat fancy vegetables, but to me that means a waste of the first twenty years. We change the world by teaching children how to make salad. Now. It's going to be awesome. Let's go. *Serves 4*

2 cups small cauliflower florets

1 teaspoon extra-virgin olive oil

Kosher salt

1 cup Brussels sprouts leaves

1 head butter lettuce, cored

½ cup thinly sliced radishes

½ cup thinly sliced young carrots

½ cup dried currants

1 cup Cider Vinaigrette (page 64)

1 Preheat the oven to 450°F.

2 Place the cauliflower florets in a large cast-iron sauté pan, toss with the olive oil, and season with a couple pinches of kosher salt. Roast the cauliflower in the oven for 12 minutes, or until cooked and golden brown on one side. Remove from the oven, transfer the cauliflower to a plate, and let it cool.

3 Meanwhile, place a large saucepan filled with water over high heat and bring to a boil. Season it with salt until it's nicely salty. Prepare an ice water bath and place it nearby. Add the Brussels leaves to the boiling water and blanch for 15 to 30 seconds, just until the leaves turn bright green. Drain the leaves and shock them in the ice water. Drain on a paper towel.

4 In a large salad bowl, arrange the cauliflower, Brussels sprouts leaves, lettuce, radishes, and carrots, keeping each ingredient somewhat separated from the others. Sprinkle the salad with a couple pinches of kosher salt and the currants. Tuck the well-shaken vinaigrette, still in the jar, into the bowl so guests can mix and dress as they like.

BUTTER LETTUCE
WITH ROASTED
CAULIFLOWER
AND BRUSSELS
SPROUTS

1 Pour the apple cider into a small pot and place it over medium-high heat. Reduce the cider to ¼ cup. Let it cool to room temperature.

2 Place the reduced cider in a jar and add the mustard, cider vinegar, olive oil, parsley, a big pinch of kosher salt, and black pepper to taste. Shake well and use.

SIMPLE MISO VINAIGRETTE

This vinaigrette is Japanese in inspiration but worldly in versatility. It's my kids' favorite. The ratio is cut down a bit in favor of more acidity because of the lesser punch of rice vinegar. The salt is also reduced because of the presence of soy sauce. This will keep for about a week in the fridge. *Makes 1 cup*

¼ cup finely grated yellow onion

1 tablespoon soy sauce

1 teaspoon grated orange zest

2 tablespoons freshly squeezed lime juice

2 tablespoons rice vinegar

1 teaspoon white miso

½ cup grapeseed oil

Pinch of kosher salt

Place all the ingredients in a jar, seal it tightly, and shake. Done. Use.

JULIA'S VINAIGRETTE

Based on the Julia Child classic, this vinaigrette just delights every time. If we can teach this country that good food is this easy, we'll have a better world. (Please continue to come to restaurants, though; that's how I pay my mortgage.) It's a 3 to 1 ratio of oil to acid. From that you can do almost anything. This makes enough to keep in the fridge for multiple salads. It stays fresh for about a week. *Makes 1 cup*

2 tablespoons freshly squeezed lemon juice

2 tablespoons red wine vinegar

1 teaspoon mustard powder

1 tablespoon minced fresh tarragon leaves

¼ cup extra-virgin olive oil

½ cup grapeseed oil

¼ teaspoon kosher salt

Freshly ground black pepper, to taste

Place all the ingredients in a jar, cap it firmly, and shake it up. Use.

CIDER VINAIGRETTE

Makes 1 cup

1 cup nonalcoholic apple cider

1 teaspoon whole-grain mustard

¼ cup cider vinegar

½ cup extra-virgin olive oil

2 tablespoons chopped fresh flat-leaf parsley leaves

Kosher salt

Freshly ground black pepper

PECANS

Pecans, no matter the pronunciation (*peeeecan, pecaahn, pecaaan*), are big business down here in the South, and have been for over a century. To me they are the most wonderful nut, even if they really are a drupe and not a nut. A drupe is a husky fruit with a single seed. In the case of the pecan, the seed is what you eat. There are plenty of varieties to look out for in the pecan world, but I particularly love the tiny round Elliotts.

PECAN, LEEK,
SOURDOUGH, AND
CELERY STUFFING

PECAN
PRALINES

PECAN GRANOLA WITH
MAPLE AND OATS

PECAN PRALINES

When we think of Southern candies, it is hard not to put pecan pralines at the top of the list. Have patience and a good wooden spoon? You are halfway to the quintessential gift to a new neighbor: Southern hospitality made right with our Southern nut. *Makes 2 dozen pralines*

3 cups packed light brown sugar

1 cup heavy cream

¼ pound (1 stick) unsalted butter

2 tablespoons sorghum molasses

1 teaspoon pure vanilla extract

Pinch of cayenne pepper

2 tablespoons toasted benne or sesame seeds

2 cups pecan halves, toasted

Combine the brown sugar, cream, butter, and sorghum in a medium pot. Place it over medium heat and bring it up to 236°F, stirring all the way and following the progress on a candy thermometer. When the temperature has been reached, remove the pot from the heat and let the mixture cool to 150°F, then stir in the vanilla, cayenne, benne seeds, and pecans. Spoon onto wax paper in tablespoon-size mounds and let cool. Store in an airtight container for up to 5 days.

PECAN GRANOLA WITH MAPLE AND OATS

The only time I remember enjoying the school bus when I was young was a trip to the sugar shacks of the Gatineau mountains east of Ottawa. The steamy vats of slowly cooking maple syrup, the drizzling of hot syrup onto cups of snow, the maple candies, the cans of syrup all lined up . . . I may live in pecan country now, but that love of maple hasn't left me. It's what's for breakfast. *Makes about 3 pints*

3 cups rolled oats

1 cup cooked long-grain white rice

2 tablespoons packed light brown sugar

½ teaspoon ground cinnamon

¼ teaspoon kosher salt

1 teaspoon pure vanilla extract

½ cup maple syrup

2 tablespoons vegetable oil

1 cup pecan pieces, toasted

½ cup dried cranberries

1 Preheat the oven to 325°F. Line a rimmed baking sheet with parchment paper.

2 Place the oats in a large bowl and add the cooked rice, brown sugar, cinnamon, salt, and vanilla. Toss well. Then add the maple syrup and vegetable oil, and toss well

again. Spread the mixture out on the prepared baking sheet and bake for 20 minutes. Then remove it from the oven and let it cool. As the granola cools, stir and break it up once in a while so you don't end up with one giant granola bar. When it is cool, you can break up larger chunks with your hands.

3 Add the pecans and cranberries, and mix well. Store, at room temperature, in sealable quart or pint jars to keep it fresh.

PECAN, LEEK, SOURDOUGH, AND CELERY STUFFING

The old stuffing-versus-dressing debate is still very active in the South. To me stuffing is made of larger chunks of bread than dressing, and stuffing is redolent with celery and herbs, toasted bread, and full-flavored chicken stock. It's crispy on the exterior but soft underneath, and it likes quiet walks on the beach with its close friend gravy. Dressing is finer, wider in ingredient choices, from cornbread to oysters, and its lineage is decidedly Southern. It has never graced the interior of a turkey, and gets made in Pyrex containers that get redistributed to family members by the small masking tape name tags on their bottoms. Stuffing graced the interior of a bird until the powers that be told us not to do this as we were potentially poisoning our ilk, at which point it started being baked in Pyrex containers as well. You can call them whatever you want but that's my take on it. *Serves 4 to 6 as a side*

3 tablespoons unsalted butter, plus more for the pan

1 quart cubed sourdough bread (½-inch cubes)

¼ cup extra-virgin olive oil

Kosher salt

2 cups minced leeks, white and light green parts

2 cups minced celery

½ tablespoon chopped fresh thyme leaves

½ teaspoon chopped fresh tarragon leaves

2 tablespoons chopped fresh flat-leaf parsley leaves

1 bay leaf

½ cup pecan halves, toasted

2 cups chicken stock (see page 22)

2 large eggs

1 Preheat the oven to 375°F. Lightly butter an 8 × 8-inch baking dish and set it aside.

2 Put the bread cubes in a large bowl and add the olive oil. Toss well to coat the bread, and then season with kosher salt to taste. Pour the bread onto a baking sheet,

spreading it out, and toast in the oven until nicely golden brown, about 10 minutes. Remove the bread from the oven and set it aside. Leave the oven on.

3 Heat a large pot over medium-high heat and add the butter. When it bubbles and froths, add the leeks and celery, sprinkle with a few pinches of kosher salt, and cook for 5 minutes. Add the thyme, tarragon, parsley, and bay leaf. Stir well, add the toasted bread and the pecans, and continue cooking for 2 minutes. Remove the pot from the heat and let cool for 8 minutes. Remove the bay leaf.

4 In a mixing bowl, whisk together the stock and the eggs. Making sure the pot of stuffing is not so hot that it will scramble the eggs, pour the mixture over the stuffing. Stir well to moisten all the bread, and then pour the stuffing into the prepared baking dish. Place it in the oven and bake for 30 minutes, or until golden brown and piping hot.

SORGHUM AND MILK–BRAISED PORK LOIN WITH PECAN FARRO RISOTTO

Milk-braised pork is a classic, with the curds slowly separating from the whey, the wonderful aroma of sage and shallot, and the golden meat slowly cooking in its aromatic bath. Wonderful stuff that is far easier than you would think. *Serves 4 to 6*

2 pounds boneless pork loin	1 medium yellow onion, cut into ½-inch-thick slices
Kosher salt	
¼ teaspoon freshly ground black pepper	12 fresh sage leaves
	2 tablespoons sorghum molasses
1 tablespoon extra-virgin olive oil	
	1 quart whole milk
1 teaspoon unsalted butter	Pecan Farro Risotto (start this 30 minutes before the pork is done; recipe follows)

1 Season the pork all over with kosher salt to taste and the black pepper. Heat the olive oil in a large braising pan over medium-high heat, and add the butter. When the butter has foamed, carefully lower the pork into the pan, fat side down, and let it sear and caramelize for 10 minutes. Turn the pork over and sear on the other side for 10 minutes, until very nicely browned. Remove the pork and set it aside.

2 Add the onion slices and sage leaves to the pan and sweat the onions over medium heat for 5 minutes, until softened but not colored. Return the pork to the pan, spoon in the sorghum, and pour in the milk. Season lightly with kosher salt and black pepper, as the liquid will concentrate as it cooks. Bring the milk to a simmer, then reduce the heat to low, cover the pan, and cook for 1½ hours, turning the pork once halfway through the cooking time.

3 Remove the pork from the braising pan and set it on a clean cutting board. Raise the heat to medium and reduce the milk by half. The curds will become more apparent and your house will smell awesome. Curds are a good thing.

4 Slice the pork and arrange the slices over the farro risotto, with the braising liquid spooned over the top.

PECAN FARRO RISOTTO
Serves 4 to 6 as a side

4 cups chicken stock (see page 22)	Kosher salt, to taste
	½ cup pecans, toasted and crushed
1 tablespoon extra-virgin olive oil	
	¼ cup grated Parmigiano-Reggiano cheese
1 shallot, minced	
1 cup farro	2 tablespoons unsalted butter
1 bay leaf	

1 Pour the chicken stock into a small pot and set it on a back burner on low heat.

2 Warm the oil in a medium saucepan over medium heat, and add the shallot. Cook the shallot down for 3 minutes, until it is very aromatic, and then add the farro. Stir well to coat, and lightly toast the farro for about 5 minutes. Add the bay leaf to the farro. Then start gradually adding the warm chicken stock, about 1 cup every 5 minutes or so. As each addition cooks down, stir a lot, and when the stock is almost fully incorporated, add more stock. Taste the farro after 20 to 25 minutes of cooking; cook until it is just tender and quite wet, wetter than a risotto would be if it came to your table at an Italian restaurant.

3 Season the risotto with kosher salt and then add the pecans. Stir to incorporate, and then vigorously stir in the Parmigiano-Reggiano and the butter.

SORGHUM AND MILK-
BRAISED PORK
LOIN WITH PECAN
FARRO RISOTTO

PERSIMMONS

Persimmons grow well in South Georgia, and it's a delight to see them come into season. They grace the windowsill, ripening from firm little orange orbs to soft, sweet treats. The Fuyu variety gets particularly sweet and the nice thing about nonastringent varieties like Fuyu is that they can also be eaten while still firm. The astringent varieties of persimmon need to fully ripen and soften a bit before being edible.

PERSIMMON "POP-TARTS"

I never had Pop-Tarts growing up. I still to this day have never eaten a Pop-Tart, except ones I have made myself. So this may or may not be Pop-Tart-like. All I really know is it's good. *Makes 4 pastries*

FOR THE FILLING
1 tablespoon unsalted butter
2 cups finely diced persimmons
1 tablespoon sugar
1 tablespoon rice vinegar
½ teaspoon pink peppercorns
¼ teaspoon ascorbic or citric acid powder, or ½ teaspoon freshly squeezed lemon juice

FOR THE DOUGH
2 cups all-purpose flour, plus more for dusting
1 tablespoon sugar
1 teaspoon kosher salt
1 cup cold unsalted butter, cubed
2 large eggs
2 tablespoons whole milk

1 Prepare the filling: In a small sauté pan over medium heat, melt the butter until it bubbles and froths and then add the diced persimmons. Continue cooking for about 15 minutes, until the fruit is soft and jamlike. Add the sugar, vinegar, peppercorns, and ascorbic acid, and cook until the filling is almost dry, about 3 minutes more. Remove from the heat and transfer to the refrigerator to chill while you make the dough.

2 While the filling is chilling, make the dough: Combine the flour, sugar, and salt in a mixing bowl. Cut in the remaining cup of cold butter until the mixture resembles coarse sand. In a small bowl, whisk together 1 egg and the milk. Add this to the flour mixture, and stir until thoroughly combined. Shape the dough into a disk, wrap it in plastic wrap, and chill it in the refrigerator for 1 hour.

3 On a floured surface, roll out the dough with a rolling pin to form a ¼-inch-thick rectangle, continuously dusting the bottom and top of the dough to ensure it doesn't stick. Cut out 4 rectangles, each roughly 4 × 6 inches. Spoon the filling evenly onto the rectangles, keeping it off-center toward the right side, leaving enough room for the dough to be folded over. Whisk the remaining egg, and lightly brush the right side of the dough with some of this egg wash (reserve the remainder). Fold the left side of the dough over the right, and using a floured fork, crimp the edges to seal them. Make sure that there are no air pockets inside each tart. Place the tarts on a baking sheet and chill in the refrigerator for 20 minutes.

4 Meanwhile, preheat the oven to 325°F.

5 Brush the top of the tarts with the remaining egg wash, and bake for 20 minutes, or until golden brown.

LOBSTER SALAD WITH PERSIMMON, CRISP BLACK RICE, MIZUNA, AND GINGER VINAIGRETTE

Mizuna is another fall delight that Woodland Gardens grows for us. It looks like a sharp-edged dandelion leaf and is a wonderfully crisp green well worth seeking out. If you can't find it from a local farm, go to a Korean or Japanese grocer, which will likely have it. If you don't have that resource, use spinach or arugula. If you don't have those, make something else. *Serves 4 to 6*

¼ cup peanut oil
1 cup cooked black rice
1 Fuyu persimmon, peeled and diced
¼ cup Ginger Vinaigrette (recipe follows)

2 live lobsters (1¼ pounds each), cooked, shelled, and cut into large pieces (see page 59)
2 cups mizuna leaves
Kosher salt

1 Place a medium saucepan over medium-high heat and add the peanut oil. When the oil is quite hot, add the cooked rice and cook, stirring often, for about 3 minutes, until the moisture is gone and the rice is crisp. Pour the rice onto absorbent towels and set aside.

2 In a large bowl, combine the persimmon with the vinaigrette. Add the lobster meat and the mizuna, and toss well. Season with a few pinches of kosher salt and toss again. Arrange the salad on a platter and then sprinkle the crisp rice over the top.

GINGER VINAIGRETTE

This recipe makes more than you need for the lobster salad, but that'll just make you eat more salads. *Makes 1 cup*

1 teaspoon grated fresh ginger
½ teaspoon finely minced orange zest
1 teaspoon mustard powder

⅔ cup grapeseed or canola oil
¼ cup rice vinegar
2 tablespoons dry sake

Combine all the ingredients in a mason jar, cap it, and shake it up just before using. The vinaigrette will keep in the refrigerator for up to a week.

PERSIMMON
"POP-TARTS"

LOBSTER
SALAD WITH
PERSIMMON,
CRISP BLACK
RICE, MIZUNA,
AND GINGER
VINAIGRETTE

GRILLED PORK BELLY WITH PERSIMMONS AND SPICY SOY VINAIGRETTE

Buying pork belly is easier than it used to be. Most farmers' markets have plenty of Berkshire, Red Wattle, Mangalitsa, or Duroc to choose from, and if you get to know that farmer, he or she will teach you all about the wonderful beasts. If you just want a regular cut of belly, from a regular old pig, go find a great Korean grocer, which will have those bellies all laid out in different cuts, wrapped up in even-steven lines. I tend to go for the single-pound rectangle, skin off. It won't pack the flavor of a Red Wattle, but it won't disrupt your finances so much either. My Korean grocer of choice in Atlanta (and beyond) is a chain of large stores called Super H Mart, bustling places with great produce, pork, beef, and fish. Go and find your own equivalent and get to know those aisles. *Serves 4*

1 pound pork belly, skin off

½ teaspoon fennel seeds

½ teaspoon cumin seeds

¼ teaspoon black peppercorns

½ teaspoon coriander seeds

¼ cup kosher salt

2 tablespoons sugar

1 tablespoon extra-virgin olive oil

1 small yellow onion, diced

1 carrot, cut into small dice

1 celery stalk, peeled and diced

1 tablespoon minced fresh ginger

½ hot Hungarian or Fresno chile, seeded and minced

3 cups chicken stock (see page 22)

4 tablespoons Simple Miso Vinaigrette (page 64)

2 watermelon radishes, thinly shaved

¼ pound arugula leaves

4 Pickled Pearl Onions (page 89), sliced

2 ripe persimmons, peeled and cut into wedges

1 Place the pork belly in a baking dish and set it aside.

2 In a dry cast-iron skillet, combine the fennel seeds, cumin seeds, peppercorns, and coriander seeds and toast over medium-high heat for 2 minutes, until toasty but not burned. Grind the toasted spices in a spice grinder, and then combine them with the salt and the sugar. Generously sprinkle the spiced salt over all sides of the pork belly, cover the baking dish with plastic wrap, and chill in the fridge for at least 8 hours and up to 24 hours.

3 Preheat the oven to 325°F.

4 Remove the pork belly from the cure, rinse it quickly under cold water, and pat it dry. Place a heavy, lidded braising pan over medium-high heat and add the olive oil. Add the pork belly and sear it off for 3 minutes per side, for a total of 6 minutes. Remove the pork belly.

5 Add the onion, carrot, celery, ginger, and chile to the braising pan and cook for 5 minutes, until the mixture is aromatic and the vegetables are starting to soften. Return the pork belly to the pan, add the chicken stock, and bring to a boil. Cover the pan, place it in the oven, and braise until the meat is tender, about 2 hours.

6 Remove the belly from the braising liquid and cut it into slices.

7 To serve, crisp the slices of pork in a hot skillet for 1 minute, and then transfer them to individual plates. Using a spoon, dress the pork with the vinaigrette, radishes, arugula, pickled pearl onions, and persimmons.

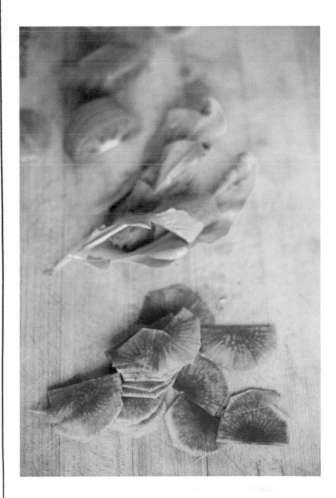

SUNCHOKES

Also known as Jerusalem artichokes, sunroots, or topinambours, these little potato-like gems rule. Sometime in your life, go to a local farm and watch actual sunchoke flowers flow in the wind. A relative of the sunflower, they are really tall, stunning plants. The season is short but the eatin' is good, like a sweeter, earthier, nuttier potato.

Wash them well. I use a clean toothbrush on mine and scrub away all the dirt under cold running water.

POACHED EGGS OVER
SUNCHOKE HASH
(PAGE 80)

PICKLED
SUNCHOKES

FOIL-ROASTED
SUNCHOKES

PICKLED SUNCHOKES

Sunchokes are really versatile, but this little pickle is that good on its own, or with a chicken curry, or with bacon and eggs. *Makes 1 quart or 2 pints*

⅔ cup white wine vinegar

2 teaspoons pickling salt

1 tablespoon sugar

1 teaspoon ground turmeric

½ teaspoon ground ginger

1 teaspoon coriander seeds

¼ teaspoon crushed red pepper flakes

1 bay leaf

1 pound sunchokes

1 In a nonreactive saucepan, combine 1⅓ cups of water with the vinegar, pickling salt, sugar, turmeric, ginger, coriander seeds, red pepper flakes, and bay leaf, and bring to a vigorous boil. After boiling for 1 minute, reduce the heat and simmer over medium-low heat for 5 minutes. Then keep hot over low heat.

2 Peel the sunchokes and slice them into ⅛-inch-thick rounds. Pack the sunchokes into a clean 1-quart pickling jar (or 2 pint jars), leaving 1½ inches of headspace at the top. Pour the hot brine over the sunchokes, leaving 1 inch of headspace at the top but fully covering the sunchokes. Cap with the lid and band, and let cool for 2 hours.

3 Process according to the jar manufacturer's directions to keep for up to 10 months on the shelf; unprocessed pickles can be stored in the refrigerator for 10 days.

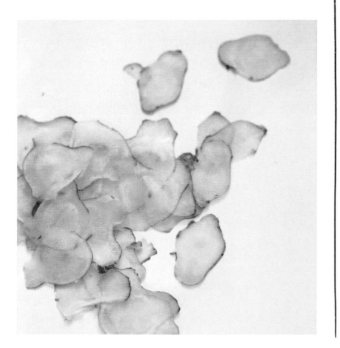

FOIL-ROASTED SUNCHOKES

I love the whole campfire bundle-of-food-in-foil concept. Toss it in the coals, or your oven, and the results are awesome. Easy cleanup, too! *Serves 4 as a side*

1 pound sunchokes, unpeeled but scrubbed

2 tablespoons extra-virgin olive oil

2 sprigs fresh marjoram

1 sprig fresh rosemary

4 long strands of lemon zest, removed with a vegetable peeler

½ teaspoon kosher salt

Freshly ground black pepper, to taste

¼ cup chicken stock (see page 22)

1 Preheat the oven to 400°F.

2 Place a 16-inch-long piece of foil on the countertop. Arrange the sunchokes on half of the foil, drizzle with the olive oil, and tuck in the marjoram, rosemary, and lemon zest. Season the pile with the salt and some pepper, then bunch up the foil a little to create a rim before pouring in the stock, so it doesn't go all over the place. Fold the other half of the foil over the sunchokes, and crimp all the edges to seal.

3 Place the package on a small baking sheet, and bake in the oven for 40 minutes. Remove from the oven, open the foil carefully to avoid the steam, set it on a plate, and serve.

POACHED EGGS OVER SUNCHOKE HASH

Hash is such a simple medium but is so rewarding. It can be beets, potatoes, yams, turnips, or, in this case, sunchokes. Poaching eggs perfectly is something you should learn how to do, just like riding a bike and swimming. Read up on perfectly poached eggs on page 184. *Serves 2 to 4*

½ pound sunchokes

½ teaspoon freshly squeezed lemon juice

Kosher salt

1 large leek

1 tablespoon unsalted butter

2 ounces bacon, finely diced

1 tablespoon chopped fresh flat-leaf parsley leaves

½ teaspoon chopped fresh thyme leaves

1 teaspoon Dijon mustard

1 large egg, beaten

1 tablespoon extra-virgin olive oil

4 poached eggs (see page 184)

1 Peel the sunchokes and cut them into ½-inch dice. Place them in a small pot, add the lemon juice, and cover with cold water. Add a few pinches of kosher salt and bring to a boil. Then turn the heat down and simmer for 5 to 7 minutes, until mostly tender. Drain the sunchokes and divide them into 2 equal portions. Pulse one portion in a food processor or blender until it becomes a chunky paste. Stir this back into the other sunchokes and set aside to cool.

2 Cut the leek in half lengthwise and rinse it well under cold water to dislodge any dirt that sits between the layers. Cut the white and light green parts into a small dice (save the dark green and root ends of the leek for a stock or soup). Place a medium sauté pan over medium-high heat and add the butter. When it bubbles and froths, add the leek and the bacon. Cook until the leeks are soft and the bacon is just beginning to crisp, about 5 minutes.

3 Add the leek-bacon mixture to the cooked sunchokes, and then add the parsley, thyme, mustard, and kosher salt to taste. Add the egg to the mixture; combine well to fully bind the ingredients. Form into 4 "pucks."

4 Place a large sauté pan over medium-high heat and add the olive oil. Carefully add the sunchoke hash "pucks" and crisp them off for about 4 minutes per side—be careful to keep them whole when turning them over, since they are fragile. Transfer to plates, and top each one with a poached egg. Eat.

SWEETBREADS WITH SUNCHOKE PUREE, RAISINS, AND LEMON

I adore sweetbreads for many reasons but mostly because they are the beginner's offal. I can fool anyone into eating a thymus gland. This is one of those recipes that, yes, takes time and involves a fair number of steps. And yes, you will be wondering if this is all worth it. I promise you it is. *Serves 4*

½ cup Madeira

½ cup raisins

1 pound veal sweetbreads

¼ cup diced carrot

¼ cup diced onion

¼ cup diced peeled celery

1 sprig fresh thyme

¼ teaspoon yellow mustard seeds

¼ teaspoon coriander seeds

Kosher salt

1 cup buttermilk

1 cup Wondra flour

¼ cup extra-virgin olive oil

1 lemon, thinly sliced

1 cup Sunchoke Puree (recipe follows)

½ cup arugula leaves

1 Combine the Madeira and raisins in a small pot and place it on a back burner over low heat; let the raisins warm until they're plumped up, then turn off the heat.

2 Rinse the sweetbreads under cold running water, pat them dry, and set them aside. Place a medium pot with 6 cups of water over high heat, and add the carrot, onion, celery, thyme, mustard seeds, and coriander seeds to the water. Bring to a boil, then immediately turn to a low simmer. Add enough kosher salt to make the water pleasantly salty, and then add the sweetbreads. Poach the sweetbreads for 10 minutes.

3 Meanwhile, prepare an ice water bath and set it near the stove.

4 When the sweetbreads are done, drain them and submerge them in the ice water to stop the cooking. Pull the cooled sweetbreads out of the ice water, pat them dry, and get a cutting board ready to clean them up.

5 Cleaning sweetbreads is essential. To do this, pull away the membrane and connective tissue that you see, so you end up with small, grape-size kernels of clean sweetbreads. Discard the connective tissue that you have worked so hard to pull away.

6 Put the sweetbreads in a small bowl and season with kosher salt. Pour the buttermilk over the sweetbreads and stir gently. Place the flour in a shallow bowl. Strain

SWEETBREADS WITH
SUNCHOKE PUREE,
RAISINS, AND LEMON

the sweetbreads from the buttermilk and then dredge them in the flour. Line up all the dredged sweetbreads on a clean baking sheet.

7 Take the plumped raisins and puree half of them with some of the Madeira in a small food processor. Set the remaining whole plumped raisins and the puree aside in two separate containers.

8 Place a large sauté pan over medium-high heat and add the olive oil. When it is hot, add the sweetbreads and crisp them up for 1½ minutes on each side, for a total of 3 minutes. Remove the sweetbreads from the pan, blot them on a paper towel, and season immediately with kosher salt. Add the lemon slices to the pan and sear them until they are nicely caramelized, about 2 minutes. Remove from the heat and line them up next to the crisp sweetbreads.

9 Arrange your plates: Warm the sunchoke puree and dollop it equally on each plate. Stud the puree with the sweetbreads, and then make a little swirl of raisin puree around the sunchoke puree. Garnish with the arugula leaves, crisped lemon slices, and plumped raisins.

FROM PORTUGAL WITH LOVE: MADEIRA

Madeira can be an endless topic of discussion, but the short of it is this: it is a fortified wine that is fully oxidized, made on the island of Madeira, off the coast of Portugal. Because it is oxidized, you can keep an open bottle on the shelf for a long time and it will pretty much taste the exact same as the day you opened it. Madeira is a very important product in the history of the South, as the ports of Savannah and Charleston were key to its import from Europe. To me it tastes like a caramelized sherry with some vibrant port overtones. It is wondrous stuff. Look for the Rare Wine Company's line of Madeiras named for important port cities. For some reason I find a kinship to the "Charleston" and "Savannah" in that line of wonderful elixirs.

SUNCHOKE PUREE

Sunchokes oxidize quickly, so I add a touch of ascorbic acid to the cooking water, ensuring a vibrant, fresh-looking puree instead of a sad murky-looking one. If you can't find ascorbic acid, which is commonly sold at health food stores and better groceries, you can use half a teaspoon of lemon juice to achieve the same results.

Serves 4 to 6 as a side

1 pound sunchokes
½ pound Yukon Gold potatoes
¼ teaspoon ascorbic or citric acid powder, or ½ teaspoon freshly squeezed lemon juice
½ teaspoon kosher salt, plus more to taste
1 sprig fresh thyme
1 bay leaf
¼ pound (1 stick) cold unsalted butter, cubed

1 Peel the sunchokes and the potatoes, and cut them into ½-inch dice.

2 Place a 2-quart saucepan over medium heat and fill it halfway with water. Add the ascorbic acid to the water. Then add the sunchokes, potatoes, salt, thyme, and bay leaf, and cover with a small round of parchment paper. Bring to a boil, reduce the heat, and simmer until the vegetables are fork-tender, about 20 minutes.

3 Strain the vegetables, saving the cooking water, and discard the thyme sprig and the bay leaf. While they are still hot, place the sunchokes and potatoes in a blender along with ½ cup of the cooking liquid. Puree at medium speed, slowly adding the butter to the spinning puree until it has been completely incorporated. If you want it thinner, add more cooking liquid. Add more salt if necessary, and serve.

SWEET POTATOES

Sweet potatoes are easy to farm, inexpensive to buy, simple to cook, and laden with good nutrients. The greens are abundant and wonderfully delicious. The Beauregard variety is particularly loved in my kitchens—sweet as can be and utterly succulent.

SIMPLE SWEET POTATOES

So easy. So good. *Serves 4 as a side*

1 pound fingerling sweet potatoes

2 tablespoons unsalted butter

2 tablespoons extra-virgin olive oil

Fine sea salt

1 Preheat the oven to 375°F. Line a baking sheet with paper towels, and set it aside.

2 Cut the sweet potatoes into ½-inch-thick slices. In a large ovenproof sauté pan over medium heat, melt the butter and cook until it is light brown and the aroma is nutty. Add the sweet potatoes in a single layer, and raise the heat to medium-high. Cook for 5 minutes, or until the slices are golden brown on the bottom. Add the olive oil and a few generous pinches of fine sea salt, and transfer the pan to the oven. Roast in the oven for 15 minutes, or until tender.

3 Drain the potatoes onto the paper-towel-lined baking sheet, and then transfer them to a serving dish.

SWEET POTATO GRATIN

This is simply layers of sweet potatoes and cream, slowly cooked. I could eat this stuff every night in the fall and winter. It reheats well, too, so if you find some time on Sunday and want to get a jump on Monday's dinner, go right ahead. Double or triple it for a crowd if you have lots of friends. *Serves 4 to 6 as a side*

1½ pounds sweet potatoes, peeled

2 tablespoons unsalted butter

¼ cup minced shallots

1 cup heavy cream

Kosher salt

¼ teaspoon freshly ground black pepper

1 Preheat the oven to 375°F.

2 Slice the potatoes very thin, using a mandoline. (No need to soak them in water—just work fast so they don't oxidize.)

3 Place a small saucepan over medium heat and add 1 tablespoon of the butter. Add the shallots to the melting butter and sauté for 5 minutes. Once the shallots are nicely browned, add the cream and cook for 2 minutes. Season the cream with kosher salt to taste and the black pepper, and set the pan aside off the heat. Take an 8-inch cast-iron sauté pan and start arranging the potatoes

in layers: Working from the middle, form a pinwheel of slightly overlapping slices until you get to the edge of the pan. After each layer is complete, add a sprinkle of salt and 2 tablespoons or so of the cream. In the end you will have about 8 layers and the depth will be about 1½ inches. Dot the top with the remaining tablespoon of butter, and cover it with a round of parchment paper. Weight down the gratin with another heavy pan, and place this whole heavy setup on a rimmed baking sheet (to make your oven cleanup easier when the cream inevitably bubbles over). Place in the oven and bake for 45 minutes to 1 hour, removing the top pan and the parchment for the last 5 minutes. The potatoes are done when they're tender when pierced with a knife.

4 Serve hot, or let it cool down, store in the refrigerator, and reheat to serve it the following day.

GLAZED SWEET POTATOES WITH MAPLE GASTRIQUE

Another example of the synergy of North and South. My veins are partially full of maple syrup and I adore the Southern staple crop of the sweet potato. Sometimes gastriques are just used as a glaze, and other times combined with a hearty stock and served as a full-blown sauce. This is of the former camp. *Serves 4*

½ cup maple syrup

½ cup white balsamic vinegar

1 pound fingerling sweet potatoes

Kosher salt

4 tablespoons (½ stick) unsalted butter, cold, cut into ½-inch cubes

1 tablespoon chopped fresh marjoram leaves

1 In a small saucepan, combine the maple syrup and vinegar and cook over medium-high heat until reduced to ½ cup, about 4 minutes. Then reduce the heat to very low.

2 Cut the sweet potatoes into ½-inch-thick rounds and place them in a medium pot. Cover with cold water, place over medium-high heat, and bring to a boil. Add a few large pinches of kosher salt, reduce the heat to a simmer, and cook until the potatoes are fork-tender, about 15 minutes. Drain and return them to the pot.

3 Whisk the butter into the gastrique, and then pour the sauce over the potatoes. Stir to coat the potatoes in the gastrique, and sprinkle in the marjoram. Place the potatoes in a shallow serving bowl. Eat.

SIMPLE SWEET
POTATOES

GLAZED SWEET POTATOES
WITH MAPLE GASTRIQUE

SWEET POTATO GRATIN

ROASTED SWEET POTATOES WITH LIME, QUESO FRESCO, CHILES, AND CILANTRO

The sweetness of the sweet potato is a perfect foil to the lime, chiles, and cilantro here. The queso fresco just makes it better. *Serves 4*

4 sweet potatoes
1 teaspoon olive oil
2 teaspoons kosher salt
1 lime, halved

3 tablespoons queso fresco
1 fresh serrano chile, sliced
¼ cup lightly packed fresh cilantro leaves

1 Preheat the oven to 325°F.

2 Rub the sweet potatoes with the olive oil and salt. Wrap them individually in aluminum foil and place on a baking sheet. Roast in the oven for 1 hour, or until soft. Unwrap the potatoes and let them cool briefly, until you can handle them.

3 Cut the sweet potatoes from end to end just to pierce the flesh, then push the ends together with a small amount of pressure to open the potatoes. Squeeze the lime over the potatoes and season with a little more kosher salt. Add the queso fresco, chile, and cilantro leaves, and serve.

CAN SWEET POTATOES SOLVE FAMINE?

I grew up watching Live Aid concerts and reading about the malnutrition and starvation caused by inequity and drought in sub-Saharan Africa. For anyone born between 1968 and 1974, this was the serious side of MTV, in between Huey Lewis videos. Africa is a continent that needs our assistance more than ever, and luckily there are groups like the ONE Campaign leading the charge with really smart initiatives designed to empower the entire continent. Founded by Bono, the lead singer of U2, ONE seeks to end extreme poverty through some very novel programs, like a recent project to advance the popularity of farming vitamin-enriched, GMO-free sweet potatoes in Africa. Like little nutritional power packs, sweet potatoes are a windfall of an inexpensive, sustainable, and eminently practical crop for the region. Platforms like these will truly make the world a better place. Go and support a cause like this that you feel good about, 'cause your voice can make a real difference. And while you're at it, cook some sweet potatoes because they can power your family . . . and maybe the world.

VIDALIA & OTHER FALL ONIONS

Fall onions have been harvested in the summer and cured a bit for sale in the fall. I think the cure just concentrates that sugar, like a late-harvest grape. Onions are the vegetable I could never live without. They provide the backbone to foundational flavors and are inexpensive, versatile, and just plain delicious. So shed a tear or two, but make them tears of joy, because you are about to eat some onions.

PICKLED
PEARL ONIONS

PICKLED ONIONS
1:1 cider vin)
water
3% sugar
2% salt
allspice   10·21·
2012

VIDALIA ONION
MARMALADE

CHARRED VIDALIA
ONION SALAD WITH
LACINATO KALE AND
PICKLED CHERRIES

VIDALIA ONION MARMALADE

This marmalade is thickened with pectin, which makes the cooking time much shorter than for a traditional onion marmalade. The result is a fresh-tasting sweet-and-sour onion jam that's a really flexible condiment. I love it on toasted bread as the base for an open-faced sandwich at lunch or adorning a nicely grilled steak for dinner. It's also great as a finishing touch to sautéed greens or as a base for a quick vinaigrette. *Makes 1 quart*

2 large Vidalia onions, cut into medium dice

1 tablespoon peanut oil

Pinch of kosher salt

3 bay leaves

¼ cup sugar cane vinegar

¼ cup sugar

1 teaspoon powdered pectin

In a large skillet over medium-low heat, sweat the onions in the peanut oil and salt, stirring constantly until the onions are soft and translucent, about 15 minutes. Add the bay leaves, vinegar, sugar, and pectin, and cook over medium-high heat for 15 to 20 minutes, until thick. Chill and store in the refrigerator.

PICKLED PEARL ONIONS

I have an argument to make when it comes to your fridge door. You have way too much stuff in there that you do not use. Fifteen hot sauces? C'mon now. You need to figure this out, 'cause you have stuff in there from the 1990s.

You probably have a jar of pickled pearl onions in there. Maybe you don't use them because they're not delicious, but I'll bet this version of them will get used—in a classic gin Gibson, or in a simple salad, or to finish a pork stew with some orange zest and chile flakes. May all condiments be this versatile . . . and tasty. *Makes 1 quart*

4 cups pearl onions

1 cup cider vinegar

2 tablespoons sugar

1½ tablespoons pickling salt

6 allspice berries

6 black peppercorns

2 whole cloves

1 Pack the onions in a clean 1-quart jar, leaving 1 inch of headspace.

2 Combine the vinegar, 1 cup of water, and the sugar, pickling salt, allspice berries, peppercorns, and cloves in a small nonreactive saucepan. Bring to a boil over high heat. Reduce to a simmer and cook for 5 minutes. Then carefully pour the hot brine over the onions, leaving ½ inch of headspace, and secure the lid and band. Let cool for 2 hours. Then process according to the jar manufacturer's directions to store up to 10 months on the shelf, or store in the refrigerator for 10 days.

3 Think about making a Gibson cocktail and garnishing it with your own onions!

CHARRED VIDALIA ONION SALAD WITH LACINATO KALE AND PICKLED CHERRIES

This is a very modern salad with pickled cherries and Lacinato kale. It shows the flexibility and versatility of the sweet onion, in this case charred to a deep hue, the caramelization providing the apex of flavor as the sugars get pulled out and shown off. It is a recipe that is easy to prepare if you have some pickled cherries, some kale, and fifteen minutes to wow the family. *Serves 4 as a side or an appetizer*

1 Vidalia onion, cut in half from root end to sprout end

Kosher salt

Freshly ground black pepper, to taste

16 small leaves Lacinato kale, torn into bite-size pieces

1 cup fresh flat-leaf parsley leaves

6 Pickled Cherries (page 269), cut into quarters

2 tablespoons Pickled Cherry Miso Vinaigrette (recipe follows)

1 Slowly caramelize the onion halves, cut side down, in a cast-iron skillet over medium-low heat for 30 to 45 minutes. No need to turn them or flip them—just let them cook on the one side. Remove the onions from the pan and let cool to room temperature. They will be nicely charred.

2 Slice the onion halves lengthwise into ½-inch-thick slices, and season with kosher salt and black pepper to taste. Combine the sliced onion with the kale, parsley leaves, and pickled cherries. Lightly dress the salad with the vinaigrette and arrange on a platter.

PICKLED CHERRY MISO VINAIGRETTE

Makes ¾ cup

3 tablespoons juice from
Pickled Cherries (page 269)

3 tablespoons red wine vinegar

1½ teaspoons blonde miso

6 tablespoons extra-virgin
olive oil

Combine all the ingredients in a jar, cap it with a lid, and shake vigorously. Will keep, refrigerated, for up to 2 weeks.

SWEET ONION SOUP WITH CARAWAY AND CROUTONS

I have always adored onions. Like some of my favorite people in the world, they are not so likable at first, but if you break through the bitter armor, you find they are sincerely sweet underneath. The trick to making something as simple as an onion into an amazing soup is in using a bit of butter and slow-cooking the onions to bring out their natural sugar. Your nose will tell you how you're doing, as it often does with good cooking. Trust your senses, young Jedi. *Serves 6*

¼ pound (1 stick) unsalted
butter

1½ pounds sweet onions, cut
into ½-inch-thick slices

1 cup minced celery

1 sprig fresh thyme

1 sprig fresh flat-leaf parsley

1 bay leaf

3 cups chicken stock
(see page 22)

1 cup heavy cream

Kosher salt

1 cup finely diced rye bread

1 tablespoon extra-virgin
olive oil

1 teaspoon caraway seeds,
toasted

1 In a heavy, medium pot, melt the butter over medium heat, and when it bubbles and froths, add the sliced onions. Cook the onions for 30 to 40 minutes, stirring regularly, until they have colored a bit, but most important, until they smell truly delicious. Add the celery and cook for 5 more minutes. Then bundle up the thyme, parsley, and bay leaf in some kitchen twine and toss that in, too. Add the chicken stock, increase the heat to bring to a boil, and turn the heat down to simmer for 10 minutes. Stir in the cream. Season with kosher salt to taste, and remove the herb bundle. Remove the pot from the heat and get ready to puree.

2 Set up your blender with a clean pot next to it, and rest a conical sieve in the pot. Arm yourself with a small ladle for pushing the soup through the sieve into said clean pot. Puree the soup in batches, and pour it through the sieve into the pot. (You can omit the straining if you want to go in a more rustic direction.) Taste the soup and adjust seasoning with salt if necessary.

3 In a small bowl, toss the bread cubes with the olive oil. Place them in a small sauté pan and toast over medium-high heat until crisp. You will want to watch this process closely, because the difference between cooking croutons to a successful golden brown and burning the heck out of them is nary a minute or so. When they are done to your liking, remove from the heat and reserve.

4 Ladle the hot soup into bowls, and garnish each one with toasted caraway, some croutons, and more parsley, if you like. Eat.

WINTER

What Winter Means to Me
SNOWBIRD EDITION

Let us realize that winter can be so much more than cabbage and potatoes. You just have to revel in the deep greens or pale colors that winter specializes in: salsify, parsnips, hardy greens, onions, bok choy, broccoli and cauliflower, rutabagas and turnips. Now I am hungry just from writing that list, and it's December so I will do what I can. I survey my larder and there are two lonely rutabagas, big ones, crying out for attention. The house needs aromas, wafts and warmth, and the anchor of that sensory link is butter and onions. So I put a heavy pot on the stove and add some chopped onion. I let it slowly grow in flavor, coaxing out the sugars from the onion. I add some caraway, coriander, and orange zest, all staples of my December larder, and then add the rutabaga and some stock. I cut a little vented parchment top and let the mixture cook until everything is tender. I season and blend and add some yogurt or cream, depending on my mood and what's in the fridge. In under an hour, I have celebrated the season. And the house smells great.

Depending on where you live, winter can be a soft nudge of cooler weather or an icy and prolonged figure-four leg lock. What you have to do is to realize that your kitchen is the place you need to be, basking in the sunshine of dark green leafy stuff, highlighted with bright citrus, anchored with roots and brassicas. Realize as you thinly slice radishes while looking out the frosty window that this cold will end, and when it does you will have a pang of remorse—sometime in June—when you actually miss broccoli. So grab that broccoli by its florets and get cooking.

BOK CHOY, TATSOI, CHARD & OTHER TASTY WINTER GREENS

Oh, the greens. They abound in the winter. Luckily a hot pan and some olive oil wilts them into tasty submission, but they can be more versatile than that—raw, cooked, or pickled. We can do so much with greens, starting with the following recipes.

PICKLED CHARD STEMS

Nose-to-tail philosophy has gone to the vegetables, too, and chefs have figured out how to use every last inch of everything. Once upon a time we'd throw out the thick stems of the chard, but I find pickling them gives me a great condiment to use anywhere I might want a crisp-tart bite. *Makes 1 pint*

2 cups finely sliced chard stems

1 teaspoon pickling salt

2 teaspoons sugar

1 teaspoon yellow mustard seeds

1 cup distilled white vinegar

¼ teaspoon chile powder

1 Pack the chard stems into a clean pint jar, leaving 1 inch headspace.

2 Combine the pickling salt, sugar, mustard seeds, vinegar, chile powder, and 1 cup of water in a nonreactive pot and bring to a boil. Reduce the heat to low and simmer for 5 minutes. Then carefully ladle the hot mixture into the jar, leaving ½ inch of headspace. Cap the jar with its lid and band, and let cool for 2 hours. The jar can be stored in the refrigerator for up to 3 weeks, or processed according to the jar manufacturer's directions to store on the shelf for up to 10 months.

SAUTÉED SWEET POTATO GREENS

We do also look beyond our yard for inspiration, and this is an ode to Chinese cookery. Even with the massive amounts of sweet potatoes grown in our vicinity, the leaves are just now becoming popular for eating, though they're very common in Africa and Asia. They are wonderfully rich in vitamins A and K and in polyphenols, and have a magical way of hitting that hot pan and wilting into a beautiful pile of silky goodness in a minute's time. It is a very efficient way to get your vitamins, and a kind respite from the ubiquity of spinach. Find a farmer who grows the tubers and get her to sell you some leaves. That farmer will be happy to oblige, as they were probably just going in the compost pile anyhow. *Serves 4 as a side*

1 tablespoon grapeseed oil

1 pound sweet potato greens, stems finely chopped and leaves torn

Kosher salt

1 teaspoon freshly squeezed lemon juice

1 teaspoon cold unsalted butter

Pinch of crushed red pepper flakes

Place the largest sauté pan you have on the stove, or use a wok. Crank up the heat to high, and when the pan is blazing hot, turn on the hood vent and turn off the smoke detector if it's a touchy one. Add the grapeseed oil and swirl it around in the pan. When the first wisps of smoke waft off the oil, add the greens. Cook them for 1 minute, as you would spinach, quickly stirring them around halfway through. Season with kosher salt while they are cooking, and then add the lemon juice, butter, and red pepper flakes, stirring well to combine. Remove the pan from the heat and transfer the greens to a paper-towel-lined plate. Blot off the excess moisture and serve immediately.

SIMPLE BOK CHOY WITH BENNE AND SOY BUTTER

Benne, a variety of sesame seed native to Africa and brought to the South, makes everything better. Buy it often, making sure it's fresh. *Serves 4 as a hearty side*

1 tablespoon peanut oil

2 bunches bok choy, chopped

2 teaspoons benne or sesame seeds, toasted

2 tablespoons Soy Butter (recipe follows)

3 tablespoons thinly sliced scallions

1 Put the peanut oil in a large pan or wok and set it over high heat. When the pan is very hot, reduce the heat to medium-high, add the bok choy, and sauté until all the leaves start to wilt. Remove the pan from the heat and add half the benne seeds, all the soy butter, and the scallions. Stir until the soy butter is melted and has emulsified. Drain the bok choy on a baking sheet lined with paper towels.

2 Place the bok choy on a platter, and sprinkle with the remaining benne seeds.

SAUTÉED SWEET
POTATO GREENS

SWEET
POTATO
GREENS

BENNE SEEDS
AND OIL

PICKLED
CHARD
STEMS

SOY BUTTER

Makes ½ cup

¼ cup (½ stick) unsalted butter at room temperature

2 tablespoons soy sauce

1 tablespoon freshly squeezed lemon juice

Combine the butter, soy sauce, and lemon juice in a small bowl and mix until well blended with a small wire whisk or fork. Scrape out with a spatula and set aside until ready to use.

TATSOI SALAD WITH CITRUS-SOY VINAIGRETTE AND PICKLED RADISHES

No tatsoi? No problem. Use spinach or bok choy leaves, or even spring greens. This is just a great salad, period. That said, tatsoi is a lovely addition to your salad bowl, bringing a full-flavored member of the brassica family into the mix. Resplendent in vitamin A and tastes great. Tatsoi is where it's at. *Serves 4*

2 bunches tatsoi

¼ cup Citrus-Soy Vinaigrette (recipe follows), or to taste

Kosher salt, to taste

2 tablespoons chopped Pickled Radishes (recipe follows)

If the tatsoi leaves are small enough, leave them whole. Tear larger leaves into quarters. In a large mixing bowl, lightly dress the greens with the citrus vinaigrette and kosher salt. Divide the dressed greens among individual plates, and add the pickled radishes as a garnish.

CITRUS-SOY VINAIGRETTE

Vinaigrettes are a foundation to build a good meal from. Having many of them in your arsenal of cooking skills is a good thing. This one is so simple but so lively and delicious. You can zest the citrus prior to making this and save that lovely zest for a marmalade or a limoncello.

Makes 1 pint

2 medium oranges

1 grapefruit

1 lime

1 lemon

1 tablespoon Dijon mustard

1 tablespoon soy sauce

1 tablespoon honey

1 teaspoon finely chopped fresh ginger

1 cup peanut oil

1 teaspoon light sesame oil

1 teaspoon kosher salt, or to taste

1 Juice the oranges and grapefruit, and strain the juice into a small saucepan. Place the pan over medium heat and reduce the orange/grapefruit juice to measure ⅓ cup. Set aside to cool slightly.

2 Juice the lime and lemon. In a blender or mini food processor, combine the lime and lemon juices with the reduced orange/grapefruit juice, mustard, soy sauce, honey, and ginger. Turn the blender on high and slowly drizzle in the peanut oil to create an emulsion. Finish the dressing with the sesame oil and salt. The dressing will keep for a week in the fridge.

PICKLED RADISHES

I adore radishes, and radishes adore being pickled. This recipe uses Cherry Belles, but it will work with just about any radish you have in season. D'Avignon, White Icicles, Fakirs, Pink Beauties . . . bring them on.

Makes 1 quart

1 bunch Cherry Belle radishes, greens removed

1 cup cider vinegar

2 tablespoons honey

1 bay leaf

1 teaspoon black peppercorns

1 sprig fresh thyme

1 Clean the radishes very well and cut them in half from top to bottom, or in 1 × ½-inch pieces. Place the radishes in a clean 1-quart mason jar, leaving 1 inch headspace.

2 Pour 2 cups of water into a small nonreactive saucepan, and add the vinegar, honey, bay leaf, peppercorns, and thyme sprig. Bring to a boil, reduce the heat to low, and simmer for 5 minutes. Carefully ladle the hot pickling mixture into the jar, leaving ½ inch of headspace. Cap the jar with the lid and band, and let cool for 2 hours. The jar can be stored in the refrigerator for up to a month, or processed according to the jar manufacturer's directions to store on the shelf for up to a year.

TARTINE OF MUSTARD GREENS, PARMIGIANO-REGGIANO, CARAMELIZED ONIONS, AND OLIVE TAPENADE

Though mustard greens have their own section elsewhere in this chapter, they are too good to just have that one spot. I cook them a lot, or adorn little plates of food with their delicate brethren, the Scarlet Frills variety, as done here on a simple open-faced sandwich. *Serves 4*

2 Vidalia onions

1 tablespoon peanut oil

Kosher salt

4 1-inch-thick slices sourdough bread

5 tablespoons olive oil

½ cup Olive Tapenade (recipe follows)

½ pound mustard greens (Scarlet Frills is especially great)

¼ pound Parmigiano-Reggiano cheese, shaved into thin slices

1 Cut the onions with the grain (lengthwise) into about ⅛-inch-thick slices.

2 Place a medium saucepan over low heat, add the peanut oil and a generous amount of kosher salt, and slowly cook the onions, stirring frequently so they cook evenly, until they have fully caramelized. This should take about 45 minutes.

3 While the onions are cooking, preheat the oven to 425°F.

4 Place the sourdough slices on a baking sheet. Drizzle each slice with 1 tablespoon of the olive oil and season with kosher salt. Toast in the oven for 5 to 7 minutes, or until golden brown.

5 To assemble the tartines, spread the tapenade in a thin, even layer over the toasted sourdough slices. Top with a layer of the caramelized onions, followed by the mustard greens. Finish with the shaved Parmigiano-Reggiano, and drizzle the tartines with the remaining tablespoon of olive oil.

OLIVE TAPENADE
Makes 2 cups

1 teaspoon orange zest

2 tablespoons freshly squeezed orange juice

1 shallot, minced

1 tablespoon rinsed and minced anchovies

1 tablespoon capers, minced

1 tablespoon finely chopped fresh flat-leaf parsley leaves

¼ cup olive oil

1½ cups Kalamata olives, pits removed

Kosher salt

1 Combine the orange zest and juice, shallot, anchovies, capers, parsley, olive oil, and olives in a food processor and pulse until smooth. Season with kosher salt, but make sure you taste it first because a tapenade contains a lot of salty ingredients.

2 This will stay fresh, tightly covered, in the fridge for 10 days.

BROCCOLI

Broccoli has a tough road to travel. It has never really been high-end restaurant food, and has basically been relegated to the vegetable your kids eat if cooked in the simplest ways imaginable. But good broccoli has a green crispness, a natural sweetness, and tastes great. The past ten years have seen some rise in "fancier" broccoli varieties, and raabs, sprouting broccolis, and leaf broccoli are seeing a comeback. May broccoli reign supreme.

ROASTED BROCCOLI RAAB
WITH PECANS, CHILE
THREADS, AND MUSTARD
VINAIGRETTE

ROASTED BROCCOLI RAAB WITH PECANS, CHILE THREADS, AND MUSTARD VINAIGRETTE

So simple but so rewarding. Raab has a punchy acidity that works well with the rich pecans. The vinaigrette is a great CYWU (Condiment You Will Use). Chile threads are available through fine spice stores like Terra Spice in Chicago. *Serves 4 as a side*

2 tablespoons peanut oil

2 bunches broccoli raab, trimmed and washed

½ cup pecans, toasted and coarsely chopped

Sea salt, to taste

¼ cup Mustard Vinaigrette (recipe follows)

Chile threads, to finish (optional)

1 In a large sauté pan, heat the peanut oil over high heat until it is just about to smoke. Add the broccoli raab and reduce the heat to medium. Caramelize the broccoli raab on one side, 3 to 4 minutes. Add the pecans, season with sea salt, toss, and cook until the raab is crisp-tender, about 4 minutes more. (Cook in batches if the pan is overcrowded.) Drain the mixture on a baking sheet lined with paper towels.

2 Divide the broccoli raab and pecans among individual plates, drizzle with the mustard vinaigrette, and garnish with the chile threads, if using.

MUSTARD VINAIGRETTE

Makes 1 cup

2 teaspoons Dijon mustard

1 tablespoon whole-grain mustard

1 teaspoon chile powder

½ teaspoon kosher salt, or to taste

3 tablespoons cider vinegar

½ cup olive oil

Combine the mustards, chile powder, salt, and vinegar in a mixing bowl. Whisking vigorously, slowly drizzle in the olive oil until emulsified. Will keep, refrigerated, for a week.

CAST-IRON BROCCOLI WITH ANCHOVIES AND OLIVES

High heat wins this recipe. The broccoli stays crisp but gets a good amount of lovely charred color to it. The anchovies provide an umami punch that makes sense. *Serves 4 to 6 as a side*

3 tablespoons peanut oil

2 heads broccoli, cut into 2-inch spears

Kosher salt

6 salt-packed anchovy fillets, rinsed and coarsely chopped

¼ cup capers

1 cup Niçoise olives, pitted and coarsely chopped

4 garlic cloves, thinly sliced

Juice of 1 lemon

½ tablespoon olive oil

1 Heat a large cast-iron skillet over medium-high heat. Add 2 tablespoons of the peanut oil and bring to a slight smoke. Then add the broccoli spears, making sure they are spread out evenly in the skillet. (Cook in batches if it doesn't all fit.) Let the broccoli caramelize, turning it after 3 minutes, or when nicely browned. Season with a pinch of kosher salt, and toss. Cook for an additional 3 minutes and then turn the heat to low.

2 Add the remaining tablespoon of peanut oil along with the anchovies, capers, olives, and garlic. Cook until the garlic is toasted, and then finish with the lemon juice.

3 Arrange the broccoli on plates, and drizzle with the olive oil.

BROCCOLI SOUP WITH ROASTED CHICKEN

This is comfort food at its finest, and a great way to use up that chicken you roasted last night. Soup for dinner is a fun break; make it a meal with a salad on the side, a great loaf of bread, and a fine piece of cheese. *Serves 6*

2 tablespoons kosher salt, plus more to taste

1 pound broccoli, cut into large florets

1⅓ cups unsalted butter

1 large Vidalia onion, halved and thinly sliced

¼ cup chopped celery

¼ cup chopped leek (white and light green parts)

2 garlic cloves, chopped

1 cup dry white wine

1 quart chicken stock (see page 22)

2 cups heavy cream

½ pound roasted chicken, cut into medium dice and warmed

¼ cup shaved Parmigiano-Reggiano cheese (shaved with a vegetable peeler)

2 tablespoons julienned fresh ginger

¼ cup plain yogurt

1 tablespoon Urfa or Aleppo chile powder

1 Prepare a large ice water bath and set it near the stove.

2 Add the 2 tablespoons salt to a gallon of cold water in a large pot, and bring to a boil. When the water boils vigorously, drop in the broccoli and cook for 1 minute; use a slotted spoon to transfer the broccoli to the ice water bath. (This will set the chlorophyll in the broccoli and preserve the fresh green color for the finished soup.) Remove the cooled broccoli from the ice water and set it aside.

3 In a soup pot, melt the butter over medium heat. Add the onion, celery, leek, and garlic and cook gently until tender, about 10 minutes. Add the white wine and reduce by half, 3 to 5 minutes. Then add the chicken stock, bring to a boil over medium-high heat, and reduce to a simmer. Cook for 15 minutes. Then add the heavy cream and bring the soup back to a simmer. Add the broccoli, bring just back to a simmer, and remove from the heat.

4 Working in small batches, puree the soup in a blender. Season with kosher salt to taste. Spoon the soup into individual bowls, and garnish with the roasted chicken, Parmigiano-Reggiano, ginger, yogurt, and a sprinkle of chile powder.

BRUSSELS SPROUTS

I, full of malapropisms, always called them "brussel" sprouts, until recently. "No, no, no," Mary corrected. "It's Brussels." I had never connected the maligned little sprouts to the land of the Flemish and the Walloons. I thought they were Californian.

It was the Romans who were responsible for the sprouts happening in the land of Tintin, having brought them northward from the Mediterranean. Those crafty Romans got around, sometimes leaving good in their wake. It does seem strange that the little orbs got the moniker. Some things are famously Belgian: bungled programs in colonial Africa, Smurfs, chocolate, women tennis players, a manly martial arts actor, fries, and waffles, but these little green leafy balls have to show their passports to be believed—at least to me.

From September to February we get truly magnificent Brussels sprouts from Woodland Gardens. The leaves cling tightly to the small head; the color is beautifully pale green with no yellow; the smell is fresh and bright. In my head the smell matches with many things, but cream, bacon, chestnuts, thyme, chile flakes, eggs, barley, chicken, and rye bread take leadership roles.

TOASTED RYE WITH BOILED EGGS, CELERY REMOULADE, AND BRUSSELS SPROUTS

A simple yet elegant open-faced sandwich. It'll wow your brunch guests or make a happy start to a winter dinner. *Serves 2*

2 large eggs

Kosher salt

½ teaspoon distilled white vinegar

1 tablespoon olive oil

1 cup Brussels sprouts, each cut into 8 wedges

2 slices rye bread

1 tablespoon salted butter

¼ cup Celery Remoulade (recipe follows)

1 Place the eggs in a small pot and cover with cold water. Bring to a boil over high heat, add ½ teaspoon kosher salt and the vinegar, and then reduce the heat to medium-low. Simmer for 1 minute. Remove the pot from the heat, cover it, and let the eggs sit in the hot water for 12 minutes. Then run the eggs under cold water, peel, and reserve.

2 Warm a medium skillet over medium-high heat, and then add the oil. When the oil is hot, add the Brussels sprouts and cook for 3 minutes, or until they take on a nice caramelized color, a hue that looks yummy. Stir the sprouts around and season with kosher salt to taste. Remove from the heat and set aside.

3 Toast the bread, and butter each slice. Place a dollop of remoulade on each plate, just off center. Slice the boiled eggs in an egg slicer. Place a piece of toast on each plate, somewhat covering the remoulade, and arrange the egg slices on the toast. Place another dollop of remoulade over the eggs, and pile on the Brussels sprouts. Eat.

CELERY REMOULADE

Makes ¾ cup

½ cup mayonnaise

1 teaspoon whole-grain mustard

1 teaspoon cider vinegar

1 teaspoon freshly squeezed lemon juice

Pinch of cayenne pepper

2 teaspoons drained tiny capers, chopped

2 tablespoons finely minced celery

1 tablespoon finely minced fresh dill

Kosher salt, to taste

Freshly ground black pepper, to taste

Combine all the ingredients in a small bowl and stir well. It keeps, refrigerated, for 5 days.

FRIED BRUSSELS SPROUTS WITH LIME VINAIGRETTE

This is an awesome way to eat Brussels sprouts. Crisp wins a lot of hearts. *Serves 4 as a side*

1 quart peanut oil

1 pound Brussels sprouts, outer leaves removed

1 teaspoon grated lime zest

¼ cup freshly squeezed lime juice

2 tablespoons Asian fish sauce

1 tablespoon rice vinegar

1 shallot, finely minced

Sea salt

2 tablespoons olive oil

½ cup coarsely chopped cilantro

2 teaspoons thinly sliced Pickled Peppers (page 310)

1 In a large pot, heat the peanut oil over medium-high heat until it reaches 350°F. When the oil is hot, it will be shimmering a bit but not smoking. If you drop a Brussels leaf in it, it will dip down and then float to the top very quickly. If it sinks slowly, the oil is not hot enough. If the oil is smoking, it is too hot and the sprouts will taste like burnt oil. Best way to tell? Buy a deep-fry thermometer, available at every grocery store I have ever been to.

2 While the oil is heating, quarter the Brussels sprouts. Set aside. In a small bowl, combine the lime zest and juice with the fish sauce, vinegar, shallot, sea salt to taste (if needed), and olive oil.

3 Once the oil reaches 350°F, fry the Brussels sprouts, in batches, until they are golden brown around the edges, 2 to 3 minutes. Remove them from the oil and drain on a baking sheet lined with paper towels.

4 In a bowl, toss the fried sprouts with a little sea salt and dress them with the vinaigrette to taste. Arrange the cilantro and pickled peppers on each plate, and top with the Brussels sprouts.

TOASTED RYE WITH
BOILED EGGS, CELERY
REMOULADE, AND
BRUSSELS SPROUTS

FRIED
BRUSSELS
SPROUTS
WITH LIME
VINAIGRETTE

EGG IN A HOLE,
CRISPED BRUSSELS
SPROUT LEAVES, AND
SHAVED GRUYÈRE

CRISPED BRUSSELS
SPROUT LEAVES

ROASTED CHICKEN
THIGHS OVER BARLEY
AND BRUSSELS
SPROUT RISOTTO
(PAGE 110)

EGG IN A HOLE, CRISPED BRUSSELS SPROUT LEAVES, AND SHAVED GRUYÈRE

How to get kids to eat Brussels sprouts? Put them over an egg in a hole. (This also works for adults.) Is this another recipe for eggs, bread, and Brussels sprouts? Similar, sure, but whatevs. *Serves 2*

2½-inch-thick slices good white bread

2 teaspoons unsalted butter

2 eggs

Kosher salt

1 cup Crisped Brussels Sprout Leaves (recipe follows)

4 ounces cave-aged Gruyère cheese, shaved with a vegetable peeler

½ teaspoon cider vinegar

1 teaspoon olive oil

1 Use a 3-inch round cookie cutter to cut the center out of each slice of bread, keeping the centers.

2 Place the butter in a large nonstick skillet over medium heat. When it has melted, add the bread slices and the rounds to the skillet, and then crack an egg into each hole. Season the eggs evenly with kosher salt. Cook for 3 minutes, until the bread is toasted and the egg is set on the bottom. Turn over and cook for another 1½ minutes, or longer if you like your egg yolk firm. Transfer the egg-filled toasts to 2 plates. Remove the bread rounds from the skillet as well and set them aside.

3 In a small bowl, combine the Brussels sprouts, Gruyère, cider vinegar, and olive oil. Toss well and arrange over the eggs in the holes. Garnish with the bread rounds.

CRISPED BRUSSELS SPROUT LEAVES
Makes about 4 cups

16 Brussels sprouts

2 tablespoons olive oil

½ teaspoon kosher salt

1 Preheat the oven to 450°F.

2 Take a paring knife and carefully core all of the Brussels sprouts. Pull the leaves away from the heads and place the individual leaves in a medium bowl. Add the olive oil and salt, and toss well. Place the sprout leaves in one layer on a baking sheet, without crowding them, and roast in the hot oven for 4 to 5 minutes, until well toasted. The process will go from beautiful to disaster in about 30 seconds, so keep an eye on them. Remove the sprout leaves from the oven when they are nicely crisped and brown around the edges but still have some nice bright green to them. Eat or use in a recipe.

HOW I FEED MY KIDS

I get a lot of questions about how my kids eat. They are two years apart—two tweens—but they have always eaten well, within reason. They still get really excited about wolfing down a pillowcase of refined sugar at Halloween. They still jones for fast food, particularly a very divisive chicken sandwich here in the South. They like to eat snacks ten times a day as opposed to three balanced, healthier meals. But they do eat their vegetables.

We started young. Brussels leaves, raw carrots, stewed cabbage, celery, spinach just barely wilted, tomatoes, onions, sweet peppers—all of these appeared on their plates. We made no demands; we just presented the offerings as dinner. We didn't make a line in the sand, anchoring them to their chairs until the food was eaten. In my experience as a child trapped at the dining room table, my food was inevitably fed to the dog or wrapped in a napkin for a trip to the garbage. As a stubborn young fellow, rarely did I lose that battle, so as a parent, I wanted to see a way around those forced-march tactics.

I think it's important not to carve food into smiley faces, or to make food into a game. Leave that to food that is so crappy that they have to put a "Happy" box around it. For the real food I make for my family, I want them to learn that food is beautiful, tasty, and makes you feel good in its natural state. Our kids eat vegetables on a regular basis because the vegetables have always been on our table.

We just get the food out there and don't overly explain it. We avoid the 5 p.m. snacks of junk that will quell any hopes of voracious appetites when they are given the good stuff at dinner. We lay out a spread family-style and let our kids make their own meals. If they are hungry, well-exercised, well-cared-for kids, reared on the goodness of vegetables, they will make a great meal of it.

ROASTED CHICKEN THIGHS OVER BARLEY AND BRUSSELS SPROUT RISOTTO

The trick to roasting chicken thighs really well is to leave them be in that medium-heat pan. Don't jiggle the pan; don't poke and prod the thighs. Just let the fat render away and crisp the skin to a golden sheet. Get used to slowly crisping proteins on your stovetop while you do other things. If you want to control the mess, get a grease splatter screen to put over the pan as the chicken cooks.

This dish is a matter of cadence. From start to finish it should take 45 minutes, but it's really only about 20 minutes of work, unless you count stirring something once every 2 minutes as work. *Serves 4*

Kosher salt

½ pound Brussels sprouts, cut into small wedges (about 8 per sprout)

3 tablespoons olive oil

4 chicken thighs, bone in, skin on

Freshly ground black pepper

1½ cups chicken stock (see page 22)

¼ cup minced yellow onion

¼ cup minced fennel bulb

½ cup pearl barley

1 tablespoon unsalted butter

1 tablespoon freshly grated Parmigiano-Reggiano cheese

8 small Tokyo or hakurei turnips, with a couple of green turnip leaves

1 teaspoon freshly squeezed lemon juice

1 Preheat the oven to 375°F.

2 Place a medium pot of water on the stove and bring to a boil. Prepare an ice water bath and set it near the stove.

3 Add enough kosher salt to the boiling water to make it taste pleasantly salty. Then add the Brussels sprouts and cook for 1 minute. Remove the sprouts from the boiling water and shock them in the waiting bowl of ice water. When they are chilled, remove from the water and set aside.

4 Place a medium ovenproof sauté pan over medium heat and add 1 tablespoon of the olive oil. Season the thighs all over with kosher salt and black pepper. Add the thighs to the oil, skin side down. Make sure there is space between them and that the heat is not too high. Slowly crisp and render the chicken skin, cooking it for about 15 minutes. Remember not to touch the thighs; just let the skin crisp and the fat render.

5 While the chicken is crisping, start the risotto: Combine 1 cup of water and the chicken stock in a small pot and set the pot on a back burner on low heat. Take a heavy 3-quart pot, place it over medium heat, and add 1 tablespoon of the olive oil. When the oil is hot, add the onion and fennel and cook for 3 minutes, until softened. Add the barley, stir and toast for 1 minute, and then slowly add about 1 cup of the stock mixture. Cook, stirring often with a wooden spoon, until the barley begins to look a little dry; then add more stock. Repeat, gradually adding the remaining stock mixture. Risotto likes moisture but doesn't want to be drowned.

6 When the chicken skin is very crisp, turn the thighs over and place the pan in the oven. Roast for about 10 minutes, until cooked through.

7 Slowly but surely you will have cooked the stock into the barley. After 20 or 25 minutes you will be just about finished. The barley should be tender but still a touch toothsome at this point. Season with kosher salt to taste, and add the butter, Parmigiano-Reggiano, and reserved blanched Brussels sprouts. Stir well, partially cover, and set aside on the stovetop, but removed from the heat, to keep warm.

8 Remove the chicken from the oven and let it rest for about 5 minutes.

9 Meanwhile, slice the turnips into thin disks and place them in a bowl. Season the turnips with the remaining tablespoon of olive oil and the lemon juice. Chop up the turnip greens and add them to the bowl. Toss well.

10 Arrange the barley risotto on a small platter and top it with the chicken thighs and the turnips. Eat.

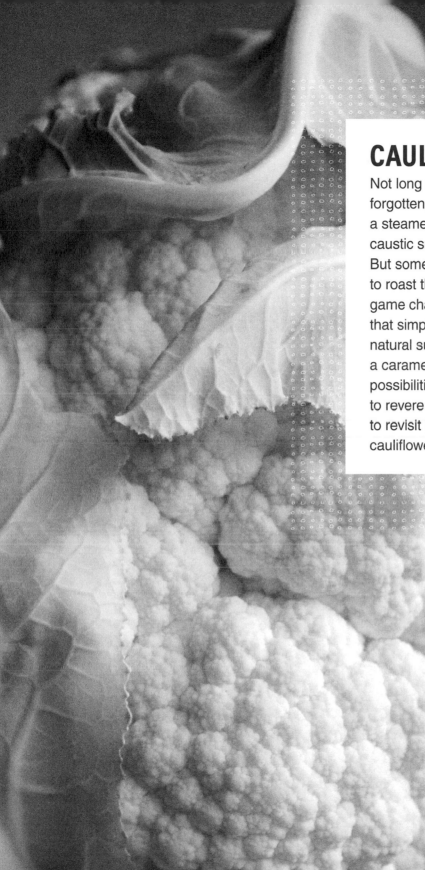

CAULIFLOWER

Not long ago cauliflower was neglected and forgotten, a sad part of the crudité platter, a steamed side lacking flavor and vigor, a caustic smell more than a beautiful offering. But sometime, somewhere, a chef decided to roast the fractal delight and the whole game changed. The new approach took that simple head of florets and brought the natural sugars to the forefront, highlighting a caramelized goodness and showing new possibilities. Sometimes that's all it takes to revere something again. So here we are to revisit all the wonderful ways to cook cauliflower.

CAULIFLOWER GRATIN

CARAMELIZED CAULIFLOWER WITH RADISH, NASTURTIUM, MINT, AND CITRUS VINAIGRETTE

CAULIFLOWER GRATIN

The French are onto something and it's not just the full month of vacation they get every year. They also have a penchant for taking full-flavored vegetables, enriching them with cream, and browning them in the oven. This is one of those times when you confit the duck, crisp the Brussels, gratin the cauliflower, and open a bottle of Cornas. Then you murmur sweet nothings in French and eat with aplomb. *Serves 4 to 6 as a side*

2 cups heavy cream
2 garlic cloves
Kosher salt
Freshly ground black pepper
1 tablespoon olive oil

1 head cauliflower, cut into florets
1 cup fresh bread crumbs, toasted
2 ounces Parmigiano-Reggiano cheese, grated (about ⅓ cup)

1 Pour the cream into a small saucepan, add the garlic cloves, and cook over medium heat until reduced by half, about 10 minutes. While it is cooking, keep a close eye on it and use a rubber spatula to scrape the sides of the pan to prevent the cream from burning. Season the cream mixture with kosher salt and black pepper to taste.

2 Preheat the oven to 425°F.

3 In a large sauté pan set over high heat, heat the olive oil and bring it to a light smoke. Add the cauliflower and caramelize it on one side for 5 minutes. Season with a little kosher salt. Remove the pan from the heat and add the garlic-cream mixture. Scatter the bread crumbs on top, season with kosher salt and black pepper, and toss.

4 Place the mixture in a medium casserole dish and bake for 20 minutes. Remove from the oven, sprinkle the Parmigiano-Reggiano on top of the cauliflower, and bake for 10 more minutes, until browned and bubbly.

CARAMELIZED CAULIFLOWER WITH RADISH, NASTURTIUM, MINT, AND CITRUS VINAIGRETTE

This is a salad or a side, but maybe it's more than that. It takes earthy cauliflower and marries it with the peppery taste of nasturtium, the crispness of radish, and the vivacity of mint. *Serves 4 as an appetizer or a side*

1 tablespoon freshly squeezed orange juice
½ teaspoon grated orange zest
1 tablespoon freshly squeezed lime juice
½ teaspoon ground sumac
Kosher salt

4 tablespoons olive oil
2 cups small cauliflower florets
½ cup thinly sliced radishes
¼ cup fresh mint leaves
1 cup nasturtium flowers and leaves
Freshly ground black pepper

1 First, make the vinaigrette: Combine the orange juice, zest, lime juice, sumac, and ¼ teaspoon kosher salt in a small bowl. Whisk in 3 tablespoons of the olive oil and set aside.

2 Place the remaining tablespoon of olive oil in a large cast-iron pan and heat it over medium-high heat until it comes to a light smoke. Add the cauliflower florets and cook for 3 minutes, until they are a little brown and caramelized but still have some crunch to them. Remove the pan from the heat, add the radishes, mint, and nasturtium flowers and leaves, and toss well. Add half of the vinaigrette. Season with kosher salt and black pepper to taste.

3 Divide the cauliflower mixture among individual plates, and douse with some of the remaining vinaigrette. If you don't use all the vinaigrette, it will stay fresh in the fridge for a week.

LEEK AND CAULIFLOWER PUREE

This is a simple side that will marry with so many things—like scallops, roasted chicken, duck . . . Really, the possibilities are endless. *Serves 4 to 6 as a side*

2 medium leeks, dark green parts removed

2 tablespoons unsalted butter

Kosher salt

1 head cauliflower (about 1¾ pounds)

2 garlic cloves, coarsely chopped

2½ cups chicken stock (see page 22), plus more if needed

1 Slice the leeks lengthwise, and then into half-moons. Wash them thoroughly and drain.

2 Melt the butter in a large saucepan over medium-low heat. Add the leeks and season with 1 teaspoon kosher salt. Slowly cook the leeks for about 15 minutes, stirring often to avoid caramelization.

3 While the leeks are cooking, core and cut the cauliflower into 1-inch pieces.

4 Add the garlic and the cauliflower to the leeks and continue to cook for 5 minutes. Add the chicken stock, raise the heat to high, and bring the liquid to a boil. Reduce the heat to medium-low and simmer, covered, until the cauliflower is cooked all the way through, about 15 minutes.

5 Place all the contents of the pot into a blender and puree on high speed. If needed, add more chicken stock to thin the puree. The consistency should be slightly looser than polenta. Season with kosher salt to taste, and serve.

ROASTED ROMANESCO CAULIFLOWER WITH RAISINS, VIN COTTO, CAPERS, AND PARSLEY

I adore the beauty of Romanesco, with its spiral heads and lime green color. This dish marries sweetness, acidity, and salinity in a perfect gustatory three-way. *Serves 4 as a side*

2 small heads Romanesco cauliflower, cut into florets

3 tablespoons olive oil

Sea salt

¼ cup raisins

2 tablespoons Vin Cotto (recipe follows)

1 tablespoon capers

2 tablespoons finely chopped fresh flat-leaf parsley leaves

Juice of 1 lemon

1 Preheat the oven to 400°F.

2 In a bowl, toss the Romanesco with the oil and a few generous pinches of sea salt. Spread it out on a baking sheet and roast in the oven for 15 minutes, or until it's dark brown around the edges. Place the roasted florets in a mixing bowl and toss with the raisins, vin cotto, capers, and parsley. Add lemon juice to taste. Serve.

VIN COTTO

Vin cotto is a spiced cooked wine, and though you can buy it at a specialty Italian food shop, it is really easy to make.
Makes 1 cup

2 cups good Chianti

½ cup sorghum syrup or honey

1 tablespoon balsamic vinegar

1 cinnamon stick

4 whole cloves

¼ teaspoon ground mace

¼ teaspoon ground nutmeg

Combine the wine, sorghum, vinegar, cinnamon stick, cloves, mace, and nutmeg in a small pot and cook over medium heat until reduced to 1 cup of liquid, about 10 minutes. Stir occasionally so the sorghum doesn't burn. Strain the vin cotto into a clean mason jar and store it in the fridge for up to 1 month.

ROASTED ROMANESCO
CAULIFLOWER WITH
RAISINS, VIN COTTO,
CAPERS, AND PARSLEY

COLLARD & MUSTARD GREENS

Collards are a hearty, vitamin-rich green with a long history and tradition in the South. Mustard greens are their spicy brethren; they don't take as long to cook and pack a wallop of pungent heat when raw. Both should be staples on your table, as they are inexpensive, nutritious, abundant, and tasty.

SEARED SCALLOPS WITH CREAMED MUSTARD GREENS AND MUSTARD

Find a great fishmonger from whom to buy scallops. You just have to demand the best for something so perishable. Scallops are kind of like the sales contest in *Glengarry Glen Ross*, where the top prize is a Cadillac, the second prize is a steak knife set, and the third is that you get fired. Second place won't do when it comes to scallop quality—only the best will wow the palate. Look for scallops that smell fresh like the ocean and are pretty dry to the touch, not slimy at all. *Serves 4*

Kosher salt	Freshly ground black pepper
1 pound young mustard greens, chopped	1 pound (U12 size) dry-packed sea scallops (12 scallops would be perfect; make sure they are preservative free)
2 tablespoons unsalted butter	
½ cup minced sweet onion	2 tablespoons olive oil
½ cup heavy cream	2 teaspoons Dijon mustard
¼ teaspoon finely grated nutmeg	

1 Prepare an ice water bath. Bring a large pot of water to a vigorous boil and add enough salt to taste pleasantly salty. Add the mustard greens, in batches, cooking each batch for 1 minute. As soon as they are blanched, remove the greens with a slotted spoon and submerge them in the ice water. Drain the greens, squeeze the excess water out of them, and set aside.

2 In a medium sauté pan, melt 1 tablespoon of the butter over medium-high heat. Add the onion and cook until quite limp, and then let it brown, about 7 minutes in all. Add the cream and cook down for 5 minutes, or until the cream is quite thick. Season with the nutmeg and add the mustard greens. Stir well, heat through, season to taste with salt and pepper, and set aside in a warm place.

3 Pat the scallops dry and season them with kosher salt. Place a large sauté pan on high heat and add the oil. When the oil is shimmering, place the scallops in the hot pan and sear them on one side for 3 minutes, until they are nicely browned. Add the remaining tablespoon of butter, and when it has melted, spoon the butter over the scallops to baste them. Turn the scallops over and cook for another 2 to 3 minutes, until just cooked. Remove the scallops from the pan and set them aside to rest for a couple of minutes.

4 Spoon ½ teaspoon of the mustard on each of 4 plates. Spread the mustard out with the back of a spoon, and arrange the creamed mustard greens on top of the mustard. Top the greens with the scallops and serve immediately.

VEGETARIAN COLLARD GREENS

I get asked a lot whether collards can be made vegetarian. Sure they can! The traditional ham hock and chicken stock can be taken away, but you still need a little sweet and sour to complete the flavors that people expect when you say "collards." This recipe solves that with aplomb. *Serves 4 as a side*

1 pound trimmed collard greens (weighed after the ribs have been removed)	2 yellow onions, cut into small dice
	Kosher salt
2 garlic cloves, thinly shaved	1 tablespoon honey
1 tablespoon unsalted butter	2 tablespoons cider vinegar

1 Stack the collard greens on top of each other, roll them up, and slice the roll into ½-inch-wide strips. Submerge the greens in a bowl of cold water and then lift them out into a colander. Drain for a couple of minutes and then dry on paper towels.

2 In a large saucepan, slowly sweat the garlic in the butter over medium-low heat.

3 When the garlic is very aromatic, add the onions. Season the onions with kosher salt, and sweat for 15 minutes, until translucent and soft.

4 Raise the heat to medium, add the collard greens and cook for 10 minutes, stirring occasionally. Stir in the honey and vinegar, and cook for 10 more minutes, or until the collards are tender but still have some chew. Adjust the seasoning with more kosher salt, honey, or vinegar, if needed, and serve.

SEARED
SCALLOPS
WITH CREAMED
MUSTARD
GREENS AND
MUSTARD

VEGETARIAN
COLLARD
GREENS

TURKEY, ANDOUILLE,
SHRIMP, AND COLLARD
GREENS GUMBO

KIMCHI CREAMED COLLARD GREENS

Collards really cook down a lot, so don't be fooled into buying some puny little bunch. I like my collards on the smaller, younger side of life. (The younger the collards, the shorter the cooking time.) The addition of kimchi gives the classic creamed greens an umami bite that I adore. *Serves 6 to 8 as a side*

3 tablespoons olive oil

1 large yellow onion, minced

½ pound slab bacon, minced

2 pounds collard greens, trimmed and torn into bite-size pieces

¼ cup sherry vinegar

1 tablespoon sorghum or maple syrup

2 cups chicken stock (see page 22)

Kosher salt

1 cup heavy cream

1 cup finely chopped Classic Cabbage Kimchi (page 200)

1 Place a large pot over medium heat and add the olive oil. Add the onion and sauté until it has some color. Add the bacon and cook for 10 minutes, or until fully rendered.

2 Add the collards and sauté until a bit limp, 4 to 5 minutes. Add the vinegar and cook down until almost dry. Add the sorghum, stock, 2 cups of water, and kosher salt to taste. Simmer, covered, for about 45 minutes, until the collards are tender.

3 While the collards are cooking, get the kimchi cream ready to roll: In a small saucepan, cook the cream over medium heat, watching it closely, until it has reduced by one-third, 4 to 5 minutes. Add the chopped kimchi.

4 When the collards are tender, stir the kimchi cream into the greens and cook to marry the flavors, about 10 minutes. Serve.

TURKEY, ANDOUILLE, SHRIMP, AND COLLARD GREENS GUMBO

I adore gumbo, but cooking it opens the door to all sorts of criticism. The roux experts suddenly line up to judge the color of your base, the richness of the broth, the complexity of the end product. Just make it how you want, because the thing about gumbo is that everybody makes it a little different. So just make it. Get the rice cooking and the finishing flourish of filé ready. Roux your world. *Serves 8*

1 pound boneless turkey breast

1 pound turkey drumsticks

Kosher salt

2 tablespoons peanut oil

½ pound Andouille sausage, cut into large dice

¼ pound (1 stick) unsalted butter

¾ cup all-purpose flour

½ cup medium-diced sweet onion

½ cup medium-diced red bell pepper

½ cup medium-diced fennel bulb

½ medium turnip, cut into medium dice

½ cup medium-diced celery

2 bunches collard greens, stacked, rolled up, and sliced into 1-inch-wide strips

2 quarts chicken stock (see page 22)

1 pound small shrimp, peeled and deveined

2 teaspoons Worcestershire sauce

1 teaspoon cayenne pepper

1 teaspoon freshly cracked black pepper

2 teaspoons gumbo filé powder

4 cups cooked rice, for serving

1 Season the turkey breast and drumsticks with 1 teaspoon kosher salt. Heat a large, heavy-bottomed pot over medium-high heat. Add the peanut oil, and when it comes to a light smoke, add the turkey breast, skin side down. Sear until the skin is golden brown and crisp, about 4 minutes. Turn it over and brown the other side, another 4 minutes. Place the breast on a paper-towel-lined baking sheet and set it aside.

2 Repeat the same process with the drumsticks, adding more oil, if needed.

3 Keep the pot on the heat and add the diced Andouille sausage. Brown the sausage, 4 to 5 minutes, and transfer it to a paper-towel-lined plate. Reduce the heat to medium-low and add the butter. Once the butter has melted, add the flour to make the roux: Using a wooden spoon, constantly stir the mixture, making sure not to burn the butter, until the roux is an even, nutty brown, the color of lightly roasted coffee. This process will take up to

30 minutes. Be patient and it will pay off. Be careful—it is extremely hot.

4 Once the roux is richly browned, add the onion, bell pepper, fennel, turnip, and celery. Slowly cook the vegetables until they become translucent, roughly 10 minutes. Season with 1 teaspoon kosher salt. Add the collard greens and cook for another 5 minutes. Add the chicken stock and raise the heat to bring the liquid to a boil. Make sure that you are constantly stirring so that there is no sticking. Once the liquid has reached a boil, reduce the heat to a simmer.

5 Cut the turkey meat into a large dice and add it to the gumbo. Simmer until the turkey is tender, about 1 hour.

6 Add the shrimp, Worcestershire, cayenne, and black pepper. Cook until the shrimp are just cooked through, just 2 to 3 minutes. Pull the pot off the heat, add the filé powder, stir well to combine, adjust the seasoning with more kosher salt if necessary, and serve with a ½ cup scoop of cooked rice per person.

ROUX

As I learned my craft I was taught a very important lesson by my chef in Hull, Quebec, at a seminal restaurant called Henri Burger. There were no burgers and no shortcuts at Henri Burger. It was a fancy French joint, with everything made from scratch at a time when most fine-dining restaurants were using soup bases and powdered stocks. For some reason we were always steered away from thickening with roux, that doing so was a simply a shortcut to actually reducing and concentrating flavors.

For years I avoided roux. It wasn't until living in the South for years that I actually even thought about making a gumbo. And that's when I realized the beauty of a roux.

You see, what I didn't like about the flour thickener was the flour taste, chalky and dusty, maligning the purity of whatever I was making. But it turns out that I just wasn't cooking the roux long enough, wasn't giving it a chance to develop the flavor that is so important to a gumbo. I wouldn't say I am fully sold on the place of roux in many foods, but I sure am sold on using it to make a classic gumbo. You have to be patient with roux, and when you cook it right, it is the opposite of a shortcut. It takes precision in temperature, a lot of time, and a wooden spoon to achieve that dark mahogany color that gives a gumbo its charm.

Whether it is oil or butter, the ratio is about the same: One part flour to one part fat, cooked over low or medium heat, stirring constantly. The time is the key to showing roux's wide spectrum of flavor. In 15 minutes you will have a blond roux; with 30 you will have an amber to mahogany; and with 45 minutes you will have a fully dark roux. (This is the one time in cooking where you *shouldn't* taste as you go, lest you'd like to cook your mouth.) If you make too much, it freezes well, so use your time wisely and make twice as much as you need.

ENDIVES, CHICORIES & RADICCHIOS

Bitterness in food is becoming more beloved than before, and I hope this continues. I see Treviso at the store now. We sell more endive salads than ever before. This is a good trend to see because when you really immerse yourself in the bitter greens family, you realize that they are pretty darned addictive. I can eat a whole head of frisée all by my lonesome, but I don't want to be lonesome.

BITTER GREENS SALAD WITH CRAB, APPLE, AND PISTACHIOS

This appetizer takes just five minutes to put together and is a great late winter starter. I love bitter greens with the richness of crab. The yogurt lightens it all up, too. *Serves 4 as an appetizer*

½ pound blue crabmeat, picked over for cartilage and shells

1 teaspoon whole-grain mustard

1 teaspoon freshly squeezed lemon juice

3 tablespoons plain Greek yogurt

Kosher salt

2 tablespoons shelled unsalted pistachios, chopped

2 cups chopped Treviso or other variety of radicchio

1 cup arugula leaves

1 tablespoon olive oil

1 teaspoon red wine vinegar

1 crisp apple

1 In a small bowl, combine the crab, mustard, lemon juice, yogurt, and a couple pinches of kosher salt. Stir delicately to avoid breaking up the crab too much. Set aside while you build the rest of the salad.

2 In a medium bowl, combine the pistachios, Treviso, arugula, olive oil, and red wine vinegar. Cut the apple into very thin slices and add them to the salad. Season with a pinch of kosher salt and toss well.

3 Divide the crab evenly among 4 plates. Top with equal amounts of the salad and serve.

WARM FRISÉE WITH HOT PICKLE–MISO VINAIGRETTE, CAULIFLOWER, AND SEAWEED

The food I love to cook keeps showing more influences from around the world, because the world is becoming a wonderfully small place. This dish is dotted with influences from Japan, with the miso, seaweed, and sesame. It's a great warm salad. *Serves 4 to 6 as an appetizer or a side*

3 ounces dried wakame seaweed

½ small to medium cauliflower

1 teaspoon peanut oil

Kosher salt

3 heads frisée lettuce

¼ cup Hot Pickle–Miso Vinaigrette (recipe follows)

1 tablespoon toasted sesame seeds

1 Using kitchen scissors, cut the dried seaweed into inch-long pieces. Soak the pieces in cold water for 20 minutes; then drain, rinse vigorously, and soak for another 20 minutes.

2 Meanwhile, preheat the oven to 425°F.

3 Cut the cauliflower into small bite-size florets. In a bowl, toss the florets with the peanut oil and kosher salt to taste. Spread them out on a baking sheet and roast in the oven for 10 minutes, or until the edges are golden brown. Remove the baking sheet and set it aside to cool to room temperature.

4 Prepare a bowl of ice water. Remove the stem ends of the frisée, and submerge the greens in the ice water to wash them. Remove the greens from the water and dry thoroughly on paper towels.

5 In a small saucepan, warm the pickle-miso vinaigrette over medium-low heat. When you heat an emulsification, it will break, and that's fine here. Drain the wakame and pat it dry. In a mixing bowl, dress the frisée and wakame with a pinch of kosher salt and the hot vinaigrette.

6 Arrange the greens on plates, top with the reserved cauliflower, and sprinkle with the sesame seeds.

HOT PICKLE–MISO VINAIGRETTE
Makes 1 pint

3 spicy dill pickles

1 shallot

1 teaspoon Dijon mustard

1 tablespoon white miso

¼ cup rice vinegar

¾ cup peanut oil

1 Finely dice the spicy pickles and the shallot.

2 In a small mixing bowl, combine the mustard and miso and whisk until smooth. Continue whisking while you add the vinegar, then slowly drizzle in the peanut oil. Stir in the pickles and shallots. Will keep, refrigerated, for a couple of weeks.

HOT-SMOKED TROUT,
SHALLOT, AND FRISÉE
WITH BUTTERMILK
DRESSING

HOT-SMOKED TROUT, SHALLOT, AND FRISÉE WITH BUTTERMILK DRESSING

Hot-smoking is putting food over direct heat and smoke. Cold-smoking is smoldering the wood in a box and funneling that smoke into a separate box, where it smokes the food without adding heat. Both are wonderful, but hot-smoking is more achievable for the home. This brief cure and hot smoke are a great way to eat some beautiful river trout. *Serves 4*

6 shallots, cut into ¼-inch-thick slices	¼ cup sugar
½ cup red wine vinegar	1 teaspoon ground white pepper
½ cup dry red wine	1 teaspoon grated lemon zest
1 teaspoon kosher salt	1 teaspoon grated lime zest
1 bay leaf	1 teaspoon grated orange zest
4 rainbow trout fillets (5 to 6 ounces each), skin on	2 heads of frisée, trimmed and cut into bite-size pieces
½ cup sea salt, plus more to taste	¼ cup Buttermilk Dressing (page 28)

1 Place the shallots in a heatproof bowl.

2 In a small saucepan, combine the vinegar, wine, ½ cup of water, the kosher salt, and the bay leaf. Bring the mixture to a boil, remove from the heat, and carefully pour over the sliced shallots. Set aside in the refrigerator to chill.

3 Clean the trout of any connective tissue or fat. Remove the pin bones from the fillets with small needle-nose pliers. In a mixing bowl, combine the sea salt, sugar, and white pepper. Add the lemon, lime, and orange zests, and mix the ingredients until completely incorporated. Spread an even layer of about half of this salt cure mix on a rimmed baking sheet, and arrange the trout fillets in a row on top. Add the remaining cure mix to the tops of the fillets to completely cover the fish. Allow the fish to cure for 1 hour at room temperature.

4 About 30 minutes into the curing process, prepare a fire on a charcoal grill outside. I use pecan wood and a Weber grill. Light four small pieces (about 6 × 3 × 3 inches) of hickory wood on the fire and let them burn for about 30 minutes so the heat subsides and they fully burn to a charcoal black. Install the grill grate, and place a brick on the grate to elevate your trout away from the heat. Wash the fish under cold water, and press the fillets dry between paper towels. Place the dry fish, skin side down, on a roasting rack. Place the rack of trout on the brick and cover the grill, closing the top vent. Hot-smoke the fish for 4 minutes, until just cooked, and then remove it from the heat and let it cool a bit before placing it in the fridge. Once the fish is cold, peel off the skin and carefully flake the fish into bite-size pieces.

5 In a mixing bowl, lightly dress the frisée with the buttermilk dressing and season with sea salt. Place the frisée greens on individual plates, and arrange the pickled shallots and smoked trout on the salad.

NEW YORK STRIP WITH ONION SOUBISE AND SUGARLOAF ENDIVE

Soubise is a thick pureed onion sauce that just makes me happy. Sugarloaf endive makes me even happier. It is probably my favorite green. It can be eaten raw in a bitter salad or quickly cooked as a side. Here it shows off with a great steak. If you can't find Sugarloaf endive, you can use Belgian endive in its place. *Serves 4*

Two 12-ounce New York strip steaks	1 sprig fresh thyme
Sea salt	¼ teaspoon ground white pepper
½ teaspoon fennel seeds, toasted and ground	1 tablespoon olive oil
5½ tablespoons unsalted butter	2 cups chopped Sugarloaf endive
1 yellow onion, diced	1 tablespoon chicken stock (see page 22)
1 teaspoon kosher salt	¼ teaspoon crushed red pepper flakes
2 tablespoons rice (Carolina Gold, if possible)	1 teaspoon freshly squeezed lemon juice
¾ cup heavy cream	

1 Season the steaks all over with sea salt and the ground fennel seeds. Let them sit at room temperature until the salt is dissolved.

2 In a medium saucepan, melt 2 tablespoons of the butter over medium-low heat. Add the onion and the salt and cook slowly for 20 minutes, stirring to make sure not to get any color. Add the rice and continue to cook for 5 minutes. Add the cream and the thyme sprig. Continue to cook until the rice is cooked all the way through, about

NEW YORK STRIP WITH ONION SOUBISE AND SUGARLOAF ENDIVE

15 minutes. Season with the white pepper and remove the thyme sprig. Place the onion-rice mixture in a blender and puree until completely smooth. Reserve in a covered container (to prevent a skin from developing on top).

3 Divide the olive oil in 2 large cast-iron sauté pans and heat over high heat. Pat the steaks dry. Once the oil comes to a light smoke, add the steaks, reduce the heat to medium-high, and cook for 3 minutes. Add 1 tablespoon of the butter to each pan and baste the steaks for 1 minute. Turn the steaks and continue to cook for 4 minutes, basting occasionally. Take the steaks out of the pans and let them rest for 5 minutes on a paper-towel-lined baking sheet.

4 In another sauté pan, melt the remaining 1½ table-spoons butter over high heat. When the butter begins to froth, add the endive. Season with sea salt to taste, and quickly sauté the endive for about 1 minute. Add the chicken stock, red pepper flakes, and lemon juice to glaze the endive. Remove from the heat and get those plates out.

5 Cut the steaks into neat slices, against the grain. Place a small dollop of the onion soubise on each plate and gently smear it to cover one-quarter of the plate. Place the sautéed endive to the side, and fan out the steak next to the greens, somewhat covering the soubise.

KALE

Kale was once considered a decorative winter plant and now it propels us to make smoothies! I love kale because it doesn't seem like a food I need to eat for my health, rather a food I want to eat because it tastes awesome. Green, fibrous, and fulfilling are attributes that I like in food, and kale brings that all together. But to all the naysayers, I give you four varieties that will make you love kale: Red Russian, Lacinato, Redbor, and Beira. Buy some of these, or some seeds, and you'll see that I was right.

SAUTÉED FLOWERING KALE WITH GARLIC AND LEMON

You know how we just let the garden run ragged once in a while 'cause we get bogged down in those things we call work, family, and "other than homesteading" activities? Well, kale is one of those things that is actually great when it's cooked whole, flowers and all. It's also absolutely beautiful and has become a bit of a staple on finer restaurant menus, which means more availability in your CSA box or at your market, should you not have access to a garden of kale gone to bolt.

Serves 4 as a side

1 tablespoon olive oil

1 garlic clove, very finely sliced

1 pound flowering kale, roughly chopped

¼ cup chicken stock (see page 22)

1 tablespoon unsalted butter

Kosher salt

½ lemon, for juicing

Place a large sauté pan on medium-high heat, and when it gets hot, add the olive oil. When the oil shimmers, add the garlic and cook for about 15 seconds, until aromatic. Then add the kale and stir it around to wilt it down some, cooking for about 3 minutes. Add the stock, and when the liquid is reduced by half, add the butter and stir it vigorously to gloss the kale. Season to taste with kosher salt, and finish with a squeeze of lemon juice. Serve immediately.

IS THERE REALLY A BACKLASH AGAINST KALE?

We fought so hard. We finally get a wave to ride and that wave was the salad. It was a heady time with people getting all healthy and vitamins being dosed around, not as additives to chocolate milk but naturally occurring in a food. Now you call it over and call for its demise? I don't get it.

Was kale salad really just "last year's trend"? This isn't a Kale Patch Doll or a Talking Elmo; this is a real vegetable. We listen to the lament about people needing to eat better. We encourage them to do so and then have an inkling of success and some people call it yesterday's fad. We have to fight for the goodness. We have to fight for kale. I can deal with a backlash against the kale chips and the kale bumper stickers, but keep your paws off of my salad. I worked too hard to get people eating more vegetables to have you malign it. You hear me? You can have my kale when you pry it from my cold, dead salad bowl.

KALE SALAD WITH CRISP SHALLOTS AND CAPER DRESSING

Yes, kale salad. Do not run away from this. It is too good for you to be rash. You eat it and then tell me what you think. Then eat it again, 'cause you will.

Serves 2

1 cup peanut oil
2 shallots, sliced into thin rings
½ cup Wondra flour
Kosher salt, to taste

12 leaves Lacinato kale, cut into bite-size pieces
½ cup Caper Dressing (recipe follows)
2 ounces Parmigiano-Reggiano shaved into thin slices

1 Pour the peanut oil into a small saucepan and place it over medium-high heat. Using a deep-fry thermometer, monitor the temperature. You want it to reach 350°F.

2 Meanwhile, in a small bowl, dredge the shallot slices in the flour. Shake off the excess flour.

3 Once the peanut oil has reached 350°F, fry the shallots until they are golden brown, about 2 minutes. Remove the shallots with a slotted spoon, and let them drain on paper towels. Season the fried shallots with a few pinches of kosher salt.

4 In a mixing bowl, dress the kale with half the caper dressing. Spoon some more dressing on the bottom of a large serving platter. Arrange the dressed kale on the platter and top with the shaved Parmigiano-Reggiano and fried shallots.

CAPER DRESSING

Makes ¾ cup

1 egg yolk
1 teaspoon Dijon mustard
1 tablespoon freshly squeezed lemon juice
½ teaspoon kosher salt

½ cup peanut oil
1 tablespoon cider vinegar
1 tablespoon capers, chopped
½ teaspoon grated lemon zest

1 In a blender combine the egg yolk, mustard, lemon juice, and salt. Blend at medium speed, and with the blender running, slowly add the peanut oil to create a strong emulsion—the vinaigrette will thicken.

2 Pour the dressing into a small mixing bowl and whisk in the cider vinegar, capers, and lemon zest. Thin with 1 tablespoon of water. The dressing will keep, covered and refrigerated, for 1 week.

RED RUSSIAN KALE SALAD WITH ROASTED SWEET POTATO AND APPLE

This salad has everything I love for a hearty main-course salad. Don't fall prey to the people who insult the pedigree of a great kale salad. Kale rules. *Serves 4 as a side*

3 tablespoons olive oil

¼ pound fingerling sweet potatoes, thinly sliced

Sea salt

1 pound Red Russian kale, cut into bite-size pieces

Grated zest and juice of 1 lemon

1 apple

½ cup pecans, toasted and chopped

1 Heat 2 tablespoons of the olive oil in a large cast-iron sauté pan over high heat. Once the oil is hot but not smoking, add the sweet potatoes. Reduce the heat to medium and caramelize the potatoes for 1½ minutes per side, making sure not to burn them. Season with sea salt to taste. Transfer the potatoes to a baking sheet lined with paper towels, and reserve.

2 In a large mixing bowl, dress the kale: Beat the kale up a little bit as though you are giving it a Swedish massage. This will soften the kale and let the flavors seep in as you add sea salt to taste, the lemon zest, and lemon juice to taste, along with the remaining tablespoon of olive oil.

3 Core and slice the apple, and add it to the kale. Toss to coat with the dressing. Arrange the kale and apples on plates, and top with the sweet potatoes and the chopped pecans.

LAMB MEATBALLS WITH KALE, CUMIN YOGURT, AND RICE

Lamb meatballs appear in various forms across the Middle East. We are lucky here in the United States, where we can get great lamb from people like Craig Rogers at Border Springs Farm in Patrick Springs, Virginia, and John Jamison at his namesake Jamison Farm, in Latrobe, Pennsylvania. We also have great farms producing local and organic kale, wonderful dairies producing yogurt, and a burgeoning staple crop in the return of rice to our agrarian landscape. This is a simple dish, to be had on a colder evening. It just feels good as you break through the meatballs and scoop up the rice, the greens, the yogurt. And it tastes even better. *Serves 4*

FOR THE MEATBALLS

½ teaspoon cumin seeds

½ teaspoon fennel seeds

¼ teaspoon yellow mustard seeds

¼ teaspoon crushed red pepper flakes

¼ teaspoon coriander seeds

¼ teaspoon chile powder

3 tablespoons olive oil

1 cup minced yellow onion

2 garlic cloves, minced

½ cup cornbread crumbs or regular fresh bread crumbs

1 pound ground lamb

1 egg

Kosher salt

½ cup chicken stock (see page 22)

2 cups finely chopped Red Russian kale (or any kale will do)

FOR THE CUMIN YOGURT

½ cup plain yogurt

½ teaspoon cumin seeds, toasted and ground

1 tablespoon freshly squeezed lemon juice

Kosher salt

TO FINISH

2 cups cooked rice (I like Carolina Gold), hot

2 tablespoons pine nuts, toasted

2 tablespoons torn fresh mint leaves

8 leaves Roasted Kale (recipe follows)

1½ tablespoons finely chopped Preserved Lemon (page 172)

1 Prepare the meatballs: Combine the cumin seeds, fennel seeds, mustard seeds, red pepper flakes, and coriander seeds in a small cast-iron sauté pan. Toast over medium heat, gently shaking the pan, until just beginning to smoke. Remove from the heat, let cool, and then grind to a fine powder in a spice grinder. Mix with the chile powder and set aside.

2 Place the same pan over medium heat and add 1 tablespoon of the olive oil. When the oil is hot, add the onion and cook for 5 minutes, or until it is translucent and slightly caramelized. Add the garlic and cook for 2 more minutes. Then remove from the heat and let cool.

3 In a medium mixing bowl, combine the cooled onion and garlic, the spice mixture, the bread crumbs, and the lamb. In a small bowl, lightly whisk the egg with a few generous pinches of kosher salt. Add the egg to the lamb, mix well, and form into meatballs, slightly more than 1 ounce each, about the size of a Ping-Pong ball. You should have about 16 meatballs once you are done. Season the outside of the meatballs with kosher salt.

4 Heat the remaining 2 tablespoons olive oil in a large sauté pan over medium-high heat, and when the oil is shimmering, add the meatballs. Cook for about 3 minutes to brown them, and then gently turn the meatballs to cook on the opposite side for 3 more minutes. Add the chicken stock, the chopped kale, and some more kosher salt. Cover and cook for 4 minutes, until the meatballs are cooked through.

5 Let the meatballs rest off the heat while you prepare the cumin yogurt: In a small bowl, combine the yogurt with the ground cumin and lemon juice, and season with a pinch of kosher salt.

6 Find 4 bowls for serving, and spoon 2 tablespoons of the cumin yogurt into each one. Scoop ½ cup of the hot cooked rice on top of the yogurt. Place 4 meatballs

in each bowl, and distribute the kale and some of the cooking liquid evenly. Sprinkle each bowl with toasted pine nuts, torn fresh mint, and then with roasted kale leaves and chopped preserved lemon. Serve immediately.

ROASTED KALE LEAVES

These crisp leaves are a great garnish or a simple snack. *Serves 1 ('cause you won't want to share) as a snack*

8 long Lacinato kale leaves **¼ teaspoon kosher salt**
1 tablespoon olive oil

1 Preheat the oven to 400°F.

2 In a mixing bowl, dress the kale leaves with the olive oil and the salt. Arrange the leaves on a large baking sheet so they have space between them. Place in the oven and bake for 5 to 7 minutes, until they are lightly browned and quite crisp. Carefully move them from the sheet to a baking rack and let them cool at room temperature. Use the same day or store in an airtight container for a couple of days.

PARSNIPS

Parsnips are the lonesome pale taproot usually found hanging out with the rutabagas. What that parsnip doesn't know is that it is a versatile leader of the crisper drawer, a charismatic roaster, full of flavor and able to get along with just about anyone. Vote parsnip.

PARSNIP PUREE

Great as a base for a dish, like a roasted chicken or a hearty steak, or as a side all its own. *Serves 4 to 6 as a side*

2 tablespoons cold unsalted butter

1 small yellow onion, chopped

Kosher salt

About 3 parsnips, chopped into ½-inch pieces (2 cups)

2 cups chicken stock (see page 22)

2 tablespoons heavy cream

Juice of 1 lemon

Diced apple (optional)

Fresh thyme leaves (optional)

1 In a medium saucepan over medium heat, melt 1 tablespoon of the butter until it begins to froth and bubble, then add the onion. Reduce the heat to medium-low and slowly sweat the onion, stirring to prevent any color from developing. Add a pinch of kosher salt. Once the onion is soft, after about 5 minutes, add the parsnips and cook for 5 minutes. Then add the chicken stock and the cream. Bring to a simmer, and cook until the parsnips are soft and tender, about 20 minutes.

2 Place the contents of the pan into a blender and carefully puree on high speed. With the blender running, add the remaining tablespoon of cold butter and the lemon juice. Season with kosher salt to taste, garnish with apple and thyme, if using, and serve.

SAUTÉED PARSNIPS WITH COUNTRY HAM, PARSLEY, AND BASIL

This is a mélange, a flavor mix, a stack of edible Legos. Vegetal + salty succulence + herby crisp + herby tender.

When you cook you have to think in this way, of how things work together. This is a simple dish that will make you realize how easy it is to make great food. In a matter of minutes. Get to the stove and gittir dun. *Serves 4 as a side*

2 tablespoons olive oil

About 3 parsnips, sliced into ¼-inch-thick disks (2 cups)

Sea salt

1 tablespoon minced shallot

½ cup julienned country ham

2 tablespoons coarsely chopped fresh basil leaves

2 tablespoons fresh flat-leaf parsley leaves

1 tablespoon white balsamic vinegar

In a large sauté pan, heat the olive oil over high heat. When the oil comes to a light smoke, add the parsnips. Reduce the heat to medium-high, add a few pinches of sea salt, and cook for 5 minutes, stirring constantly to prevent burning. Add the shallot and cook for 30 seconds. Add the ham, basil, parsley, and vinegar. Stir to combine. Adjust the seasoning with more sea salt if needed, and serve.

OAT RISOTTO WITH OXTAIL, ROASTED SHALLOT, AND PARSNIPS

If you don't have a pressure cooker, you should get one. When you braise in a pressure cooker, the results are succulent and really, really tender.

Oh, and by the way, Anson Mills oats are amazing. They just taste totally different, with natural nuances of cinnamon and spice and a hearty texture. This is miles from instant oatmeal. Get some soon at AnsonMills.com. *Serves 6*

FOR THE OXTAILS

2 pounds oxtails, cut into thick joints, trimmed of excess fat

Kosher salt

2 tablespoons olive oil

1 tablespoon unsalted butter

1 medium yellow onion, cut into 1-inch pieces

2 medium carrots, cut into 1-inch lengths

1 cup coarsely chopped celery

1 head garlic, cut in half, exposing the cloves

1 bouquet garni: 1 sprig fresh marjoram, 2 sprigs fresh thyme, and 2 sprigs fresh parsley, tied into a bundle

½ cup dry red wine

3 cups chicken stock (see page 22)

FOR THE OAT RISOTTO

3 cups chicken stock (see page 22)

2 tablespoons unsalted butter

3 shallots, quartered

Kosher salt

1 tablespoon olive oil

1 leek, white and light green parts, well washed and sliced into thin half-moons

1 cup heirloom steel-cut oats

¼ cup hearty red wine

¼ cup very finely grated Parmigiano-Reggiano cheese

2 parsnips, shaved with a mandoline into paper-thin rounds

Fresh chervil (optional)

1 To cook the oxtails: Season the oxtails all over with kosher salt. Heat a large sauté pan over medium-high heat. Pour the olive oil into the pan, and when it shimmers, add the oxtail pieces. Sear for 4 minutes, until the oxtails are nicely browned, then turn and sear for another 4 minutes. Set aside.

PARSNIP
PUREE

SAUTÉED PARSNIPS
WITH COUNTRY HAM,
PARSLEY, AND BASIL

OAT RISOTTO WITH
OXTAIL, ROASTED
SHALLOT, AND PARSNIPS

2 Place a pressure cooker pot over medium heat and add the butter. When it has melted, add the onion and cook until it is translucent and soft, 5 minutes. Then add the carrots, celery, garlic, and bouquet garni. Cook for 5 minutes, and add the red wine. Reduce the liquid by half. Add the chicken stock and the seared oxtail pieces. Seal the lid of the pressure cooker, turn the heat to high, and when the pressure is built up in the pot, reduce it to medium heat and cook for 45 minutes.

3 Cool the pressure cooker by running it under cold water until the steam lock disengages. Open the lid and transfer the oxtails to a dish to cool. Strain the braising liquid, discarding the solids. Pour the braising liquid into a small pot, place it over medium heat, and reduce to 1 cup. Set aside.

4 When the oxtails are cool enough to handle, pick off the meat, discarding the bones and cartilage. Set aside the oxtail meat, covered.

5 To make the oat risotto, preheat the oven to 400°F.

6 Combine the chicken stock and the reserved oxtail braising liquid in a saucepan, and place on a back burner on low heat. (Risotto likes to be made with warm stock.)

7 Place a small ovenproof sauté pan over medium heat and add 1 tablespoon of the butter. Place the quartered shallots in the pan and cook for 5 minutes without disturbing to caramelize. Toss, then transfer the pan to the oven and finish cooking the shallots, 15 minutes. When they are soft, remove the pan, season the shallots with kosher salt, and set them aside.

8 Heat a large sauté pan over medium heat, add the olive oil, and then add the leek. Cook for 5 minutes, until very aromatic. Then add the oats, and stir well with a wooden spoon to fully enrobe the oats in the leeks and oil. Deglaze the pan with the red wine, and cook the wine down to just about dry. Then gradually add the chicken stock, about 1 cup at a time, adding it when the oats have fully absorbed the last addition, stirring all the while with a wooden spoon. The oats will take about 20 minutes from start to finish, so get used to the rhythm of stirring and slowly adding stock. Season with kosher salt as the oats are cooking.

9 When the oats are tender with a little bite still to them, finish the risotto with the remaining tablespoon of butter and half of the Parmigiano-Reggiano cheese. Fold in the oxtail meat and the shallots, and garnish with the remaining cheese, parsnips, and chervil, if using.

SALSIFY

Salsify is like the black swan of cooking. It looks menacingly earthy, but when you clean it up and peel away the exterior, it is angelically pale, harboring a clean, creamy oyster flavor that comes out in stews or when sautéed. But why stop there when you can also fry, blanch, or shave it into salads?

FRIED SALSIFY

If you fry it, they will eat it. Crunch means a lot in the world of food, and this is no exception. Salsify just revels in a simple frying process, with very little work or adornment. This should be the new snack for the kids. *Serves 2 to 4 as a snack*

4 stalks salsify

4 cups neutral vegetable oil

Fine sea salt, to taste

1 Peel the salsify thoroughly with a vegetable peeler, and cut off ½ inch at both the top and the bottom. Then, with a clean peeler, shave lengths of the salsify by running the peeler down the stalk. Place the long shavings into a bowl of cold water as you work. Once you are done prepping, let's get the fryer set up.

2 Pour the oil into a deep cast-iron pan or a tall saucepan, and bring it to 350°F over medium-high heat.

3 As the oil heats, drain the salsify shavings and pat them completely dry with paper towels.

4 Carefully add the salsify, in batches, to the fryer and cook for 30 to 45 seconds, until they are crisp and golden brown. Remove with a slotted spoon and place on a bed of paper towels. Season with fine sea salt while still hot.

5 If you want to keep the fried salsify crisp, let it cool to room temperature, place it in a sealable container, add a small pouch of food-grade silica (those little pouches that read DO NOT EAT), and seal the container. (You can buy food-grade silica packs online or just save them from the packs of toasted seaweed, as I do.) Store at room temperature.

SALSIFY AND OYSTER STEW WITH TOAST

Salsify and oysters are made for each other. This is an ode to the classic oyster stew, simple and clean with beautiful flavors that just make sense. It's great for a crowd, too, so feel free to double it up. This recipe calls for merkén, a specialty type of Chilean chile powder that is a little hard to find but is worth it if you can find it. If you can't, just use regular chile powder. *Serves 4*

2 to 3 stalks salsify

Distilled white vinegar or freshly squeezed lemon juice (optional)

1 teaspoon olive oil

2 ounces slab bacon, cut into thin strips

¾ cup thinly sliced leek, white and light green parts

1 garlic clove, minced

1 sprig fresh thyme

¼ cup dry white wine

¼ teaspoon merkén or regular chile powder

¼ teaspoon ground ginger

¼ teaspoon chile threads (see page 103; optional)

1 cup chicken stock (see page 22)

20 oysters, shucked, liquor reserved

½ cup heavy cream

2 tablespoons crème fraîche

Kosher salt

Freshly ground black pepper

¼ cup coarsely chopped fresh flat-leaf parsley leaves

2 slices white sourdough bread, toasted

1 Peel and thinly slice the salsify, reserving the slices in a bowl of cool water, preferably with a few drops of vinegar or lemon juice added.

2 Place a 2-quart saucepan over medium-high heat, and add the olive oil and bacon. Cook the bacon for about 4 minutes, until just beginning to crisp. Add the leeks and cook for 3 minutes, until soft. Drain the salsify and add it, along with the garlic and thyme sprig, and stir well. Add the wine and deglaze the pan, stirring vigorously with a wooden spoon to loosen all the particles from the bottom. Cook the wine down for about 2 minutes, until it has reduced by half. Add the merkén, ginger, and chile threads, if using, to the pot. Then add the chicken stock and ½ cup of the reserved oyster liquor (add more chicken stock if you don't have much oyster liquor). Reduce the heat to medium and cook for 5 minutes. Stir in the cream and the crème fraîche, and cook for 5 more minutes.

3 Your base is done, and now you just need to poach the oysters in the broth and season the stew: Add the oysters to the pot and reduce the heat to low. Cook for about 4 minutes, until just cooked through, and then season with kosher salt and black pepper to taste. Remove the thyme sprig and stir in the parsley.

4 Serve in bowls, with half a piece of toast tucked into each serving.

FRIED SALSIFY

SALSIFY AND OYSTER
STEW WITH TOAST

COUNTRY HAM WITH
CURED EGG YOLK,
ROASTED SALSIFY,
AND ARUGULA

PEARL BARLEY, SALSIFY, AND SWEET POTATO STEW

This is really what the future of food has in store. Good grains and healthy tubers mingle well here in a really warming stew. This would be great on its own or with a simple roast chicken. *Serves 4 as a side, 2 as a main dish*

1 tablespoon olive oil

1 sweet onion, diced

Sea salt

½ cup pearl barley

1½ cups chicken stock (see page 22)

2 stalks salsify

½ cup diced sweet potato (½-inch dice)

2 cups chopped sweet potato greens

1 tablespoon unsalted butter

2 teaspoons freshly squeezed lemon juice

1 In a medium pot, warm the olive oil over medium heat. Add the onion and a generous amount of sea salt, and cook until translucent, roughly 10 minutes. Add the barley and cook for 5 more minutes. Add the chicken stock and bring to a boil over high heat. Once the liquid reaches a boil, reduce the heat and simmer, stirring often, for 30 to 35 minutes, until the barley is tender but still retaining a touch of interior firmness.

2 While the barley is cooking, peel the salsify and slice it into ½-inch-thick coins. As you work, drop the slices into a bowl of cool water.

3 When the barley is almost but not quite tender, drain the salsify and add it, along with the sweet potato, to the pot. Continue to cook until the veggies are almost cooked through, about 10 minutes. Then add the sweet potato greens and stir to combine; they should take just a minute or so to cook. Finish the stew by removing the pot from the heat and stirring in the butter and lemon juice, and additional sea salt to taste, if necessary.

COUNTRY HAM WITH CURED EGG YOLK, ROASTED SALSIFY, AND ARUGULA

Curing egg yolks is pretty cool. The results yield a bright yellow yolk that can be Microplaned into ethereal snowflakes to adorn a salad, or sliced really thin to add an opulent, concentrated salinity. It's kind of like a close kin of bottarga, the cured fish roe of Italy. In this recipe the yolk acts as a foil to the rich salsify and a compatriot to the country ham. I use an eighteen-month-old ham from Allen Benton, in Madisonville, Tennessee, a man whose hams and bacons I enjoy immensely. But you could use some great prosciutto or speck if a wonderful Benton ham is not in the realm of possibility. *Serves 4 as a side or an appetizer*

3 stalks salsify

2 tablespoons unsalted butter

Kosher salt

1 tablespoon white wine vinegar

¼ cup chicken stock (see page 22)

Freshly ground black pepper, to taste

¼ pound arugula, preferably Astro

¼ pound shaved country ham, prosciutto, or speck

2 Cured Egg Yolks (recipe follows), thinly sliced

1 Preheat the oven to 375°F.

2 Quickly peel the salsify, cut the stalks in half lengthwise, and then cut them to 3-inch lengths, ending up with half-moon-shaped cylinders. Place a large cast-iron sauté pan over medium heat and add 1 tablespoon of the butter. When the butter foams, add the salsify and cook for 4 minutes. Season with a pinch of kosher salt, turn the salsify over, and place the pan in the oven. Roast for 5 minutes, or until tender and golden brown.

3 Remove the pan from the oven and place it over medium heat. Deglaze the pan with the vinegar and stock, and cook until the liquid has reduced by half. Then add the remaining tablespoon of butter and stir well to emulsify the butter into the liquid. Season to taste with kosher salt and black pepper, but realize that the cured yolks will give a fair bit of salinity to the dish in the end.

4 Arrange the arugula, country ham, and roasted salsify on a platter, and drizzle with some of the buttery cooking liquid. Garnish with the sliced egg yolk and serve immediately.

CURED EGG YOLKS

Makes 6

1 cup kosher salt   **6 egg yolks**
1 cup sugar

1 Combine the salt and sugar in a small bowl, and pour
half of the mixture into a shallow rectangular container
with a tight-fitting lid. Carefully nestle the yolks into
the salt-sugar mix and cover them with the remaining
mixture. Cover the container. Chill the yolks in the fridge
for a week.

2 Pull the yolks out of the cure and rinse them
lightly under cold water. Pat them dry, wrap them in
cheesecloth, and hang them up in the fridge to air-dry for
4 days.

3 You can either thinly slice the cured egg yolks or grate
them on a rasp. Like bottarga, they will stay fresh a long
time, about 3 months, if wrapped tightly in plastic wrap
and stored in the fridge.

SHIITAKES (OR OTHER WINTER MUSHROOMS)

If a porcini is the god of mushrooms, and morels and chanterelles are the king and queen, then the shiitake is the hardworking soul that keeps the kingdom going. Shiitakes don't cost much, but they exude flavor and show their earthy beauty in stunning ways. If you use dried shiitakes, soak them for a while, carefully getting rid of the silt that collects in the bottom of your soaking bowl.

Though this section really shows off the glories of the shiitake, you will also find maitake, oyster, enoki, and chicken of the woods mushrooms in the winter months. They can all be used in much the same way. Most are cultivated mushrooms that just like a little chill in the air.

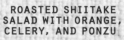
ROASTED SHIITAKE
SALAD WITH ORANGE,
CELERY, AND PONZU

DUXELLE

Duxelle is a stock-and-butter-enriched cooking of finely chopped mushrooms into a mesmerizingly luxurious paste with many uses. It's one of the staples of my French training. I explain to cooks at my restaurants that it should be cooked like a risotto, pretending that the mushrooms are the rice so their juices slowly concentrate and they absorb the flavors of the stock. Once cooked, it can garnish a roast, can be a luxe finish to a simple risotto, or can act as a base for a beautiful poached fish. *Serves 4 as a side or a lavish garnish*

1 pound fresh shiitakes, stemmed and brushed clean (do not rinse them)
2 tablespoons unsalted butter
2 shallots, finely minced
Kosher salt

1 cup chicken stock (see page 22)
Leaves from 2 sprigs fresh thyme, finely chopped
Freshly ground black pepper

1 Mince the shiitakes with a large chef's knife until very fine. If you're short on time you can pulse them in a food processor, but this is a little rough on the poor things.

2 Heat a large, heavy frying pan or braising pan over medium-high heat, and add the butter. When the butter begins to foam, add the minced shallots and cook for 3 minutes, stirring every 30 seconds or so. When the shallots are translucent and aromatic, add the mushrooms and sauté, stirring every once in a while, until they are lightly browned, 5 minutes; season lightly with kosher salt after they have browned. Reduce the heat to medium, add about ¼ cup of the chicken stock, and stir. Cook until the mushrooms seem dry, then add another ¼ cup of the stock. Repeat this process until all the stock has been added. Then reduce the heat to medium-low and cook until the consistency is moist but not liquid, like a soft polenta, about 10 minutes. Add the thyme, and season with kosher salt and black pepper.

3 Remove the pan from the heat, and using a rubber spatula, scrape the duxelle into a bowl. Serve immediately or cool, cover, and refrigerate until ready to use in a recipe.

ROASTED SHIITAKE SALAD WITH ORANGE, CELERY, AND PONZU

This is so much more than a simple cold salad—it turns a grilled steak, a poached fish, or a roasted bird into a meal with very little work. Kombu is an edible seaweed that is the base flavor for dashi, the mother stock of Japan, and is commonly available at any worldly grocery. Ponzu is a simple but delicious sauce made from dashi, soy sauce, and citrus, and is a great building block to have at your culinary disposal. *Serves 4 as a light appetizer or a side*

3 cups stemmed fresh shiitakes, brushed clean (do not rinse them)
2 tablespoons olive oil
Kosher salt
2 tablespoons Citrus Ponzu (recipe follows)

2 medium navel oranges, peeled, halved lengthwise, and cut into ½-inch-thick half-moons
1 cup finely chopped peeled celery, with leaves

1 Preheat the oven to 450°F.

2 In a medium bowl, toss the mushrooms with 1 tablespoon of the olive oil and season with kosher salt to taste. Place the mushrooms in a roasting pan or on a baking sheet, and roast in the oven for 10 minutes, until they are cooked and golden brown. Remove from the oven and return the mushrooms to the bowl. Add the ponzu, the oranges, and the celery. Transfer to a platter and finish with the remaining tablespoon of olive oil.

CITRUS PONZU
Makes 2 cups

1 2-inch piece dried kombu
1 cup soy sauce
¾ cup freshly squeezed orange juice

2 tablespoons freshly squeezed lime juice
½ cup dried bonito flakes
¼ cup rice vinegar

1 In a small nonreactive pot, combine the kombu, soy sauce, orange juice, and lime juice. Bring to a simmer over medium heat, and then remove from the heat. Add the bonito flakes and rice vinegar, and let sit at room temperature for 3 hours.

2 Strain the mixture, discarding the kombu and bonito. The sauce will stay fresh, covered, in the fridge for 10 days.

PAN-ROASTED COD, SHIITAKES, BUTTERNUT SQUASH, AND SOY BROTH

This dish is my mental image of a Japanese farmhouse meal I have never had. I picture a coastal scene and a Japanese man in a fisherman's sweater cooking this dish with me. Then I realize that I have never been to Japan and this is probably totally a misplaced daydream. But the food is good, so whatevs.

Buy Alaskan or Icelandic cod because U.S. and Canadian East Coast cod is not at all sustainable. More than ever we need to pay attention to where all our fish is coming from, so find a fishmonger who cares and stick with him. *Serves 4*

2 tablespoons unsalted butter

2 cups diced butternut squash

10 fresh shiitake mushrooms, stemmed, brushed clean (do not rinse them), and quartered

2 cups Soy Broth (recipe follows)

4 cod fillets (5 ounces each), skin off

Kosher salt

2 tablespoons peanut oil

2 branches fresh thyme

¼ cup fresh flat-leaf parsley leaves

1 Place a large sauté pan over medium-high heat and add 1 tablespoon of the butter. Add the butternut squash and sauté for 3 minutes, until it develops a bit of color. Add the shiitake mushrooms and cook for 3 minutes. Deglaze the pan with the soy broth, reduce the heat to a simmer, and cook until the squash and mushrooms are tender, 5 to 10 minutes. Keep warm over very low heat.

2 Pat the cod fillets dry on a paper towel. Season the fish with kosher salt on both sides. In a medium sauté pan, heat the peanut oil over medium-high heat until it starts to smoke. Gently place the cod in the pan, reduce the heat to medium, gently press down on the fish with a spoon, and let it sear. Add the remaining tablespoon of butter and the thyme sprigs to the pan. Baste the fish with the butter and cook for 5 minutes on the first side. The fish will develop a golden brown crust on the bottom. Then, using a thin spatula, turn the fish over and finish

it for 2 minutes on the other side. (The fish should cook for a total of 7 minutes for every inch of thickness.) When the fish is done, remove it from the pan and let it rest for 2 minutes. Discard the thyme sprigs.

3 Add the parsley to the vegetables in the pan. Line up 4 wide bowls and ladle in the broth and vegetables. Add a fish fillet to each bowl. Eat.

SOY BROTH
Makes 2½ cups

2 cups dashi (page 37)

2 tablespoons white miso

2 tablespoons soy sauce

1 scallion, white and light green parts, minced

In a medium saucepan, combine the dashi with the miso and soy sauce. Whisk together, and warm over medium heat until steaming but not bubbling. Finish with the scallion. Hold over very low heat and whisk again just before using.

TURNIPS

"Eat your turnips" was the dreaded line spoken from the head of the table, usually at some holiday meal. They weren't quite as off-putting as the boiled rutabagas, but still, turnips had a special place in most children's crumpled-up napkins. Overcooked, huge, bulbous, and waxy, the turnips I grew up with made no friends. Fast-forward thirty years and I couldn't be happier eating three pounds in a sitting. So what happened?

Well, my first relationship with the turnip was with the wrong turnip; no one warms up to a preparation that mimics prison food from *Game of Thrones*. The turnips that I have fallen for are the hakurei and Tokyo varieties, and they are a different beast completely. They arrive fresh and whole, root to stem to tender greens. They are a treat to unpack from our produce box. I also love the purple top, scarlet, Orange Jelly, and Amber Globe—varieties that are becoming popular once again. It's time to reclaim our turnips, and here I give you some simple, delicious ways to use all three parts of a turnip.

BUTTER-ROASTED
TURNIPS AND GREENS

PICKLED
TURNIP
STEMS

PICKLED TURNIP STEMS

There is a very important movement in the food world to create little waste. This dish is an example of the nose-to-tail philosophy about meats transferred to vegetables. All too often stems go into the compost, and though I like to make the earthworms happy, this is a great keeper of a recipe. It is a versatile homemade condiment: great on fish tacos or a pork stew, wonderful in a salad of any type, or delicious as a simple adornment to grits or polenta.

The turnip stems are the stalks, the part between the bulb and the leaf (more about the leaves later!). It usually ends up as compost. I am no botanist, but these are tasty treats. *Makes 1 quart*

½ to ¾ pound small turnip stems

2 garlic cloves, cut in half

1 sprig fresh thyme

1 tablespoon pickling salt

1 tablespoon sugar

1 tablespoon yellow mustard seeds

1 cup cider vinegar

1 Clean the turnip stems well and dice to a uniform ¼ inch thick. Pack the stems, garlic, and thyme sprig into a clean quart jar, leaving 1 inch of headspace.

2 Combine the pickling salt, sugar, mustard seeds, vinegar, and 1 cup of water in a small nonreactive saucepan and bring to a boil over medium-high heat. Reduce the heat to low and simmer for 5 minutes.

3 Carefully ladle the hot pickling mixture into the jar, leaving ½ inch of headspace. Cap with the lid and band, and let cool for 2 hours. The jar can be stored in the refrigerator for 10 days, or processed according to the jar manufacturer's directions to store on the shelf for up to 10 months.

BUTTERED TURNIP GREENS

Sometimes just four ingredients achieve greatness, and this is one of those times. It is critical that the turnip greens are from young, small turnips and not those precut store-bought ones that need to cook for hours and hours. These greens are delicate and cook in a jiffy. *Serves 4 as a side*

2 tablespoons unsalted butter

8 cups chopped turnip greens (stems reserved for pickling!)

Kosher salt

¼ teaspoon caraway seeds, toasted and lightly crushed

Place a large cast-iron skillet or braising pan over medium-high heat, and melt the butter in it. When the butter bubbles and froths, add the turnip greens and cook for about 3 minutes without stirring to get a bit of color. Season with kosher salt to taste, sprinkle with the toasted caraway seeds, and stir until wilted and cooked through. Serve immediately.

BUTTER-ROASTED TURNIPS

I know. You're like *this is so simple*. It takes a stunning vegetable and puts it on a pedestal to be judged on its own. But technique is key, so don't use too much heat on the stovetop and don't cook them too long. Let's get the kids eating this! *Serves 4 as a side*

1½ tablespoons unsalted butter

1 pound hakurei turnips (about 12 small turnips), cut in half from top to bottom

Kosher salt

1 Preheat the oven to 400°F.

2 Place a large cast-iron sauté pan over medium heat. When it is hot, add the butter and let it bubble and froth. Before the butter burns, add the turnips, cut side down, and cook for 3 minutes. Then turn the turnips over, place the pan in the oven, and roast for 4 minutes, until the turnips are browning nicely but still have a crispness in the center. Remove from the oven, season with kosher salt, and transfer to a platter.

SOY-BRAISED TURNIPS

I love these turnips. They are buttery and coated with a beautiful soy lacquer. *Serves 2 to 4 as a side*

1 tablespoon unsalted butter

8 small turnips, halved from top to bottom

1 tablespoon soy sauce

3 tablespoons chicken stock (see page 22)

Tiny pinch of kosher salt

1 sprig fresh thyme

1 teaspoon toasted benne or sesame seeds

1 Warm a saucepan (one that has a lid) over medium-high heat and add the butter. When the butter has melted and foamed, add the turnips, cut side down. Let them get a little color by cooking them for about 3 minutes without turning them.

2 Add the soy sauce, stock, salt, and thyme sprig, and cover the pan. Cook for 5 minutes. Then remove the lid and reduce the liquid to a glaze. Remove the thyme sprig, transfer the turnips to a platter, and sprinkle with the toasted benne.

TURNIPS AND THEIR GREENS RISOTTO

I love the idea of using the whole turnip—stems, greens, and all. Hakureis are such a treat and so many local farms do a wonderful job nurturing them into beautiful little orbs. The greens of hakureis are very tender and wilt into a cooked state in a matter of a minute, not like those hardy turnip greens that Granny used to cook.

This risotto is a vehicle to showcase the whole turnip. Risotto is a subdued dance partner for single flavors, letting them shine. We all need a rhythm guitar player now and again, and risotto is it. *Serves 4 as a light supper*

3 small hakurei turnips

2½ tablespoons olive oil

Sea salt

4 cups chicken stock (see page 22)

½ cup minced yellow onion

1 cup Arborio rice

2 tablespoons unsalted butter

½ cup finely grated Parmigiano-Reggiano

2 cups finely chopped tender turnip greens

1 tablespoon finely sliced scallion, sliced on the bias

1 Very thinly slice the turnips. Drizzle the slices with ½ tablespoon of the olive oil and a pinch of sea salt, and set aside. These will finish the risotto.

2 On a back burner, warm the chicken stock in a medium saucepan over medium-low heat. Reduce the heat to low to keep warm and place a ladle in the pan.

3 Place a large, heavy-bottomed sauté pan over medium-high heat and add the remaining 2 tablespoons olive oil. Add the onion and cook, stirring with a wooden spoon, until it is translucent but not browned at all, about 5 minutes. Add the rice and lightly glaze it. From the moment the rice goes in, the time is about 17 minutes to completion, so keep an eye on the clock. You should be stirring a lot, but no need to stir the entire time.

4 Start adding the warm stock, about 1 cup at a time, stirring and cooking after each addition until the stock is fully absorbed, seasoning with sea salt a little at a time throughout the process. Continue adding stock, stirring and cooking until the stock is fully absorbed. After a while you will see a luxurious starchy liquid surrounding those little rice kernels. This is good; make sure there's enough liquid in there to keep that sauce nice and saucy. After about 15 minutes, taste your rice. It should have a slight al dente crunchiness to it, but you have to soothsay what it will taste like after 2 to 3 more minutes as it sits in the bowl.

5 Once you've gotten the consistency just right (you may or may not end up using all the stock), add 1 tablespoon of the butter and ¼ cup of the Parmigiano-Reggiano, and stir well to fold those beautiful finishes into the risotto. Then add the turnip greens to wilt them into the risotto. Season with sea salt to taste, stir in the remaining tablespoon of butter, and it's done. When it gets in that bowl, it will set up well.

6 Spoon the risotto into shallow bowls and garnish with the raw turnips, scallions, and remaining Parmigiano-Reggiano. Eat.

WINTER SQUASH

Some winter ingredients definitely take more time and effort, which seems apt given that everything seems more difficult in the winter. But when you break through the armor of a winter squash, a sweet, versatile prize awaits.

KABOCHA SQUASH SOUP WITH PEAR, COCONUT MILK, AND RED CURRY

Soup in winter is like a warm blanket—it just makes you feel right. This one is full of flavor and satisfies as a full meal. Kabocha squash is one of the quintessential cooking squashes that yield sweet, flavorful, smooth cubes of wonderfulness. This will work with a butternut or a red turban squash as well.

Most squash soups you see are purees, but this one keeps it fresh and brothy. It's fulfilling, and I find you notice all the flavors and textures so much more when it is not pureed. *Serves 6*

2 tablespoons peanut oil

1 yellow onion, diced

3 cups bite-size cubes Kabocha squash

1 garlic clove, minced

2 tablespoons minced fresh ginger

2 tablespoons Thai red curry paste

3 cups chicken stock (see page 22)

2 tablespoons finely sliced scallions

1 cup coconut milk

1 teaspoon Asian fish sauce, plus more if needed

½ pound firm tofu, cut into ½-inch dice

¼ cup finely chopped fresh cilantro stems and leaves

Kosher salt (optional)

2 fresh pears, cored and thinly sliced

1 Pour the peanut oil into a large saucepan or small stockpot, place it over medium heat, and sweat the onion in the oil until translucent, 5 minutes. Add the squash cubes and cook for 5 minutes, until they are just beginning to brown. Add the garlic, ginger, and red curry paste and cook, stirring constantly, until very aromatic, 3 minutes. Add the chicken stock, raise the heat to medium-high, and bring to a boil. Reduce the heat to a simmer and cook until the squash is softening, 7 minutes. Add the scallions, coconut milk, fish sauce, tofu, and half the cilantro, and stir well to combine. Simmer for another 10 minutes to bring the flavors together and finish cooking the squash. Adjust the seasoning with more fish sauce or with kosher salt, if necessary.

2 Spoon the soup into individual bowls and garnish with the remaining cilantro and the pears.

AN HOMAGE TO KEITH'S ACORN SQUASH

From age fourteen to eighteen I lived with my dad, just the two of us, in Centretown, Ottawa. My three older sisters had gone on to independent lives and Pops and I were fending for ourselves. I was in my formative years, which meant gambling my allowance, learning how to spend ten hours in a snooker hall, mastering the art of procuring beer without ID, and discovering how to forge a signature for a report card. Luckily I was being fed nutritious suppers.

We ate well. It wasn't extravagant food, certainly not foodie food, but it was healthy, mostly from scratch, and thought through. It was not about reinventing the meal but about making things in the way my dad knew how.

My dad was born in Cuba in 1940 and left before the revolution to go to boarding school in southern Ontario. He was a star athlete and a bright academic who chose economics instead of professional sports—probably a smart decision at that time as Canadian professional sports didn't pay like they do now. (Maybe the Cuban roots have something to do with the ubiquitous rice in our house, but it wasn't like he made it well; it was just usually on the table.) Earlier in life he had gone through a spell where we relied on the convenience items of the era, maybe a bit too much, but in my teens he had put aside the quick answer of fish sticks and canned yellow wax beans in favor of smart food that would be better for us. I don't know exactly why this change came about, but I think it was a mixed reaction to having more time to cook, wanting to cook in a better way, and realizing that the fish sticks and canned goods were probably not the best things for us.

One staple my dad made was something so simple and so easy but so good. It was an acorn squash, cut in half and seeded, filled with butter, brown sugar, and some thyme, covered, zapped in the microwave for four minutes, and then eaten with a spoon. The microwave wasn't a crutch, merely a device to get good food on the table effectively and quickly. He is, above all, a logical man.

I am just realizing now that those little squashes were not available year-round. They were his seasonal delight, the way some folks wait for strawberries all year long. Even an economist, who thought pinot blanc was a red wine, had bought unknowingly into the idea of seasonal goodness.

SPAGHETTI SQUASH CAPONATA

A simple caponata can really be the ideal winter condiment. It just belongs on your table. It is a lovely sweet-sour accompaniment to a vast array of foods, from a griddled piece of sourdough, to a hearty roasted duck, to a plate of rice. Think outside the box and put some caponata on it. *Serves 4 as a side*

1 spaghetti squash (about 1 pound)

2 tablespoons olive oil

Kosher salt

Freshly cracked black pepper, to taste

½ red bell pepper, cut into small dice

1 stalk peeled celery, thinly sliced

2 tablespoons honey

3 tablespoons cider vinegar

2 tablespoons dried currants

2 tablespoons capers

1 Preheat the oven to 325°F.

2 Cut the spaghetti squash in half lengthwise. Remove the strings and seeds. Drizzle the inside of the squash halves with 1 tablespoon of the olive oil, and season them with kosher salt and cracked black pepper.

3 Place the seasoned squash, cut side down, in a roasting pan and roast for 45 minutes, or until cooked through. Remove it from the oven, flip it over, and set aside to cool to room temperature.

4 Place a medium saucepan over medium heat and add the remaining tablespoon of olive oil. Add the bell pepper and celery, and lightly sweat for 5 minutes. Add the honey and vinegar to the pan, raise the heat to high, and reduce the liquid by half, about 2 minutes. Remove from the heat and set aside to cool.

5 Using a fork, very carefully flake the squash strands out of the shells onto a cutting board. The texture of spaghetti squash is, well, like spaghetti. Chop the squash into shorter strands and put them in a large bowl. Add the pepper-celery mixture, the currants, and the capers. Mix well, and adjust the seasoning with more kosher salt and cracked pepper, if desired. Serve at room temperature, or store for up to 1 week in a sealed container in the fridge.

GNOCCHI WITH BRAISED LAMB, BUTTERNUT SQUASH, AND TOMATO CONFIT

This is a great way to use the bounty of summer later on in the year. You could make a lot of tomato confit in July, process it up, and then be reliving memories of the summer past in March, while your lamb braises and the winter melts away.

Gnocchi has a dear place in my heart. I remember carrying Beatrice in a BabyBjörn on my chest as I made gnocchi, answered the phone, did the banking, made the schedule, and worked through all the butchery of the day. Bea's feet would be dusted with flour by the day's end but the gnocchi were awesome. They still are. *Serves 4 to 6*

FOR THE BRAISED LAMB

2 pounds lamb hind shanks (each shank is about a pound)

Kosher salt

2 tablespoons peanut oil

1 cup diced carrots

1 cup peeled and diced celery

2 cups diced yellow onions

10 garlic cloves, peeled and left whole

2 bay leaves

½ cup chopped scallions

1 tablespoon yellow mustard seeds

2 teaspoons crushed red pepper flakes

1 quart chicken stock (see page 22)

FOR THE GNOCCHI

3 pounds russet potatoes, washed

Kosher salt

4 egg yolks, beaten

2 cups all-purpose flour

2 teaspoons olive oil

TO FINISH

1 tablespoon unsalted butter

1 butternut squash (1 pound), peeled

Kosher salt

1 teaspoon chopped fresh marjoram leaves

2 cups chopped Tomato Confit (page 321)

Sea salt

Freshly ground black pepper, to taste

1 To cook the lamb: Preheat the oven to 325°F.

2 Pat the lamb shanks dry and season them generously with kosher salt. In a large braising pan, heat the peanut oil over medium-high heat. Once the oil gives off a light smoke, add the lamb and sear on all sides until each side is evenly browned and has a good crust. This should take about 15 minutes total. Take the shanks out of the pan and set them aside.

3 Reduce the heat to medium-high and add the carrots, celery, and onions to the pan. Cook until caramelized, about 10 minutes, stirring often to prevent burning. Once the veggies have an even color, add the garlic, bay leaves, scallions, mustard seeds, and red pepper flakes.

SPAGHETTI
SQUASH
CAPONATA

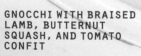

GNOCCHI WITH BRAISED
LAMB, BUTTERNUT
SQUASH, AND TOMATO
CONFIT

Cook for 2 minutes, and then add the chicken stock. Bring the liquid to a boil and add the lamb shanks. Cover the pan with a lid and place it in the oven. Cook the shanks until they are very tender, 1½ to 2 hours.

4 Take the braising pan out of the oven and let it rest for 30 minutes. Then take the shanks out of the liquid, and when they are cool enough to handle, pull the meat off the bones, removing any tough connective tissue. Reserve the clean meat in a small mixing bowl covered with plastic wrap. Strain the braising liquid through a fine-mesh sieve into a medium saucepan, place it over medium-high heat, and reduce to 2 cups. While the liquid is reducing, skim off any foam or impurities that rise to the top. Reserve the reduced braising liquid.

5 To make the gnocchi: Preheat the oven to 325°F.

6 Place the potatoes on a baking sheet and bake until fork-tender, roughly 1 hour (you can do this while the lamb is cooking).

7 Take the potatoes out of the oven and crack them open to allow the steam to release. When they are just cool enough to handle, scoop out the flesh and discard the potato skins. Pass the potato flesh through a food mill or a ricer into a bowl. Make a well in the potato and add ½ teaspoon kosher salt and the egg yolks. Combine until just incorporated, and then add 1½ cups of the flour. Lightly knead the flour into the potato, just enough to incorporate it. Cut the dough into 4 equal portions.

8 Meanwhile, in a large stockpot, bring 2 gallons of water to a boil over high heat, and season it generously with kosher salt.

9 Use the remaining flour to dust a work surface as needed. Roll each portion of dough into a long tube about 1 inch thick in diameter. Slice the tubes to create 1 × 1-inch pieces of dough. You can shape them, using a fork to create ripples in the dough, which will allow the sauce to stick to the gnocchi once cooked.

10 Prepare an ice water bath and set it near the stove. When the water has reached a boil, drop the gnocchi into the boiling water, about 15 at a time. When they float, take them out with a spider or straining spoon and place them right into the ice bath. (Keep the water hot for reheating the gnocchi later.) The blanching should take about 2 minutes per batch. Once they are all blanched, take them out of the ice water, drain, and air-dry for 10 minutes. Toss the gnocchi with the olive oil to prevent them from sticking to each other, lay them in a single layer on a sheet pan, and set them aside.

11 Preheat the oven to 400°F.

12 In a large saucepan, melt the butter over medium heat. Cut off the top section of the squash (the part without the seeds), and slice off enough of the bottom to access the seeds. Using a spoon, scoop the inside clean of the seeds. Then slice the squash into rings, about ⅓ inch thick. In the saucepan, toss the rings with the melted butter, kosher salt to taste, and the marjoram. Arrange the squash rings in one layer on a baking sheet, and roast for 10 to 15 minutes, until cooked through.

13 To finish the dish, combine the lamb meat, the braising liquid, the tomato confit, and the roasted butternut squash back in the saucepan and set it over low heat. Warm the gnocchi in a pot of boiling water, being careful not to overcook them, about 3 minutes. Drain the gnocchi and add them to the saucepan. Adjust the seasoning with sea salt and some freshly ground pepper, and serve immediately.

SPRING

SPRING IS HERE

Spring is here   *And I am singing*
The weather is near   *Winter has passed*
The birds are singing   *I am happy at last*

My sister Rachel wrote that a long time ago, when she was a smart six-year-old kid who innately understood the change that occurs in the Canadian psyche after a long winter's nap. Winter is long up there, and when spring comes we have a switch that just turns on. People walk around with a giddiness and a joie de vivre that is electrifying. Go to Montreal in early April and I guarantee you will find the happiest people on the planet.

Chefs wait for spring like no other season. Spring means ramps, morels, and English peas—things that just taste so good to a thawing world and eager palates. The CSA box that my family gets from Woodland Gardens blooms in a multicolored palette. Favas shine, tight in their lime green pods; radishes show their vast spectrum from red to black to green to white; beets parade elaborate yellow and red interiors, or even beautiful candy-striped mixes of both; asparagus runs crisp from top to bottom, a break from the grocery store's woody stems that stand in for their true seasonal glory; carrots display their resilience born from winter frosts that give them a flavor that cannot be replicated at any other time.

The land outside of our box also decrees the season. Ramps, fiddlehead ferns, spring onions, morels, and asparagus come to us from different farmers, brokers, and purveyors, and we relish their arrival. As chefs we really are as excited about ramps as our menus indicate. It's been a long winter and it is time to revel in warmth again.

ARTICHOKES

It was a brave person who first ate an artichoke, but what a find. That armor of thorns yields to that rich heart—a treasure of the culinary world. They are most certainly not local to me in Georgia, or for that matter to most Americans, but artichokes are just too good to overlook. So relish in the bounty from Castroville, California, and cook some artichokes.

STEAMED
ARTICHOKES
WITH DRAWN
THYME BUTTER

SOUTHERN
ARTICHOKE DIP

STEAMED ARTICHOKES WITH DRAWN THYME BUTTER

I was a wee little guy when Pops was doing a sabbatical in Palo Alto, at venerable Stanford University, but I remember eating egg rolls and artichokes with drawn butter. Now that may not have been in the same meal, but that's how my memory puts them: together. The egg rolls were (amazingly enough) homemade by my mum and the artichokes came from a couple hours south of us. Big, green, thistly orbs. And I fell for them—hook, line, and sinker.

Now my kids love the hunt to get to the heart of the artichoke, scraping each leaf with their teeth and getting all they can from their beauty. *Serves 4 as a side*

7 tablespoons unsalted butter	2 large globe artichokes, top 2 inches sliced off
1 cup sliced yellow onion	
1 tablespoon fresh thyme leaves	1 cup dry white wine
	Kosher salt
¼ cup fresh flat-leaf parsley leaves	1 lemon, cut into wedges

1 Place a stockpot over low heat and melt 1 tablespoon of the butter in it. Once the butter starts to foam, add the onion, half of the thyme, and the parsley, and begin to sweat the onion. While you prepare the artichokes, the onion will happily hang out over low heat.

2 Tear off the first few outer leaves from the bottom of each artichoke, as well as any attached to the stem. Using a vegetable peeler, shave the stems until you reach the white inner part. Add the artichokes to the pot, stem side up. Then add the white wine and enough water to cover the artichokes. Bring to a boil over high heat, add enough salt to make the liquid pleasantly salty, and then lower to a simmer. To keep them submerged, place a plate that's just small enough to fit inside the pot over the artichokes. Cover the pot with a lid and cook the artichokes for about 20 minutes, or until you can slide a knife into the stem with no resistance.

3 Remove the plate and then the artichokes from the liquid, and place the artichokes on a cutting board to cool. When they are cool enough to handle, use a chef's knife to carefully slice each artichoke in half, starting at the tip of the stem. This will expose the heart of the artichoke. Just above the heart you will see a fuzzy part, which is called the "choke." Using a small spoon, remove the choke. You will be left with the heart and the fleshy leaves.

4 Melt the remaining 6 tablespoons butter in a small saucepan and add the remaining thyme leaves. Once the butter is fully melted, set it aside.

5 Place the artichokes on a large platter and season with salt to taste. Garnish with the lemon wedges. Serve with the reserved melted butter for dippin'.

SOUTHERN ARTICHOKE DIP

There are some Southern staples that have become too enamored of the canned goods aisle, and artichoke dip is one of them. We can do better. Let us cook our artichokes and make the best darned artichoke dip we can. *Makes 1 quart*

4 large globe artichokes	½ teaspoon grated lemon zest
½ lemon	1 teaspoon chopped fresh thyme leaves
Kosher salt	
2 cups finely chopped Lacinato kale	2 tablespoons chopped fresh flat-leaf parsley
½ cup finely grated Parmigiano-Reggiano cheese	¼ cup minced scallions
3 tablespoons mayonnaise	1 tablespoon Louisiana-style hot sauce
3 tablespoons crème fraîche	1 baguette, sliced and toasted

1 Using a cutting board and a serrated knife, carefully cut the top 2 inches off of the artichokes, to remove the stiff tips of the leaves, and discard. Remove 1 inch from the stem ends. Then place the artichokes in a pot, and squeeze the lemon half over them. Drop the squeezed lemon into the pot as well. Cover the artichokes with water, place over high heat, and bring to a boil; then add enough kosher salt to make the water pleasantly salty. Use a plate to weight down the artichokes. Cover the pot and simmer for about 20 minutes, or until a knife can slide easily into the stems. Remove the pot from the heat, and transfer the artichokes to a plate, reserving the cooking liquid. Chill the artichokes in the fridge for about 30 minutes.

2 When the artichokes are cool, remove their tough outer leaves until you encounter the pale, tender leaves. Using a vegetable peeler, carefully whittle down the fibrous outer layer of the stems, leaving the tender inner stems intact.

3 Preheat the oven to 375°F. Prepare an ice water bath and set it near the stove.

4 Cut each artichoke into quarters from top to bottom. Using a spoon, scoop out the thistly part of the heart—the fuzzy part, or choke, that protects the best eating of all. Chop the cleaned artichoke quarters into small pieces and set aside.

5 Bring the reserved cooking water to a vigorous boil, add the kale, and blanch for 1 minute. Drain the kale, shock it in the ice water, and then squeeze out the excess water. Place the kale in a clean dish towel and ring out even more of the water.

6 In a large bowl, combine the blanched kale with the Parmigiano-Reggiano, mayonnaise, crème fraîche, lemon zest, thyme, parsley, scallions, hot sauce, and chopped artichoke quarters. Season to taste with kosher salt, and place the mixture in a medium baking dish. Bake for 30 minutes, or until bubbly and just browning on top.

7 Serve with the toasted baguette slices.

PICKLED SHRIMP, CRISP ARTICHOKES, AND BUTTER LETTUCE

The core of this dish is a timeless pickled shrimp recipe from my first book. Here you take those beautiful shrimp and turn them into a meal with sweet, crisped artichokes that will delight everyone at the table.

The ingredients list looks long, but don't let it fool you. You can just prepare the shrimp and enjoy them all by themselves if you want. *Serves 4 as an appetizer*

2 tablespoons freshly squeezed lemon juice

6 baby artichokes

½ cup olive oil

Kosher salt

1 tablespoon white wine vinegar

2 tablespoons capers, chopped

1 tablespoon salt-packed anchovies, rinsed and finely minced

½ cup chopped Pickled Fennel (page 219)

2 tablespoons thinly sliced scallions (white and light green parts)

Pickled Shrimp (recipe follows), drained, bay leaves discarded

6 leaves butter lettuce, torn in half

1 Fill a medium bowl with cold water and add 1 tablespoon of the lemon juice to it. Set it near your work area.

2 Peel off and discard the tough exterior leaves of the baby artichokes. Using a serrated knife, slice off the stiff tips of the artichokes. Then, using a paring knife, peel away the skin from the stems. Slice each artichoke in half lengthwise. Cut each half into 3 wedges. As you work through this process, place the cut artichokes in the bowl of acidulated water; this will prevent them from oxidizing and browning.

3 Once the artichokes have all been prepared, remove them from the water and thoroughly pat them dry with paper towels. Place a large sauté pan over medium-high heat. Add ¼ cup of the olive oil, and when it is shimmering hot, add the artichokes, giving them room in the pan to brown well. Cook them for about 2 minutes, turn them over, and cook for another 2 minutes, until golden and crisp. Remove from the pan and set on paper towels to drain.

4 Place the crisped artichokes in a bowl and dress them with kosher salt to taste, the remaining tablespoon of lemon juice, the remaining ¼ cup olive oil, and the vinegar, capers, and anchovies. Add the pickled fennel, scallions, and pickled shrimp, and toss gently. Add the butter lettuce, toss once, and serve.

PICKLED SHRIMP

Makes 1 pound, plus pickling liquid

2 tablespoons Old Bay Seasoning

1 pound shrimp (I like 26 to 30 count for this), peeled and deveined

½ teaspoon celery seeds

¼ teaspoon allspice berries

½ teaspoon crushed red pepper flakes

1 tablespoon sea salt

1 cup olive oil

⅓ cup freshly squeezed lemon juice

2 garlic cloves, minced

12 dry bay leaves, or 6 fresh bay leaves

¼ cup fresh flat-leaf parsley leaves, minced

½ medium Spanish onion, thinly sliced

1 Prepare an ice water bath and set it near the stove.

2 Bring 2 quarts of water to a boil in a large saucepan. Add the Old Bay and the shrimp, and immediately reduce the heat to low. Cook for about 2 minutes, or until the shrimp are pink and just cooked through. Drain, and plunge the shrimp into the ice water to cool. When the shrimp have cooled, drain them, and reserve in the fridge until you have your pickling stuff all prepped.

3 Grind the celery seeds and allspice berries together in a spice grinder. Set aside.

4 Combine the ground celery seeds and allspice, the red pepper flakes, sea salt, olive oil, lemon juice, garlic, bay leaves, and parsley in a bowl and stir to combine.

5 In a clean, nonreactive container, arrange the shrimp, onion, and pickling mixture in layers. Repeat. Cover, and let sit in the fridge for 24 hours before serving. The shrimp will keep in the fridge for 3 to 4 days.

SHAVED ARTICHOKES, BAY SCALLOPS, AND PRESERVED LEMON

Small artichokes offer a lot of versatility: You can roast them, use them in stews, poach them, and put them in salads. Or, for the easiest method of all, you can clean them, thinly slice them, and marinate them in a little lemon juice and olive oil. It's easy, but awesome.

This rendition pairs them with super-sweet and creamy bay scallops. My favorites come from Taylor Bay, Massachusetts. The scallops are quickly seared, then bathed in olive oil and herbs before being married with the artichokes, their sweetness countered by the salty tang of preserved lemon.

Serves 4 as an appetizer

6 baby artichokes	**¼ teaspoon freshly ground black pepper**
4 tablespoons olive oil	
2 tablespoons freshly squeezed lemon juice	**2 tablespoons minced fresh flat-leaf parsley leaves**
Fine sea salt	**1 teaspoon minced fresh thyme leaves**
½ pound fresh bay scallops	
1 tablespoon canola oil	**⅛ teaspoon Korean chile powder**
1 tablespoon unsalted butter	**1 tablespoon minced Preserved Lemon (recipe follows)**

1 Using a paring knife, remove the tough outer leaves of the artichokes, and then peel the skin away from the stems. Using a serrated knife, slice off the tips of the artichokes and discard them. Work quickly to avoid letting the artichokes discolor due to oxidation.

2 Thinly slice the artichokes lengthwise, and place them in a bowl. Add 2 tablespoons of the olive oil, the lemon juice, and a few pinches of fine sea salt. Toss well, and set aside at room temperature for 1 hour.

3 Pat the scallops as dry as you can with some paper towels, and season with fine sea salt on both sides. In a medium sauté pan, heat the canola oil over high heat. Once the oil comes to a light smoke, add the scallops, making sure not to overcrowd the pan. Sear the scallops, without moving them, for 1½ minutes. When the scallops start to get a golden color around the edges, turn the heat down to medium and add the butter. Baste the scallops with the melting butter for 30 seconds. Transfer the scallops to a paper-towel-lined plate and let them cool to room temperature.

4 Place the cooled seared scallops in a bowl and add the remaining 2 tablespoons olive oil, the pepper, parsley, thyme, chile powder, and preserved lemon. Toss well, and let sit in the fridge for 20 minutes.

5 Add the artichokes to the scallops. Toss well and spoon onto a large platter. Serve.

PRESERVED LEMON
Makes 1 quart

6 lemons	**12 bay leaves**
6 tablespoons sea salt	**Freshly squeezed lemon juice, as needed**
12 coriander seeds	

1 Scrub the lemons with a vegetable brush under running water, and dry them.

2 With a knife, remove the little rounded bit at the stem end of each lemon, where the fruit hung from the tree. Starting at the other end of the lemon, make a large cut by slicing downward lengthwise, stopping about 1 inch from the stem end; then make another downward slice, so you've incised the lemon with an X.

3 Pack the sea salt into the lemons where you made the X, using about a tablespoon of salt per lemon. Put the salt-filled lemons in a large clean glass quart jar with a tight-fitting lid. Add the coriander seeds and bay leaves, stuffing them down among the lemons. Press the lemons very firmly in the jar to get the juices flowing. Cover, and let stand, at room temperature, overnight.

4 The next day, press the lemons down again, encouraging them to release more juice as they start to soften. Repeat for 2 to 3 days, until the lemons are completely covered with liquid. If your lemons aren't too juicy, add more freshly squeezed lemon juice until they're submerged, as I generally have to do.

5 After 1 month, when the preserved lemons are soft, they're ready to use. Store the lemons in the refrigerator, where they'll keep for at least 6 months.

6 To use: Remove the lemons from the liquid and rinse them under cool water. Split them in half and scrape out the pulp. Slice the lemon peels into thin strips or cut them into small dice, as needed. (You may wish to press the pulp through a sieve to obtain the juice, which can be used for flavoring in small amounts as it is pretty salty; discard the pulp solids.)

ARUGULA

When it came to naming my first restaurant, I was enamored with the word "roquette," the French term for arugula. In the end the restaurant was called 5&10, an homage to the neighborhood of Five Points, where it resides, but I made an ode to arugula by giving it firm standing on the menu. It was everywhere because I loved its spicy nature and its green tenacity, adding flourish and smarts to many dishes.

Celia, of Woodland Gardens, grows us arugula that is pure and tender, not at all like the limp, uneventful, and usually shelf-aged supermarket stuff. To me, great arugula is the epitome of freshness. Find your grower and support their love of arugula.

WILTED ARUGULA WITH RAISINS AND CAPERS

I love when greens wilt. I mean purposely wilt, not wither into a green mess in your produce drawer. When you add heat to a green, briefly and with a bit of technical skill, you endow it with a completely different flavor profile. This quickly cooked arugula shines with the richness of butter, the acidity of lemon, and the sweet-earthy-salty attributes of the raisins and capers. It is a great spring side. *Serves 4 as a side*

2 tablespoons unsalted butter

Fine sea salt

1 teaspoon grated lemon zest

1 tablespoon freshly squeezed lemon juice

1 pound arugula, stemmed

2 tablespoons raisins, coarsely chopped

2 tablespoons capers, coarsely chopped

1 In a large, wide-bottomed pot, combine 2 tablespoons of water with the butter and a few pinches of fine sea salt. Place the pot over medium-high heat, and add the lemon zest and juice. Whisk it all together; the butter will melt and emulsify into the water. Remove the pot from the heat and add the arugula. Quickly stir it in and gently wilt it. The idea is to cook it but not destroy it; if you need more heat, return the pot to medium-low and stir the greens until they are tender.

2 Transfer the wilted arugula to a serving platter and top with the raisins and capers.

SPAGHETTI WITH ARUGULA PESTO, SALAMI, AND PARMIGIANO-REGGIANO

ARUGULA SALAD WITH POACHED AND PULLED CHICKEN, BUTTERMILK DRESSING, FRIED BREAD, AND OLIVES

SPAGHETTI WITH ARUGULA PESTO, SALAMI, AND PARMIGIANO-REGGIANO

Pesto should not be a forgotten fad of the '80s. It is a staple that you need to be making, at the very least to keep from watching the slow demise of freshly picked basil or arugula in your fridge. The ice in the making of the pesto will ensure that the bright green stays bright green; a burring blender produces heat through friction, and the cold will make that heat negligible.

Pesto is spring on a plate. Bring in the sunshine.

Serves 4

Sea salt

3 tablespoons pine nuts

4 cups arugula leaves

1 garlic clove

1 cup finely grated Parmigiano-Reggiano cheese, plus more for shaving

½ teaspoon freshly cracked black pepper

3 ice cubes

¾ cup olive oil

1 teaspoon grated lemon zest

1 pound spaghetti

2 ounces salami, cut into matchsticks

1 Preheat the oven to 350°F.

2 In a large stockpot, bring 4 quarts of water to a boil over high heat. Salt it so that it tastes pleasantly salty.

3 While the water is heating, toast the pine nuts in the oven until they are golden brown, about 5 minutes, but keep a close eye on them as nuts burn very quickly. Separate them into 2 tablespoons (for the pesto) and 1 tablespoon (for the pasta), and let them cool to room temperature.

4 In a blender, combine 3 cups of the arugula, the reserved 2 tablespoons pine nuts, garlic, grated Parmigiano-Reggiano, 1 teaspoon sea salt, the pepper, and the ice cubes. Blend on high speed for 20 seconds. Then, with the blender running, slowly drizzle in the olive oil. The pesto should be smooth. Scrape it into a bowl, stir in the lemon zest, and set aside.

5 Add the spaghetti to the pot of boiling water, stir immediately, and then cook until al dente. Drain the spaghetti into a colander, and return it to the pot set over low heat. Immediately add the pesto, the remaining pine nuts, and the remaining arugula, and season with sea salt. Combine the ingredients over low heat.

6 Divide the pasta among 4 bowls, and top each one with salami and shaved Parmigiano-Reggiano.

ARUGULA SALAD WITH POACHED AND PULLED CHICKEN, BUTTERMILK DRESSING, FRIED BREAD, AND OLIVES

Sadly, we're still trapped in the idea of a meal having to be four elements: a starch, a lot of protein, and two little servings of vegetables. The funny thing is that this salad, and many like it, can meet all of those needs. We just need to vary the ratios and reframe what dinner is. Here we get super-fresh arugula, peppery and crisp, with gently poached chicken, olives for an acidic punch, and some crisp bread for texture. It's a dinner you can enjoy every day. *Serves 4*

Sea salt, to taste

¼ cup sliced yellow onion

1 teaspoon fennel seeds, toasted

1 teaspoon coriander seeds, toasted

½ teaspoon cumin seeds, toasted

½ lemon

4 chicken thighs, bone in, skin off

½ cup olive oil

4 slices white bread, crust on, torn into small bites

½ pound arugula

½ cup Buttermilk Dressing (page 28)

¼ cup picholine olives, pitted and sliced into rings

1 In a medium saucepan, combine 2 quarts of water with 1½ teaspoons sea salt. Add the onion, fennel seeds, coriander seeds, cumin seeds, and the lemon half. Bring to a simmer over medium heat, and add the chicken thighs. Reduce the heat to medium-low and cook for 20 minutes. Remove the chicken thighs from the poaching liquid and allow them to cool to room temperature. (Keep the liquid as a base for a profound chicken stock.)

2 Once the chicken has cooled, carefully pull the meat off the bone and separate it into bite-size pieces, making sure that there are no pieces of connective tissue or cartilage. Place the chicken pieces in a mixing bowl and set aside.

3 In a large sauté pan, heat the olive oil over medium heat. Once the oil is hot and shimmering, add the bread. Fry for 2 to 3 minutes, until golden brown, turning the pieces once in a while to crisp both sides. (The bread will go from light to golden brown very quickly.) Transfer the bread to a plate lined with paper towels and allow it to cool.

4 Add the arugula to the bowl containing the chicken, and very lightly dress it with half of the buttermilk dressing. Season with sea salt to taste, and toss well. Drizzle the remaining buttermilk dressing on a platter, and arrange the arugula and chicken on the platter. Top with the fried bread and the sliced olives.

WARM LOBSTER SALAD WITH PANCETTA, ARUGULA, AND POTATO

Big pieces of freshly cooked lobster abound in this dish. The potatoes are roasted and the dressing is light and punchy with mustard and lemon. The arugula goes in at the end to freshen everything up with its peppery goodness. At the restaurants we have become enamored with Astro arugula, with its beautiful round edges and milder flavor, but at home I use a lot of Surrey arugula, which is more biting in its heat and has more of a kinship to wild arugula. *Serves 4 to 6*

1 tablespoon olive oil

1 cup diced pancetta

12 fingerling potatoes, halved lengthwise

Kosher salt

½ cup crème fraîche

1 tablespoon whole-grain mustard

1 tablespoon freshly squeezed lemon juice

2 tablespoons minced fresh chives

½ teaspoon freshly ground black pepper

2 live lobsters, cooked, shelled, and cut into bite-size chunks (see page 59)

2 cups arugula leaves

1 Preheat the oven to 400°F.

2 Place a large cast-iron skillet over medium heat, and add the olive oil and pancetta. Cook the pancetta until crisp, 8 to 10 minutes. Remove the pancetta from the pan with a slotted spoon and drain on paper towels. Lower the heat to medium-low, and add the potatoes to the fat in the pan. Season the potatoes with kosher salt and sear for 10 minutes, or until they turn golden in color.

Then place the skillet in the oven and roast the potatoes for 15 minutes, or until golden brown on the outside and tender in the center.

3 While the potatoes are cooking, combine the crème fraîche, mustard, lemon juice, chives, and pepper in a bowl and whisk them together. Season with kosher salt to taste and set aside.

4 When the potatoes are done, remove the skillet from the oven. Add the lobster meat and the crème fraîche dressing, and fold together. Add the pancetta and arugula at the last moment, and transfer to a platter.

ASPARAGUS

I remember my friend Nick giving his mom an asparagus cooking pot. We were about sixteen and I had no idea, even with two years of cooking in restaurants under my belt, that such a specialized device existed. But there it was, a tall narrow pot with a steamer insert, everything all gleaming stainless steel. It was a beautiful thing and she appreciated it, a lot more than she appreciated us at that age. We were trouble, but the asparagus evidently made everything better.

Asparagus equals spring. Grill it, roast it, puree it, poach it, steam it, or broil it. Just get cooking it, and look for it in the wild and at your local market, as there is nothing like asparagus cooked the same day it was picked.

PICKLED GREEN ASPARAGUS

Pickled asparagus makes a perfect complement to a Bloody Mary or, chopped up, an unusual one to finish a rib-eye steak or a perfectly roasted chicken. Any way you cut it, it's just a good thing to preserve one of the quintessential offerings of this time of year. *Makes 1 quart*

1 pound asparagus
2 sprigs fresh tarragon
1 tablespoon pickling salt
1 tablespoon yellow mustard seeds
½ tablespoon pink peppercorns
½ teaspoon crushed red pepper flakes
1 cup cider vinegar

1 Trim or snap off the woody bottoms of the asparagus. Peel the lower 2 inches of the remaining asparagus stalks with a vegetable peeler. Pack the asparagus and the tarragon sprigs into a clean quart jar, making sure there's an inch of clearance at the top, and set it aside.

2 Combine the pickling salt, mustard seeds, peppercorns, red pepper flakes, vinegar, and 1 cup of water in a small nonreactive saucepan and bring to a boil. Reduce the heat to low and simmer for 5 minutes. Remove the pan from the heat and set it aside to cool for 10 minutes.

3 Ladle the pickling mixture into the jar, leaving ½ inch of headspace at the top. The jar can be stored in the refrigerator for up to 2 months, or processed according to the jar manufacturer's directions to store on the shelf for 9 months.

SAVORY ASPARAGUS CUSTARD

Custards are so easy to make once you know how, so use this as a technique primer. The key is to understand what the simmering water is accomplishing: it is a temperature that will steam the eggs gently to a set stage without giving you scrambled eggs. Unplanned scrambled eggs are not cool. Cook on. *Serves 6 as a side*

Kosher salt
8 asparagus spears, tough ends removed, peeled if thick
3 large eggs
1 cup heavy cream
½ cup whole milk
½ cup chicken stock (see page 22)
¼ cup shaved Parmigiano-Reggiano cheese (shaved using a vegetable peeler)

1 Lightly spray 6 ramekins or teacups with cooking spray, and set them aside. Prepare an ice water bath, and set it near the stove.

2 Bring a saucepan of water to a boil, salt it generously, and blanch the asparagus in the boiling water for 1 minute. Drain the asparagus and immediately place the spears in the ice water to stop the cooking.

3 When the asparagus has cooled, drain it and cut off the top 2 inches of the spears; set them aside for later decoration. Cut the rest into ½-inch pieces.

4 Place the small cuts of asparagus in a blender, and add the eggs, cream, milk, chicken stock, and ½ teaspoon kosher salt. Blend until smooth. Then strain this custard base through a sieve into a bowl to remove the bubbles. Let it sit for 10 minutes to mellow out, and then divide it among the prepared ramekins. Tightly cover each individual ramekin with plastic wrap.

5 Pour water to a depth of 1½ inches in a large, wide-bottomed pot with a lid, and place the pot over high heat. Bring the water to a boil, and then reduce it to a gentle simmer. Carefully place the ramekins in the simmering water, cover the pot, and steam for 15 to 20 minutes. To test for doneness, give a ramekin a brief shake: if the result is a second of shaking custard and then the wiggling stops, you are good to go. If it continues to shake as though it has a lot of uncooked liquid in the center, return it to the steam bath and cook for a few more minutes. Remove the ramekins from the pot and when they have cooled slightly carefully pull off the plastic wrap.

6 Serve warm or chilled, garnished with the reserved asparagus tips and the shavings of Parmigiano-Reggiano.

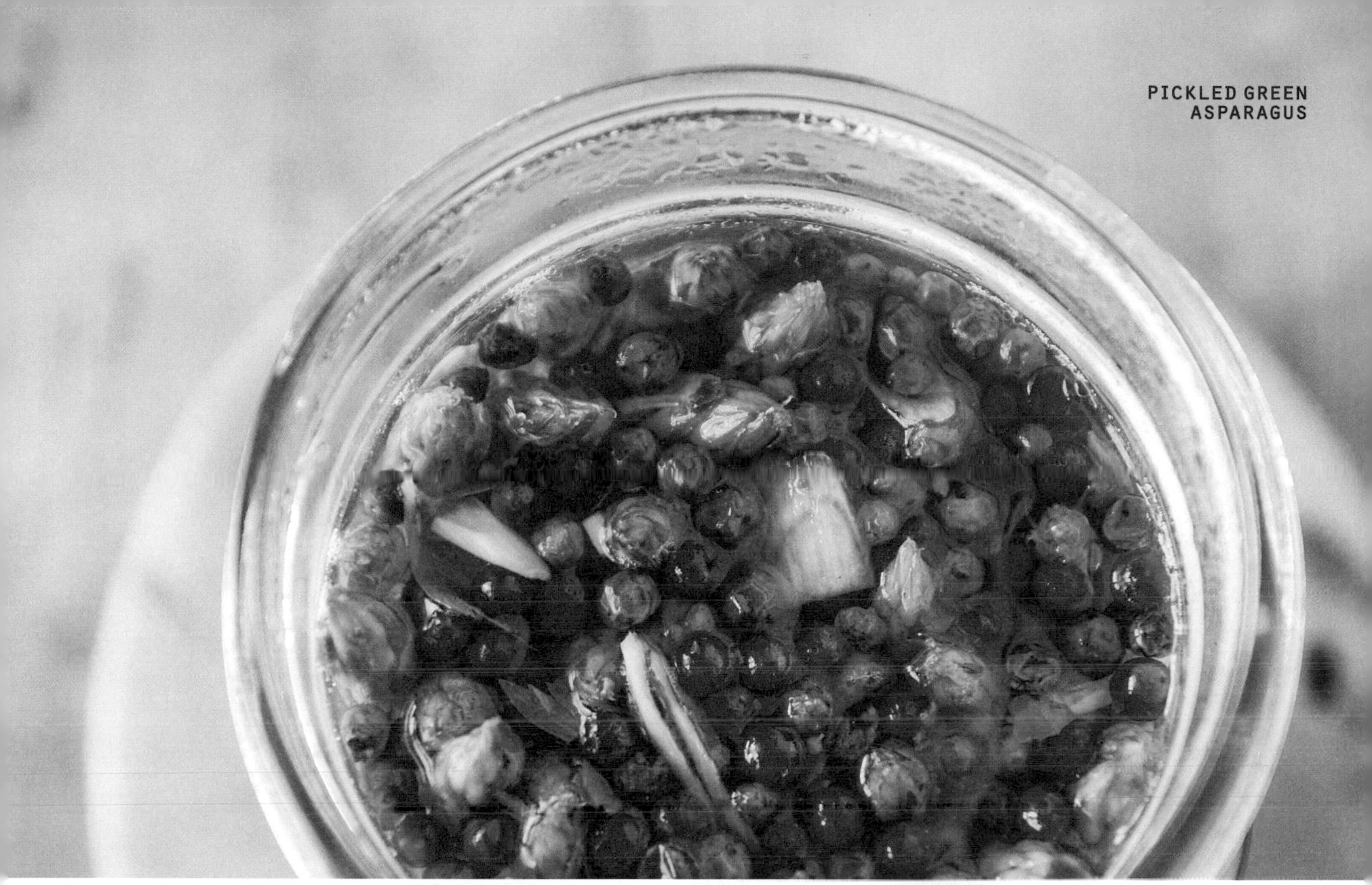

PICKLED GREEN ASPARAGUS

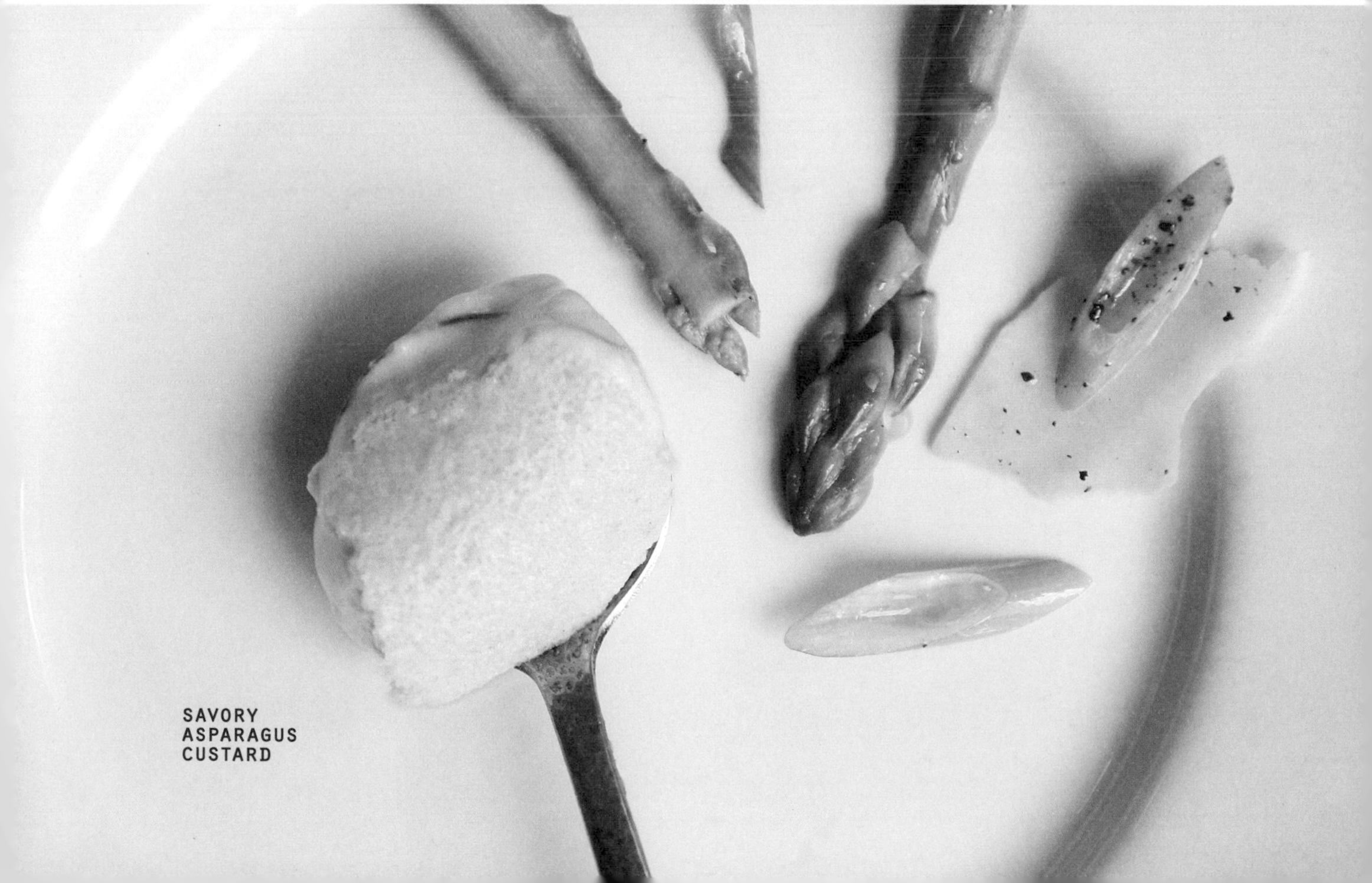

SAVORY ASPARAGUS CUSTARD

GRIDDLED ASPARAGUS,
PIPÉRADE, POACHED
EGGS, AND GRITS

SHAVED ASPARAGUS
SALAD WITH ALMONDS,
BONITO FLAKES, AND
APPLE

SHAVED ASPARAGUS SALAD WITH ALMONDS, BONITO FLAKES, AND APPLE

Raw asparagus is a winner in my book. Crunchy and bright green in flavor, it pairs here with the umami wonder of bonito flakes, the nuttiness of almonds, and the crispness of apple. *Serves 4 as a side*

1 pound asparagus

2 tablespoons olive oil

2 teaspoons freshly squeezed lemon juice

Sea salt

½ cup slivered almonds, toasted

1 apple, cored and thinly sliced

¼ cup bonito flakes

1 Snap off the woody ends of the asparagus and discard, and peel any spears thicker than a pencil. Using a mandoline or a vegetable peeler, shave the spears of the asparagus (including the heads) as thin as possible.

2 In a medium bowl, dress the shaved asparagus with the olive oil, lemon juice, and sea salt to taste. Arrange the asparagus on a serving platter with the almonds, apple slices, and bonito flakes.

GRIDDLED ASPARAGUS, PIPÉRADE, POACHED EGGS, AND GRITS

This is an ode to Spain, a culture totally infatuated with the glories of asparagus. Here the green spears are paired with a classic Basque tomato-pepper relish called *pipérade*, simple poached eggs, and grits. One of these things has no place in Spain, but you can take the boy out of Georgia but you . . . well, you know. *Serves 4*

2 cups chicken stock (see page 22)

2 tablespoons unsalted butter

Sea salt

½ cup white corn grits

½ cup heavy cream

3 tablespoons olive oil

4 garlic cloves, thinly sliced

½ cup thinly sliced shallots

1 cup julienned red bell pepper

2 roma tomatoes, peeled and coarsely chopped

2 bay leaves

1 teaspoon ground Espelette pepper

1 tablespoon sherry vinegar

½ pound asparagus, tough ends removed, spears peeled if thick

4 poached eggs (see page 184)

1 In a medium saucepan, combine the chicken stock, butter, and sea salt to taste, and bring to a boil over high heat. Whisk in the grits and stir for 1 minute with a wooden spoon. Reduce the heat to low and cook the grits, stirring often, for 20 minutes, or until they are tender. Finish the grits with the cream, add more sea salt to taste, and stir well. Cover to keep warm. (I use the waxed paper from a stick of butter for this, placed butter side down over the grits so they don't develop an unseemly crust.)

2 Meanwhile, in a medium saucepan combine 2 tablespoons of the olive oil and the garlic. Slowly cook the garlic over medium-low heat, making sure not to allow any color to develop, for about 5 minutes. Add the shallots, bell pepper, and a few pinches of sea salt. Cook for 12 minutes or until tender. Add the tomatoes, bay leaves, and Espelette pepper. Continue to cook for 15 more minutes or until the consistency is much like a thick soup. Finish with the sherry vinegar and sea salt to taste, and cover and set aside to keep warm. Remove the bay leaves prior to serving.

3 Place a large cast-iron sauté pan over medium-high heat. In a mixing bowl, toss the asparagus, the remaining tablespoon of olive oil, and a few pinches of sea salt. When the pan is giving off a light smoke, place the asparagus in the hot pan and cook for 2 minutes. Turn the asparagus over and cook for an additional 2 minutes. The asparagus should have good, even char marks all around and be crisp-tender. Remove from the heat.

4 Spoon the grits evenly onto 4 plates. Place a poached egg on each plate, and arrange the griddled asparagus and pipérade over the top.

Perfectly Poached Eggs

There are so many how-to's and recipes for poaching eggs that this seems like one more coach on the sidelines yelling at you as you try to cook: "Is the water right?" "Too much vinegar. TOO MUCH VINEGAR." Then I throw a chair onto the court and get a technical foul.

I want you to win this game without me yelling on the sidelines. So let's get some basics out of the way:

- The eggs should be at room temperature. Cooking cold ones adds a minute to this whole exercise. And I can only guess what the temperature inside your fridge is. I do know that most houses are at 70°F.

- Poach in a pot that works for you. My favorite is an All-Clad saucepan, 8 inches in diameter, 3½ inches deep, that holds 3 quarts of water.

- The swirl is important, and by that I mean the swirl you create by circulating the water before dropping the eggs in. This makes the whites tighter around the yolk and not so strung out.

- The vinegar acts as a coagulant and helps the egg whites set up correctly. Use just enough to make the eggs not taste like vinegar. This is all too common a mistake. You can omit it if you don't want the vinegar in there.

- If you don't have an instant-read thermometer, you should buy one. I have a Thermapen, and though spendy, it rules. The poaching temperature should be about 165°F.

- You need a good perforated spoon. In my restaurants we use Gray Kunz spoons, which are really swank, but at home I use one from Michael Ruhlman. It's bigger and homier.

4 eggs
1 tablespoon distilled white vinegar
1 tablespoon sea salt

1 Find 4 ramekins or teacups in your cupboard. Crack 1 egg into each ramekin.

2 Place your poaching pot on the stove, pour 2 quarts of cold water into it, and add the vinegar. Bring the liquid to a boil and add the sea salt. Reduce the heat to just below a simmer, so it's trembling, not bubbling. This will be about 165° to 170°F; take the temperature to be sure. Swirl the water a few times with a large spoon. While the water is still swirling around, gently pour each egg into the water, one by one. Start the timer. We are going for 4 minutes for a soft yolk, but if you like firm yolks, go longer. When they're done, spoon out the eggs, one by one, onto a waiting piece of paper towel. Serve immediately.

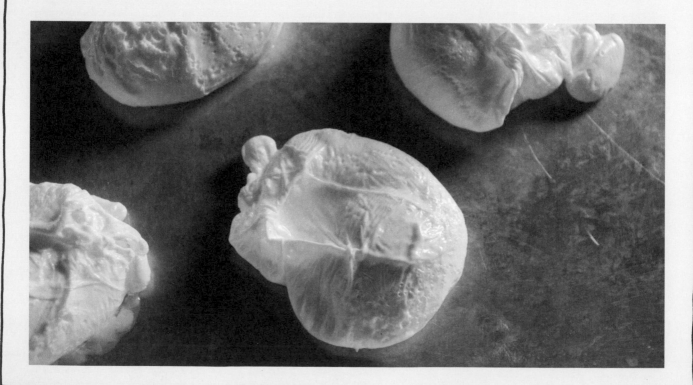

AVOCADOS

Spring is a celebration of our domestic crop of avocados, most of which are grown on family farms in California. It is good farming to support, and the results are a tasty treat. I adore avocados prepared in many ways, but often revert to the simplest way imaginable: halved, pit pulled out, sprinkled with good salt, and doused with a squeeze of lime juice. Grab a spoon and have a snack.

ROASTED POBLANO AND PECAN GUACAMOLE

I love guacamole, and this version keeps it pretty simple with the great Southern addition of toasted pecans—when you hit that toasty goodness in the pecans, it just plays up the rich, fresh flavor of the avocados. Poblano peppers offer just enough heat, yet still appeal to those shy of spiciness in food. *Makes 5 cups*

1 fresh poblano chile

1½ teaspoons olive oil

⅓ cup pecan halves

4 ripe Hass avocados

1 tablespoon freshly squeezed lime juice

½ cup minced sweet onion

¼ cup chopped fresh cilantro leaves

1 roma tomato, seeded and finely diced

¼ teaspoon toasted and ground cumin seeds

Kosher salt, to taste

Freshly ground black pepper, to taste

1 Place a small cast-iron skillet in the oven, and preheat the oven to 450°F.

2 In a small bowl, toss the poblano with a dash of the olive oil, carefully place it in the hot skillet, and roast it in the oven, turning it over when charred. When it's thoroughly blistered and charred, after about 15 minutes, place the hot pepper in a container, cover it, and set it aside to let the steam loosen the skin.

3 Turn the oven down to 400°F.

4 Place the pecans in the same cast-iron skillet, put it in the oven, and toast them for about 5 minutes—but ovens can be erratic, so keep a close eye on them. Burning nuts is a very common error, even in professional kitchens; it just happens so fast. You are looking for a nice toasty pecan, not blackened. Set the toasted pecans aside to cool, and then chop them into smaller pieces and set aside.

5 When the poblano is cool, peel, seed, and core it. Chop the flesh into small dice and reserve.

6 Cut the avocados in half and remove the pits. Cupping each avocado half in your palm, carefully score through the avocado flesh with a paring knife, creating a grid pattern. Using a soup spoon, scoop out the avocado flesh, dropping it directly into a medium bowl. Immediately toss the avocado with the lime juice to keep it from browning.

7 Add the onion, cilantro, remaining olive oil, diced tomato, cumin, kosher salt, and black pepper to the avocado. Add the pecans and poblano. Lightly mash with the tines of a large fork, and serve immediately.

CHILLED AVOCADO SOUP WITH CRAB AND YOGURT

The trick to chilled soups is to realize that flavors dull when they are cold, so you really have to put some punch into it. Lime, yogurt, cilantro stems, sautéed shallots, and tomatillos work to play a great backup to the beautiful ripe avocado. *Serves 6*

1 tablespoon olive oil

2 shallots, minced

½ cup husked and chopped tomatillos

1 teaspoon minced jalapeño

1 cup chicken stock (see page 22) or vegetable stock

¼ cup minced fresh cilantro stems

½ teaspoon grated lime zest

1 tablespoon plus 1 teaspoon freshly squeezed lime juice

2 large ripe Hass avocados

1 cup plain yogurt

Kosher salt

½ pound tomatoes, diced

½ pound crabmeat, picked over for cartilage and shells

2 tablespoons chopped fresh cilantro leaves

1 Place a small sauté pan over medium heat and add the olive oil. When the oil is hot, add the minced shallots and cook for 4 minutes, until softened. Put the shallots into a blender and add the tomatillos, half of the jalapeño, the stock, cilantro stems, lime zest, and the 1 tablespoon lime juice. Puree until smooth.

2 Pit the avocados and scoop out the flesh. Add the avocado flesh and the yogurt to the blender, and puree until very smooth. Season with kosher salt to taste. Keep the soup in the fridge until ready to serve.

3 When you are ready to serve the soup, combine the tomatoes, the remaining 1 teaspoon lime juice, the rest of the jalapeño, the crab, the chopped cilantro leaves, and kosher salt to taste in a bowl. Toss gently with a spoon. Divide the soup among individual bowls, and garnish each one with a scoop of the tomato-crab mixture. Eat.

ROASTED POBLANO
AND PECAN
GUACAMOLE

CHILLED
AVOCAOO
SOUP WITH
CRAB AND
YOGURT

ROASTED PORK TENDERLOIN WITH BOK CHOY, CURRIED TOMATOES, AND AVOCADO

Pork tenderloin is such a wonderfully easy protein to cook. Low in fat, this flexible dish really is a family-pleaser. The added bounce of the bok choy is a great addition for greenery that will make every bite that much healthier. The tomatoes and avocado marry in a classic manner that my family—and pretty much everyone—loves. *Serves 6*

2 cups cherry tomatoes, halved

Kosher salt

3 tablespoons olive oil

2 shallots, minced

2 jalapeños, thinly sliced

½ teaspoon cumin seeds, ground

1 teaspoon yellow mustard seeds, ground

4 tablespoons freshly squeezed lime juice

3 tablespoons cider vinegar

1 teaspoon light brown sugar

¼ cup chopped fresh mint leaves

¼ cup chopped fresh flat-leaf parsley leaves

3 ripe Hass avocados

2 tablespoons vegetable oil

2 pounds pork tenderloin, trimmed of all silverskin and connective tissue

3 cups thinly sliced bok choy

1 Preheat the oven to 400°F.

2 Let's make the curried tomatoes: Place the tomatoes in a medium bowl. Season them with kosher salt.

3 In a large sauté pan, bring the olive oil to a shimmer over medium-high heat. Add the shallots, then the jalapeños. Cook until tender, about 3 minutes. Add the ground cumin and mustard seeds, toast for about 1 minute, until fragrant, and remove from the heat.

4 Let the shallot mixture cool slightly. Then carefully add 2 tablespoons of the lime juice, all the vinegar, and the brown sugar, and pour the mixture over the tomatoes. Add the mint, parsley, and some more kosher salt.

5 Pit the avocados by cutting them in half and then prying out the pits. Score the flesh into ¼-inch-wide slices and scoop the slices from the shell. In a medium bowl, toss the avocado slices with the remaining 2 tablespoons lime juice, and season with kosher salt. Add them to the curried tomatoes and toss gently. Let the tomato/avocado mixture sit at room temperature for the flavors to mature while you roast the pork.

6 Place a large ovenproof sauté pan over medium-high heat and add the vegetable oil. Pat the pork dry and season it all over with kosher salt. When the oil is shimmering, carefully add the pork to the pan, and sear on all sides until golden, for a total of about 5 minutes. Then transfer the pan to the oven and roast for 7 to 10 minutes, or until the pork is a rosy medium, an interior temperature of 130°F. Remove the pork from the pan and let it rest on a cutting board for 5 minutes. While the pan is still hot, add the bok choy and simply let it wilt in the pan.

7 When the pork has rested, slice it into thin rounds, about ¼ inch thick. Arrange the pork and the bok choy on a platter, top the pork and bok choy with the tomato and avocado mixture, and serve.

BEETS

Beets are my star student. I stand by this statement: If we can get our kids to eat beets on a regular basis at three or four years old, they will be better humans and we will have a better society.

To me it's a truism that we will have a better food world if kids eat more vegetables. Farming gets better, markets get busier, diabetes rates go down with healthier eating, obesity rates go down with a palatable option to fast food and junk snacks. These are the results of a better-eating generation. A lot of people are afraid of beets because they taste earthy, but I say let beets and all their mineral sweetness be a gateway vegetable. A kid who eats beets grows up to be an adult who cares about the world of food, and that's what we need to make the world better.

PICKLED BEETS

A Southern classic and a great staple for simple salads and the pickle plate. *Makes 1 quart or 2 pints*

2 pounds small beets, without their greens

1 tablespoon kosher salt

1½ tablespoons pickling salt

2 tablespoons sugar

1 teaspoon yellow mustard seeds

½ teaspoon caraway seeds

1½ cups cider vinegar

1 Place the beets and kosher salt in a pot, add water to cover, and bring to a boil over medium heat. Then reduce the heat and simmer until tender, about 20 minutes. Drain the beets and set them aside until they are cool enough to handle.

2 Place paper towels on a cutting board (this will reduce the mess of beet juice). Peel the beets, discarding the skin, and cut them into ¼-inch-thick slices. Place the slices in a clean quart jar (or 2 pint jars), leaving ½ inch of headspace at the top, and set aside.

3 Combine the pickling salt, sugar, mustard seeds, caraway seeds, vinegar, and 1 cup of water in a small nonreactive pot and bring to a boil. Reduce the heat to low and simmer for 5 minutes. Then carefully ladle the hot pickling mixture into the jar, leaving ½ inch of headspace. Cap with the lid and band, and let cool for 2 hours. The jars can be stored in the refrigerator for up to 2 months, or processed according to the jar manufacturer's directions and stored on the shelf for up to 1 year.

FARRO WITH BEETS, DATES, AND SHAVED BEET SALAD

Farro is a beautiful grain that has been back in vogue lately. Nutty in flavor, with a nice chewy texture, it is a great starch to play around with in the kitchen and is also exceptionally good for you. Anson Mills grows a particular variety called *farro piccolo* that I love. Chile threads garnish this dish and the fiery little strands of piquant chile provide a nice textural contrast and look all pretty, too.
Serves 4 as a side dish or an appetizer

6 baby beets, with their greens, washed and dried

2 cups fresh Medjool dates

Kosher salt

1 teaspoon crushed red pepper flakes

1 cup white balsamic vinegar

2 tablespoons unsalted butter

¼ cup diced onion

1 cup farro

1 sprig fresh thyme

½ cup grated Parmigiano-Reggiano cheese, plus more for shaving

½ cup shaved baby candy-stripe beets (shaved with a mandoline)

2 tablespoons chopped fresh flat-leaf parsley leaves

1 teaspoon finely chopped fresh rosemary leaves

1 teaspoon chopped fresh mint leaves

2 tablespoons red wine vinegar

Fleur de sel or other flaky salt

8 chile threads (see page 103)

1 Peel the beets and cut them into ¼-inch cubes. Slice the beet greens into thin ribbons.

2 In a small saucepan, combine the dates, 1 teaspoon kosher salt, the red pepper flakes, and the white balsamic vinegar with enough water to just cover the dates. Bring to a boil, then lower the heat to a simmer and cook for 30 minutes, until the dates are very tender. Remove the pan from the heat and carefully strain the liquid into another small saucepan. Remove the dates from the strainer and discard the chile flakes. Reduce the strained liquid over medium heat to half its original volume. Meanwhile, remove the outer skin from the dates. When the poaching liquid is reduced, remove from the heat and set aside with the peeled dates.

3 In a wide saucepan, melt 1 tablespoon of the butter over medium-high heat. When it foams, add the onion and cook, stirring, until it is translucent, about 3 minutes. Add the farro and stir until it begins to lightly toast and the mixture is aromatic, about 2 minutes. Add the thyme sprig and 1 cup of water and stir. Let the farro simmer for about 5 minutes, then add another 1 cup of water and cook for 5 more minutes. Add the diced beets, the chopped beet greens and 2 more cups of water and cook, stirring, until the water is almost fully absorbed but the farro is still a little wet looking, about 15 minutes. Add the remaining tablespoon of butter, kosher salt to taste, and the grated Parmigiano-Reggiano. The farro should be slightly thickened. Remove from the heat, but keep warm on the stovetop.

4 In a medium mixing bowl, combine the beet shavings, parsley, rosemary, mint, and red wine vinegar. Toss lightly.

PICKLED
BEETS

FARRO
WITH BEETS,
DATES, AND
SHAVED
BEET SALAD

5 Warm the dates in the reduced poaching liquid over medium heat.

6 Divide the farro among shallow serving bowls and top with the dates, some of their poaching liquid, and the shaved beet salad. Finish each dish with a sprinkle of fleur de sel, a few shavings of Parmigiano-Reggiano, and chile threads.

ROASTED BEET SOUP WITH HARD-BOILED EGG AND CELERY CREAM

I like having a supply of homemade soup in the fridge. It makes me feel secure. Like a kid's blankie or an adult's smartphone.

Making soup is easy. This will take about an hour on a Saturday morning, but dinner is pretty much prepared after that. A simple salad, some really great bread, some nice cheese, and a big bowl of this soup will make for a happy night.

Lecithin is a water-soluble emulsifier that also gives liquids the ability to hold air, or be frothy. That is about as molecular as I get. You can buy it online, or you can skip it. *Serves 4 as an appetizer*

1 pound small beets, without their greens, washed	2 sprigs fresh flat-leaf parsley
Kosher salt	1 quart chicken stock (see page 22)
1½ tablespoons olive oil	½ cup heavy cream
2 tablespoons unsalted butter	½ teaspoon lecithin powder (optional, if you want to be fancy)
1 cup minced onion	
1 cup minced celery	4 hard-boiled eggs, peeled and sliced
2 sprigs fresh thyme	
2 bay leaves	

1 Preheat the oven to 400°F.

2 Place the beets in a saucepan, add water to cover, and bring to a boil. Salt the water generously, reduce the heat, and simmer until the beets are just tender, about 20 minutes. Remove from the heat, drain, and set the beets aside until they are just cool enough to handle. Then peel the beets, and cut them in half lengthwise. In a small baking dish, toss the beets with 1 tablespoon of the olive oil. Season them with kosher salt to taste, and roast in the oven for 15 minutes.

3 Meanwhile, melt the butter in a large saucepan over medium heat. When the butter is melted and frothing, add the onion and cook for 10 minutes, until very soft. Add ½ cup of the celery. Tie the thyme sprigs, bay leaves, and parsley sprigs in a bundle and add it to the onion. Pour in the stock and bring it to a simmer; then turn the heat down to low.

4 Remove the beets from the oven and add them to this soup base. Season the soup with kosher salt to taste, and cook for 5 minutes. Remove the herb bundle and then carefully puree the soup, in batches if necessary, in a blender. Pass it through a fine-mesh sieve into a saucepan. Set it aside until you are ready to reheat and serve.

5 For the celery cream/froth, place a small saucepan over medium heat and add the remaining ½ tablespoon olive oil. Add the remaining ½ cup celery and cook for 5 minutes, until it is softening and very fragrant. Add the cream and cook for 1 minute. Let the celery mixture cool a little, and then puree it in the blender. You can use the celery cream as a garnish, but if you want to be fancy and turn it into an airy froth, pour it into a clean plastic quart container, add the lecithin powder, and then aerate it with an immersion blender.

6 To serve, rewarm the soup and portion it into bowls. Garnish with slices of hard-boiled egg, and then spoon the celery cream—or the celery froth—on top.

BEETS WITH SERRANO HAM, YOUNG MANCHEGO, BOILED EGGS, ARUGULA, AND SMOKED PAPRIKA DRESSING

The dining world was invaded decades ago by the equation: beets + goat cheese + balsamic vinegar + greens = good.

I was quite pleased to leave that well-worn path. This salad is an ode to Spain and shows that we can always go in new directions with classic flavors.

Serves 4 as a salad or an appetizer

1 cup kosher salt, plus more to taste

6 golf-ball-size beets, without their greens

4 eggs

1 cup plain yogurt

1 shallot, minced

1 teaspoon grated lemon zest

1 tablespoon freshly squeezed lemon juice

2 tablespoons white balsamic vinegar

½ teaspoon freshly ground black pepper

2 teaspoons smoked sweet paprika (pimentón)

¼ pound arugula

3 ounces Serrano ham, sliced as thin as possible

1 ounce young Manchego cheese, thinly shaved with a vegetable peeler

1 Preheat the oven to 400°F.

2 In a small cast-iron sauté pan, create a bed of kosher salt to hold the beets. Place the beets on the salt, making sure there is space around each one. Roast the beets for 45 minutes, until they are tender but still have a little resistance when pierced with a small knife. Allow the beets to cool to room temperature.

3 Meanwhile, bring 2 quarts of water to a boil in a saucepan over high heat. Add the eggs and boil for 5 minutes. Then remove the pan from the heat, cover it, and set it aside for 5 minutes. Remove the eggs and run cold water over them to arrest the cooking process. Peel the eggs, slice them, and reserve.

4 Peel the beets and cut each one into 6 wedges. Put them in a mixing bowl and season lightly with kosher salt.

5 In a small mixing bowl, combine the yogurt, shallot, lemon zest and juice, vinegar, pepper, paprika, and kosher salt to taste. Whisk the dressing until all the ingredients are fully incorporated.

6 Smear as much dressing as you like onto a large platter and arrange the beets on top. Arrange the arugula and then the ham, Manchego, and eggs.

CABBAGE

Cabbage is such a gem of a vegetable. It is surprisingly flexible in preparation, and fast, easy, and great to prepare whether you are sautéing it, broiling it, stewing it, canning it, fermenting it, frying it . . . the list goes on. You can really do anything with cabbage, and it's all delicious and economical. Get those heads chopping

CABBAGE SAUERKRAUT

So fermentation is the hip thing all the kids are doing, and I am here to tell you where to start: sauerkraut. What's simpler than cabbage and salt? And the result is so much tastier than what you get in jars—less sour and way more complex. The basic notion is that you weigh the cabbage, use enough salt to equal 2.5% of the cabbage weight, and then the spices are to your taste. When you salt the cabbage and let it sit, you will see liquid accumulate; you push the cabbage under the liquid, and that protects it from mold. If you don't get enough liquid from the cabbage, just add some brine made by heating water and dissolving—you guessed it—2.5% of the water's weight in salt. Use a scale; it will make your life easier.

Makes a lot

6 pounds organic green cabbage, quartered, cores removed, and outer leaves discarded

½ cup kosher salt (if using Diamond Crystal brand; ¼ cup if you're using Morton's)

1 tablespoon caraway seeds

1 tablespoon black peppercorns

12 bay leaves

1½ teaspoons allspice berries

1 Wash your hands. Thinly slice the cabbage, place it in a large container, and sprinkle the salt all over it. Toss well, squeezing and beating it up a bit with your hands. Let it sit at room temperature for about 1 hour. Then add the caraway seeds, peppercorns, bay leaves, and allspice berries, and let it sit for another hour or two.

2 Pack the cabbage into clean mason jars or a ceramic crock, pushing down on the cabbage to submerge it in its juice that has exuded in the salting process. If need be, make a brine with 1 tablespoon of Diamond Crystal kosher salt (or ½ tablespoon Morton's kosher salt) to every pint of water, and top off the cabbage. Drop in a clean non-metal plate to keep the cabbage submerged.

3 The flavor will develop the longer you let it sit out; just check on it about once a day and skim off any white mold that forms. (This is normal.) After about 8 days at an ideal 65°F, you have sauerkraut, though some more adventurous people let it go for months. Taste it every few days to see how mature you like it. Once it's done, I put it into clean jars and store it in the fridge (I like to eat it within 4 weeks but it'll keep for months). Don't heat-process. Sauerkraut, like vinegar, is a live culture. You ruin any probiotic beauty if you process it.

harsch gairtopf crock

I have a Harsch Gairtopf that I bought online. The challenge with making sauerkraut is keeping the cabbage submerged in its juices during the fermentation process while still allowing the fermenting cabbage to breathe out. This ingenious crock has stone plates that nestle into the jar and hold the matter down below the liquid line to deal with the former concern, and then a beveled top that holds a moat of water, allowing air to escape but not enter the crock. It is a bit spendy, but if you use it about ten times it will pay for itself by feeding your family delicious fermented vegetables. You can buy them pretty easily online. Google dat.

CLASSIC CABBAGE KIMCHI

I love kimchi. To me, the world is a better place when we all enjoy kimchi. Fiery and fun, it gives a kick to all food. *Makes 4 quarts*

6 pounds napa cabbage

4 tablespoons kosher salt

2 tablespoons light brown sugar

⅓ cup minced garlic

⅓ cup minced fresh ginger

¼ cup hot smoked paprika (pimentón)

¼ cup Korean chile powder

1 tablespoon crushed red pepper flakes

2 tablespoons freshly squeezed lime juice

½ cup Asian fish sauce

½ cup brine shrimp (available in a jar at Asian food stores), finely chopped

2 bunches scallions, cut into ½-inch pieces (about 12 scallions)

1 Rinse the cabbage, and then quarter the heads lengthwise. Place the pieces in a large pot or bucket, and sprinkle 1 tablespoon of the salt over them. Set aside for 1 hour.

2 Rinse the cabbage under cold running water, and pat it dry. Cut the cabbage into 1-inch pieces, put them in a large bowl, and toss with the remaining 3 tablespoons salt. Let sit for 2 hours. The salt will draw out moisture from the cabbage.

3 Drain off the accumulated liquid and lightly rinse the cabbage. In a large bowl, combine the cabbage with all the remaining ingredients, and toss well. Transfer the mixture to a large crock and push the mixture down to force the liquid to rise to the top, somewhat submerging the cabbage in its spicy surroundings. Cover it with a lid and store it in a cool, dark place for 3 days to ferment and mature.

4 Once the kimchi is tasting all kinds of yummy, transfer it to clean jars (I like quarts), cap them, and store in the fridge (which will inhibit further fermentation) for up to a month. Don't heat-process. Kimchi is a live culture. You ruin any probiotic beauty if you process it.

SEA SCALLOPS WITH BUTTERED KRAUT AND PECAN BROWN BUTTER

Here scallops pair with some cabbage kraut and a pecan-laden brown butter. If you have kraut ready to roll, this takes but a minute or two to complete. *Serves 4 as an appetizer*

½ cup pecan halves, chopped

5 tablespoons unsalted butter

Sea salt

2 tablespoons sherry vinegar

8 large sea scallops, cleaned and patted dry

2 tablespoons canola oil

1 cup Cabbage Sauerkraut (page 199)

1 pinch fleur de sel or other flaky finishing salt

2 tablespoons chopped fresh flat-leaf parsley leaves

1 Preheat the oven to 325°F.

2 Spread the pecans out on a small baking sheet and toast them in the oven for 7 minutes, or until lightly browned and fragrant. Remove them from the oven and set aside.

3 In a sauté pan, melt 2 tablespoons of the butter over medium-high heat, stirring it constantly. The milk solids will start to toast and you will smell the nutty aroma. At this point take the pan off the heat and add the pecans. Lightly season the pecans with sea salt and deglaze the pan with the vinegar. Set aside.

4 Pat the scallops dry and season them with sea salt. Place a large sauté pan on high heat and add the canola oil. When the oil is shimmering, place the scallops in the hot pan and sear them on one side for 3 minutes, until they are nicely browned. Add 1 tablespoon of the butter, and when it has melted, spoon the butter over the scallops to baste them. Turn the scallops over and cook for another 2 to 3 minutes, until just cooked. Remove the scallops from the pan and set them aside to rest for a couple of minutes.

5 In a small saucepan, gently warm the sauerkraut over medium heat. Once the kraut is warm, add the final 2 tablespoons butter and mix until it has melted.

6 To finish, divide the sauerkraut among 4 plates and top it with the seared scallops. Season with the fleur de sel. Drizzle the pecan brown butter over the top and garnish with the parsley leaves.

SEA SCALLOPS
WITH BUTTERED
KRAUT AND
PECAN BROWN
BUTTER

CLASSIC
CABBAGE
KIMCHI

CRISPED PORK BELLY WITH KIMCHI RICE GRITS AND RADISHES

This dish tells the story of my Southern food. Pork is a historically common protein in our area; rice grits, or broken kernels of Carolina Gold rice, show our coastal heritage as a rice-growing region; kimchi gives a nod to a beautifully worldly populace that now calls the South home; and radishes are a simple gift from the soil, a treat that comes to us every year. *Serves 4*

2 tablespoons vegetable oil

1 pound pork belly, skin off

Kosher salt

Freshly ground black pepper

1 small onion, diced

½ cup diced carrot

¼ cup diced celery

1 bay leaf

½ teaspoon coriander seeds

4 cups chicken stock (see page 22)

½ cup thinly sliced radish

2 scallions, white and light green parts, thinly sliced

½ teaspoon sugar

1 teaspoon freshly squeezed lime juice

¼ cup unseasoned rice vinegar

1 cup Anson Mills rice grits (or long-grain rice crushed in a blender for a couple of seconds)

½ cup heavy cream

½ cup chopped Classic Cabbage Kimchi (page 200)

2 tablespoons roasted peanuts, crushed

1 Preheat the oven to 300°F.

2 Warm a medium braising pan over medium heat and add 1 tablespoon of the vegetable oil. Season the pork belly all over with kosher salt and black pepper, and add it to the pan, fat side down. Cook until well crisped, about 10 minutes per side. Remove the belly from the pan and discard all but 2 tablespoons of the rendered fat and oil.

3 Add the onion, carrot, celery, bay leaf, and coriander seeds to the pan and cook for 5 minutes, until softening and fragrant. Add 2 cups of the chicken stock, bring the liquid to a boil, return the pork to the pan, cover, and braise in the oven for about 2 hours, or until the belly is very tender. Remove the pork from the pan and place it on a plate to cool. Strain the braising liquid into a saucepan, discarding the solids. When the belly has cooled, cut it into 4 equal pieces and hold in the fridge until ready to finish.

4 Combine the radish, scallions, sugar, lime juice, and rice vinegar in a bowl and set aside to lightly pickle.

5 Now we need to start the rice grits and finish the pork belly at the same time. To cook the rice grits, combine the rice and the remaining 2 cups of chicken stock in a saucepan, and bring to a boil. Season with kosher salt to taste. Reduce the heat to a bare simmer and slowly cook the grits for about 20 minutes, until the consistency is a thick congee-like porridge.

6 While the grits are cooking, place a large sauté pan over medium-high heat and add the remaining tablespoon of vegetable oil. When the oil is hot, add the pork belly pieces and carefully recrisp and warm them.

7 When the grits are cooked through, stir in the cream and the chopped kimchi. Season if need be, and then divide among 4 plates or wide bowls. Perch the crisped pork belly over each small mound of grits, and then spoon about a tablespoon of the braising liquid over each portion of belly. Finish with some of the pickled radish mixture and the roasted peanuts.

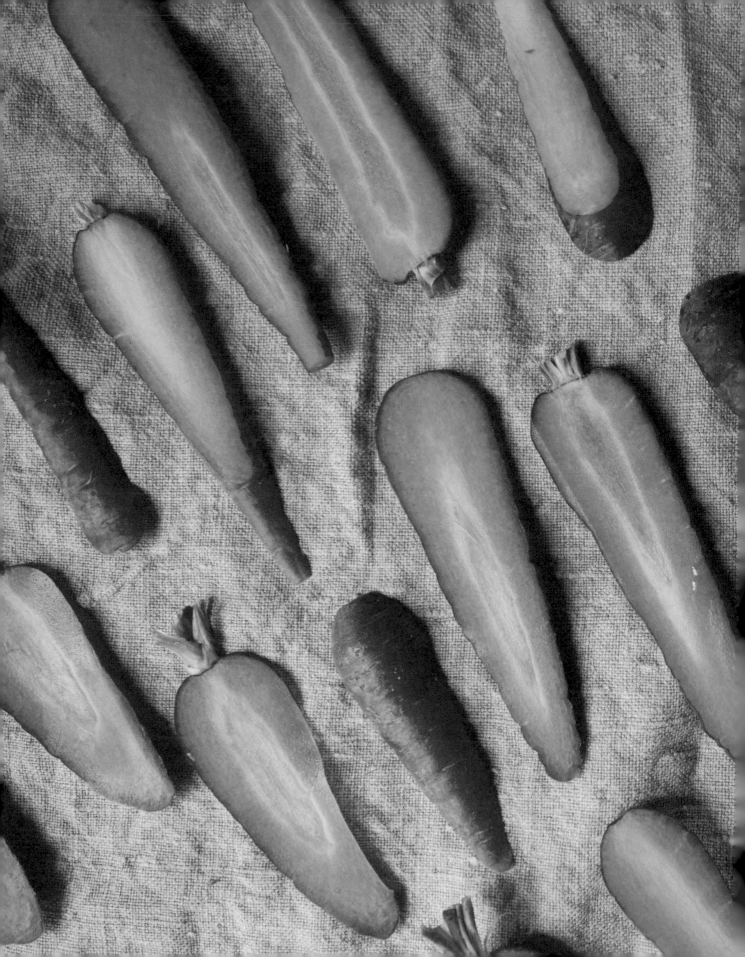

CARROTS

Carrots are my thang. They really are. Ask the cooks in my kitchen what concerns them, and it is that Hugh will eat all the carrots they have prepped. They have literally taken to setting out decoys of coarsely chopped carrots for me to snack on. My eyesight is great. (Or it was, until the inevitable need for reading glasses kicked in, reminding me of my newly minted middle-age status.) Still, I could eat a pound of carrots every day and never tire of their crisp crunch, their bright flavor, and their intense natural sweetness. They are treasures in different varieties, from Thumbelina to Nantes.

BIG BABY CARROT PUREE

This is baby food for big people, but it will still make little kids happy, too. It is a puree of the highest order, taking buttery richness and carroty sweetness and marrying them like the most powerful of food couples. *Serves 4 to 6 as a side*

2 tablespoons unsalted butter
½ cup chopped yellow onion
Sea salt

3 cups chopped carrots (from about 1½ pounds carrots)
2 cups chicken stock (see page 22)
Juice of 1 lemon

1 In a medium saucepan, melt 1 tablespoon of the butter over medium heat. Add the onion and some sea salt, and slowly cook the onion until it's soft, about 10 minutes. Add the carrots and continue to cook for 10 minutes. Add the chicken stock and bring to a boil. Then turn the heat down and simmer, uncovered, for 15 minutes, or until the carrots are completely soft.

2 Carefully pour the carrot mixture into a blender, and puree on high speed until completely smooth. While the blender is on, add the remaining tablespoon of butter and the lemon juice. Adjust the seasoning with more sea salt if needed, and serve.

FERMENTED CARROTS WITH GALANGAL AND LIME

This is a simple ferment, and your only concern is just to skim off any white mold that forms on the top. It should be done in about five days, but the longer it goes the more pronounced the flavor will be. The fermentation softens and adds salinity to the sweet carrots and gives them a really nice lactic acid charm. *Makes 1 quart or 2 pints*

1 pound carrots, peeled and sliced ¼ inch thick
1 tablespoon peeled and thinly sliced galangal or fresh ginger

1 tablespoon grated lime zest (absolutely no white pith)
2 teaspoons pickling salt

1 Pack the carrots, galangal, and lime zest in a clean 1-quart mason jar (or 2 pint jars), leaving 1 inch of headspace at the top, and set aside.

2 Combine the pickling salt and 2 cups of water in a nonreactive saucepan and heat to dissolve. Cool to room temperature.

3 Ladle the liquid into the jar, leaving ½ inch of headspace and completely covering the carrots. Cover the top of the jar with a square of cheesecloth and secure it with the jar's band. Place the jar in a dark spot that hovers between 65°F and 75°F, and leave it for 5 days, checking daily to remove any white mold that accumulates on top.

4 Remove the cheesecloth, cap the jar with the regular lid, and place in the fridge. Use it within a week.

SAUTÉED CARROTS WITH PINE NUTS, MALT VINEGAR, AND SORGHUM

Sweet and sour. Everybody loves sweet and sour. Here the sweet is sorghum and the sour is malt vinegar, the vinegar usually reserved for fish and chips. It's a great combo and an easy side that my kids adore. When I say "young carrots," I mean ones that are 4 to 7 inches in length and less than ¾ inch in diameter. The tops should be vibrant and bushy. *Serves 4 as a side*

1½ pounds young carrots, with greens
1 tablespoon plus 1 teaspoon olive oil
2 tablespoons pine nuts

1 tablespoon unsalted butter
Sea salt
1 tablespoon sorghum molasses
1 tablespoon malt vinegar

1 Prepare the carrots by removing their greens, washing them, and cutting them in half lengthwise. Wash a handful of the carrot greens, pull the leaves from the stems, and set the leaves aside to garnish the finished dish. Compost the rest of the carrot tops or reserve them for another use.

2 Place a small, heavy sauté pan over medium heat and add the teaspoon of olive oil. When the oil is hot, add the pine nuts and swirl them in the pan for a couple of minutes, until they are golden and aromatic. Depending on your medium heat, it could take far less time or slightly more, but the key to toasting nuts is that it needs your full, undivided attention. Set the pine nuts aside.

3 In a large sauté pan, heat the butter and remaining tablespoon of olive oil over medium-high heat. Once the butter melts and starts to foam, add the carrots and a few pinches of sea salt. Sauté the carrots for 5 minutes, stirring constantly. After the carrots get a little golden

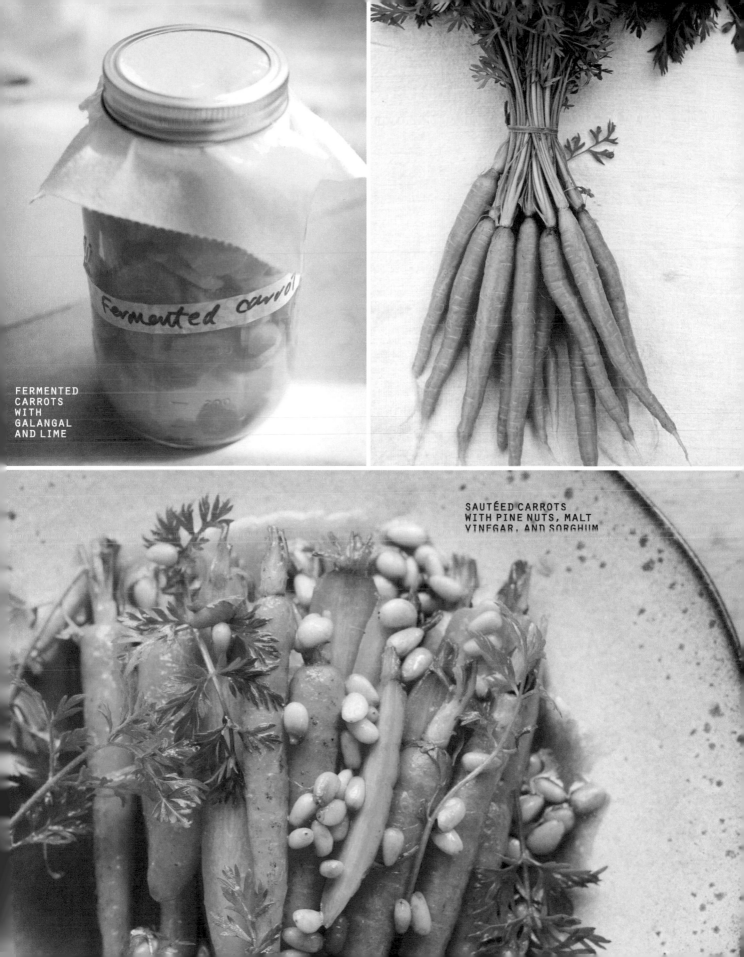

FERMENTED
CARROTS
WITH
GALANGAL
AND LIME

SAUTÉED CARROTS
WITH PINE NUTS, MALT
VINEGAR, AND SORGHUM

CARROTS VICHY

CARROT SOUP WITH
BROWN BUTTER,
PECANS, AND YOGURT

color around the edges, reduce the heat to medium. Add the sorghum and the vinegar, and stir to combine. Cook until the carrots are tender but with a little crispness in the center. Adjust the seasoning with more sea salt, sorghum, or vinegar to your taste, and remove from the heat.

4 Arrange the carrots on a serving dish, drizzle the liquid from the pan over them, and top them with the toasted pine nuts and reserved carrot leaves.

CARROTS VICHY (JUST LIKE THE BIG GUY)

The Big Guy is James Beard, one of many reasons we have advanced to the era of great food in America. Beard was a learner and a documenter, and he wrote beautifully about food with a certain disdain for people who don't care for the finer things in life. He was, shall we say, not a shy person.

JB didn't come up with this recipe, nor did I. I have changed some things, though: the herbs are fresh, the chile is added, the salt is reduced from Beard's edition. The cooking time is also a little shorter and the results are still awesome.

The original dish comes from the town of Vichy in the center of France. It's a town known for its great water, and the water is probably integral to the dish, but I am not in France and so we are using spring water from our area. Sometimes, in a pinch, I use "vegetable stock," which in my house is a code name for tap water. *Serves 4 as a side*

1 pound carrots, peeled if you roll that way, cut into ½-inch-thick rounds

¼ cup spring water

¼ cup (½ stick) unsalted butter

½ teaspoon kosher salt

½ teaspoon maple syrup

1 teaspoon chopped fresh marjoram leaves

2 tablespoons heavy cream

1 teaspoon thinly sliced fresh Hungarian or Fresno chile

½ cup chopped carrot tops

Find a heavy 2-quart pan with a lid. Place the pan over medium heat and once it is hot, add the carrots, spring water, butter, and salt. Cover and cook for 5 minutes, and then add the maple syrup, marjoram, and heavy cream. Cook for 1 more minute, or until the carrots are still crisp yet tender, too, a beautiful oxymoron in cooking. Add the chile and the carrot tops. Serve immediately.

CARROT SOUP WITH BROWN BUTTER, PECANS, AND YOGURT

The sweetness of the carrots, the acidity of the yogurt, and the nutty luxury of the brown butter make this soup a springtime favorite. *Serves 4 to 6*

1 pound carrots

4 tablespoons (½ stick) unsalted butter

1 medium yellow onion, minced

2 sprigs fresh thyme

1 red jalapeño, minced

2 tablespoons ground sesame seeds (not tahini—pulse them in a food processor or spice grinder)

1 quart chicken stock (see page 22)

Kosher salt

½ cup plus 2 tablespoons plain Greek yogurt

¼ cup crushed pecans

1 tablespoon sherry vinegar

2 tablespoons chopped carrot tops

Maple syrup, to taste

1 Peel the carrots and cut 1 carrot into very thin rounds. Cut the rest of the carrots into ½-inch pieces.

2 Melt 2 tablespoons of the butter in a medium saucepan over medium heat. Add the onion and cook, stirring occasionally, until soft, about 10 minutes. Add the thyme sprigs, jalapeño, sesame, and ½-inch cut carrots. Cook for 10 more minutes, stirring occasionally, and then add the stock and kosher salt to taste. Bring to a boil, reduce the heat, and simmer until the carrots are very tender, about 15 minutes. Remove from the heat and remove the thyme sprigs.

3 Puree the carrot mixture in a blender, taking care to secure the lid. Pour the soup back into the saucepan, stir in the ½ cup yogurt, adjust the seasoning with salt, and place the lid on it to keep it warm.

4 Melt the remaining 2 tablespoons butter in a small sauté pan over medium-high heat, and cook until the solids begin to brown. Add the pecans. Toss and toast for about 1 minute, and then remove from the heat and add the vinegar.

5 Serve the soup in bowls. Dollop each serving with the remaining yogurt and the pecan brown butter, sprinkle with the carrot tops and coins, and finish with a drizzle of maple syrup.

My Bookshelf, and How I Learn Every Day

I buy more cookbooks than my lifetime will allow me to fully read, but they still serve me well. Those books are my anchors, reminding me of where food has been and of the journey to make it better. I sit in my office and take down a copy of Michel Guérard's *Cuisine Minceur* and flip through it until something strikes a chord. I find a recipe for "Breast of Duckling with Fresh Figs" and read through for techniques that I hadn't thought of. He roasts the whole bird before removing the breasts, serving them in *aiguillettes*, or long slices. (What Michel does with the rest of the bird is not really talked about.) The breasts are finished with a sauce of wine, *fromage blanc*, and mushroom puree. It is a beautiful-sounding dish, but one that was current thirty-five years ago. What I am looking for is a way to put a similar dish into a contemporary context.

So to evolve a dish like Guérard's, I would take the bird and remove the entire breastplate so both lobes of the breast are still on the bone. I would season it with salt and rosemary, and some mustard, connecting my dish to the foresty element of Guérard's mushroom puree. I would let this cure in the fridge for a day and then pan-roast the breast, skin side down, over very low heat, finishing it in a 375°F oven to allow me to have better control of the final internal temperature. Then I would deglaze the pan with Madeira and duck stock to make a straightforward jus. I would let it rest while I made a warm fig salad with *fromage blanc* and orange confit, bringing a modern freshness. Every step is full of reverence for the flavor map that he created, but cooked through the lens of my perspective in 2014.

This is how old books make me look around and give me inspiration, and it's why it's important to have anchors in different places in culinary history.

ENGLISH PEAS & FAVAS

I remember many afternoons shelling beans when I was young. It was the kids' contribution to the table, but it was a chore that we enjoyed because for every sweet English pea that hit the bottom of the bowl, one was eaten with relish.

Spring is the time for bright green beans and peas. When buying either, look for tight pods, not too big, not too small, with shiny shells and a fresh aroma. Favas get chalky and dry when large, and English peas are just not the same when they have been sitting on the shelf for a while.

FAVA BEANS, POACHED EGG, CRISP PANCETTA, AND FOCACCIA CRISPS

Easter brunch at my house is a dish like this. It is a simple meal that is utterly fresh and reflective of the season. Just make sure you get through the fava bean shucking, blanching, and peeling early or you will have a lot of prep to do after your egg hunt. *Serves 4*

Sea salt

1 pound fava beans in the pods

½ pound thinly sliced pancetta

4 long, thin slices of focaccia or sourdough bread

2 tablespoons unsalted butter

2 tablespoons olive oil

1 tablespoon sherry vinegar

2 tablespoons finely cut fresh parsley stems

¼ cup fresh flat-leaf parsley leaves

4 eggs

1 Preheat the oven to 350°F.

2 Prepare an ice water bath and set it on the counter near the stove. Place a large saucepan of water over high heat and bring it to a boil. Season the heating water well with sea salt.

3 Remove the fava beans from their large, long pods. Add the shelled favas to the boiling water and blanch them for 1 minute, until they are bright green and just barely cooked, still crisp in texture. Drain the favas and immediately drop them into the ice water. Allow them to cool, and then remove and discard their outer skins.

4 Place the slices of pancetta in a single layer on a rimmed baking sheet, place it in the oven, and bake for 10 to 12 minutes. The fat will render out and the edges will get golden and crisp. Place the pancetta on a plate lined with a paper towel and allow it to cool.

5 Raise the temperature of the oven to 400°F.

6 Lay the focaccia out in a single layer on another baking sheet and toast the bread in the oven for about 6 minutes; it should be evenly golden brown and crisp around the edges. Spread the butter generously on the toasts.

7 In a medium mixing bowl, combine the fava beans, olive oil, sherry vinegar, and parsley stems and leaves. Season with sea salt to taste, and toss well.

8 Place the focaccia on a large serving platter and top with the fava salad. Arrange the pancetta on top of that. Set this aside.

9 Poach the eggs (see page 184), and then place them directly on the top of the dish. Serve immediately.

FAVA BEAN SALAD WITH MINT, GARLIC, ARUGULA, AND SALAMI

Simple. Favas go with mint, mint goes with garlic, garlic goes with arugula. Salami works with just about anything. This is how my cooking brain works. *Serves 4*

Sea salt

1 pound fava beans in the pods

1 head garlic, broken into cloves and peeled

1 pound arugula, stemmed

½ cup fresh mint leaves, torn by hand

2 tablespoons olive oil

1 teaspoon grated lemon zest

1 tablespoon freshly squeezed lemon juice

¼ pound dry salami, cut into very small dice

½ cup shaved Parmigiano-Reggiano cheese

1 Prepare an ice water bath and set it on the counter near the stove. Place a large pot of water over high heat and bring it to a boil. Season the heating water with a good amount of sea salt.

2 Remove the fava beans from their large, long pods. Add the shelled favas to the boiling water and blanch them for 1 minute, until they are bright green and just barely cooked, still crisp in texture. Drain the favas and immediately drop them into the ice water. Allow them to cool, and then remove and discard their outer skins.

3 In a small saucepan, cover the garlic cloves with water and bring to a boil. Season the water with ½ teaspoon sea salt, turn the heat down, and simmer for 10 minutes. Remove the garlic from the water and allow it to cool to room temperature. When it has cooled, cut each clove in half lengthwise. The garlic should taste clean, soft, and sweet.

4 When ready to serve, place the arugula, favas, garlic, and mint in a medium mixing bowl and toss lightly with the olive oil, lemon zest, and lemon juice. Season with sea salt to taste, and arrange in a beautiful heap on a platter. Sprinkle with the diced salami and finish with the shaved Parmigiano-Reggiano.

FAVA BEANS,
POACHED EGG,
CRISP PANCETTA,
AND FOCACCIA
CRISPS

FAVA BEAN SALAD
WITH MINT, GARLIC,
ARUGULA, AND SALAMI

LOBSTER WITH
PEAS AND SEARED
FINGERLING POTATOES

LOBSTER WITH PEAS AND SEARED FINGERLING POTATOES

Buying and preparing a lobster is a rite of passage to cooking from scratch. It is you against a clawed beast and you will win, because you have opposable thumbs and it just has claws. Let Darwinism guide you to a delicious lobster dinner. *Serves 4*

Kosher salt

1 pound fresh English peas, shelled

1 pound fingerling potatoes

2 tablespoons canola oil

1 cup chicken stock (see page 22)

1 shallot, thinly sliced

Juice of 1 lemon

2 1½-pound lobsters, cooked, shelled, and chopped (see page 59)

2 tablespoons unsalted butter

1 tablespoon chopped fresh chives

¼ cup pea shoots

1 Prepare an ice water bath and set it near the stove. In a medium stockpot, bring 4 quarts of water to a boil and season it well with kosher salt. Blanch the peas in the boiling water for 2 minutes, or until they are tender and bright green. Immediately drain the peas and shock them in the ice water. Allow them to chill. Then remove them from the ice water and place them on a plate lined with paper towels.

2 Place the fingerling potatoes in a small pot, and add cold water to cover and enough kosher salt so you can taste it. Place the pot over high heat and bring to a boil. Reduce the heat and slowly simmer the potatoes for 5 minutes, or until they are fork-tender. Drain the potatoes and cool them in the refrigerator. Once they are cool, dry them well and cut them into bite-size pieces.

3 In a large sauté pan, heat the canola oil over high heat. Once the oil comes to a slight smoke, add the potatoes and turn the heat down to medium. Crisp the potatoes until they are golden brown, about 5 minutes, and season them with a few pinches of kosher salt. Take the potatoes out of the pan and set them aside.

4 Pour the chicken stock into the same pan, add the shallot, and reduce over high heat until the mixture starts to thicken, about 2 minutes. Add the lemon juice, peas, lobster, and potatoes, and warm through. Reduce the heat to medium, add the butter, and stir until the butter melts and emulsifies into the sauce. Adjust the seasoning with kosher salt, and arrange on a platter. Garnish the dish with the chives and pea shoots.

BRAISED VEAL CHEEKS WITH CRUSHED PEAS AND GREEN GARLIC GREMOLATA

The cheeks of veal are so good. Working muscles yield the best braising results, and when you think about a cheek and all its chewing—that's a real worker in the muscle world. Be patient with braising and you will attain beautifully tender meat. The peas and the gremolata in this dish cut the richness beautifully. Pair it up with a nice Piedmont red and you'll have a great life. *Serves 4 to 6*

2 pounds veal cheeks, silverskin removed

Sea salt

Canola oil

1 medium yellow onion, diced

½ cup diced celery

½ cup diced carrot

1 head garlic, broken into cloves and crushed

1 large red tomato, peeled and diced

½ cup dry red wine

1 quart chicken stock (see page 22)

1 teaspoon black peppercorns

2 bay leaves

2 sprigs fresh flat-leaf parsley

¼ cup thinly sliced green garlic (sliced into rings)

¼ cup finely chopped fresh flat-leaf parsley leaves

1 tablespoon finely chopped Preserved Lemon (page 172)

2 cups shelled fresh English peas

½ cup whole milk

2 tablespoons unsalted butter

1 Preheat the oven to 325°F.

2 Pat the veal cheeks dry and season them on both sides with sea salt. Lightly coat a large braising pan with canola oil, and heat it over medium-high heat. Once the oil comes to a slight smoke, add the veal cheeks, giving them space between one another so they brown and caramelize evenly. (If they don't all fit, work in batches.) Sear the cheeks for roughly 3 minutes per side, until nicely browned. Remove the cheeks and set them aside.

3 Reduce the heat to medium and add the onion, celery, carrot, and garlic. Season lightly with sea salt, and caramelize, stirring, for roughly 15 minutes, developing some color. Add the tomato and cook for 5 minutes more, until the tomato softens. Deglaze the pan with the red wine, scraping up any browned bits with a wooden spoon, and raise the heat to high. Reduce the wine until almost dry, about 2 minutes. Add the chicken stock, bring to a boil, and add a little bit of sea salt. (The liquid will reduce by a lot, so go lightly.) Add the peppercorns, bay leaves, parsley sprigs, and the veal cheeks. Cover the pan and place it in the oven. Braise the cheeks for 1½ hours, or until they are tender.

4 Meanwhile, prepare the gremolata: Place the sliced green garlic in a small saucepan and cover with 1 cup canola oil. Heat the oil over medium-high heat, and fry the green garlic until it is lightly browned and rising to the surface of the oil. Remove the garlic, drain it on a plate lined with paper towels, and season with a few pinches of sea salt. In a small mixing bowl, toss the fried green garlic with the chopped parsley and the preserved lemon. Set this aside for later, and save the garlic-infused oil for another use.

5 Take the cheeks out of the braising liquid and set them aside on a plate. Strain the braising liquid into a saucepan and simmer it over medium-high heat, skimming any foam or fat from the top, until reduced by three-quarters. Set it aside.

6 Prepare an ice water bath and place it near the stove. In a pot, bring 2 quarts of water to a boil. Season the water with sea salt, and blanch the peas in the boiling water for 2 minutes. Drain the peas and immediately put them into the ice bath to shock them and retain their bright green color.

7 In a small saucepan, heat the milk and 1 tablespoon of the butter over medium heat. Add the peas, smash them with a fork or potato masher, and season to taste with sea salt. Remove from the heat, but keep warm on the back of the stove.

8 Rewarm the braising liquid and veal cheeks over medium-low heat. Add the remaining tablespoon of

butter to finish the liquid, which should be thick enough to coat the back of a spoon.

9 Arrange the smashed peas on a platter, top with the veal cheeks, spoon the liquid over the top, and finish with the gremolata.

FENNEL

Fennel abounds for much of the year in my neck of the woods, but I find it's best during the early break of spring. Fennel is great raw, braised, fried, stewed, pickled, or roasted. It is, like the carrot, another really versatile vegetable with a beautifully sweet but intense flavor. The bulb is the prized part, but make sure to core it if the bulb is larger than a baseball, as the center will be a bit too tough. With young fennel bulbs the core is pretty tender and can be left intact.

CARAMELIZED
FENNEL

FENNEL SALAD WITH
ANCHOVIES, LEMON,
AND ROASTED TOMATOES

GRITS WITH
SPECK AND
CARAMELIZED
FENNEL

PICKLED FENNEL

A versatile condiment for your refrigerator door. Mince them onto a piece of poached salmon, finish a gravy for chicken, put in salads, or garnish a gin and tonic. *Makes 1 quart or 2 pints*

3½ cups thinly sliced fennel bulb

2 tablespoons thinly sliced celery

2 tablespoons chopped fresh dill

1 cup rice vinegar

2 teaspoons pickling salt

1 tablespoon sugar

1 teaspoon celery seeds

¼ teaspoon crushed red pepper flakes

1 bay leaf

1 Combine the fennel, celery, and dill in a bowl and toss well. Pack the mixture into a clean quart jar (or 2 pint jars), leaving 1 inch of headspace, and set aside.

2 In a small nonreactive saucepan, combine 1 cup of water with the vinegar, pickling salt, sugar, celery seeds, red pepper flakes, and bay leaf. Bring to a vigorous boil and then simmer over medium-low heat for 5 minutes. Pour the hot brine over the fennel, covering the vegetable but leaving ½ inch of headspace in the jar. Cap the jar with the lid and band, and set it aside to cool for about 2 hours and then refrigerate.

3 The fennel is ready to eat in 48 hours and will stay good for weeks in the fridge. Or process it according to the jar manufacturer's directions and store it for up to 9 months on the shelf.

GRITS WITH SPECK AND CARAMELIZED FENNEL

Speck is a lean smoked ham from Italy that reminds me of our finest country hams. It pairs perfectly with fennel and, in this case, the goodness that is ground nixtamalized corn kernels, or grits. This is yet another example of the synergy between Italian food and Southern food, both of which revel in the beauty of simplicity. *Serves 4 as a side*

Sea salt

1 cup hominy grits (preferably from Anson Mills)

1 tablespoon canola oil

2 baby fennel bulbs, sliced in half lengthwise

¼ cup heavy cream

1 tablespoon unsalted butter, cut into 4 pieces

¼ pound speck, very thinly sliced

1 Preheat the oven to 350°F.

2 In a medium saucepan, bring 4½ cups water and 1 teaspoon sea salt to a boil over high heat, and then slowly whisk in the grits. Continue to stir the grits and turn the heat down to low. Cook the grits on low heat for 30 minutes, stirring often with a wooden spoon to avoid any chance of burning them or having them stick to the bottom of the pan.

3 While the grits are cooking, heat a medium ovenproof sauté pan over high heat. Once the pan is hot, add the canola oil. When it smokes, add the fennel, cut side down, and turn the heat down to medium. Caramelize for 2 minutes, and sprinkle sea salt to taste over the fennel. Place the pan in the oven and bake for 5 minutes, or until the fennel is tender enough to easily pierce with a small knife. Remove the pan from the oven.

4 Finish the grits by stirring in the heavy cream, and adjust the seasoning with more sea salt if needed.

5 Divide the grits among 4 bowls. Top the grits with the small tabs of cold butter, the sliced speck, and the caramelized fennel.

FENNEL SALAD WITH ANCHOVIES, LEMON, AND ROASTED TOMATOES

Fennel + anchovies + lemon + tomatoes. It's a lovely combination that just works. Also lovely is if the fennel for this salad is really thin, super light. If you want the fennel to be really thin, you need to use a mandoline. I like the Benriner brand out of Japan; they are inexpensive and fine little devices, but they want to cut you, so be very careful—using the finger guard that comes with most mandolines is much advised! *Serves 4 as a side*

1 fennel bulb, cored and thinly shaved across the grain

Sea salt

2 tablespoons plus 1 teaspoon olive oil

1 tablespoon freshly squeezed lemon juice

4 roma tomatoes

¼ teaspoon freshly cracked black pepper

1 sprig fresh thyme

1 garlic clove, very thinly sliced

1 tablespoon chopped fresh fennel fronds

8 Spanish marinated anchovies

½ lemon, thinly sliced

1 Set the oven to broil.

2 Place the shaved fennel in a mixing bowl. Add a few pinches of sea salt, the 2 tablespoons olive oil, and

the lemon juice, and combine. Set the mixture aside to marinate at room temperature.

3 Cut the tomatoes in half lengthwise and cut off the stem ends. In a small bowl, dress the tomatoes with sea salt to taste, the cracked black pepper, and the remaining 1 teaspoon olive oil. Place the tomatoes, cut side up, in a cast-iron sauté pan. Place the pan in the oven and broil for 8 minutes. Take the pan out, add the thyme sprig and the sliced garlic, and broil for 1 more minute. Remove the pan from the oven and let the tomatoes cool to room temperature.

4 Add the fennel fronds to the marinating fennel, and place half of the mixture on a platter, saving any liquid in the bowl. Top the fennel with the roasted tomatoes, and add the rest of the marinated fennel on top of the tomatoes. Garnish the salad with the anchovies and the sliced lemon. Combine any tomato juices with the remaining fennel liquid and drizzle over the salad to finish.

SHRIMP, OCTOPUS, CLAM, AND FENNEL STEW WITH FARRO

This recipe comes from Kyle Jacovino, a young chef whom I adore. He helms The Florence in Savannah and is a smart chef who just has a natural way with food. It comes easily to him. This is a wonderfully aromatic seafood stew that is a meal in itself with the fennel and the farro. Kyle, to me, is the perfect person to meld the beauty of Southern food with the wonderful simplicity of southern Italy. *Serves 6*

1 whole octopus (1½ pounds)

Kosher salt

1 cup farro (I love Anson Mills's *farro piccolo*)

2 tablespoons unsalted butter

½ cup sliced yellow onion

4 garlic cloves: 3 minced, 1 halved

1¼ tablespoons crushed red pepper flakes

1 cup diced fennel bulb

½ cup sliced leeks, white and light green parts

½ cup diced butternut squash

½ cup diced celery

½ cup dry white wine (one that you would want to drink)

1½ cups San Marzano tomatoes or your own preserved tomatoes, and their juice

1 quart chicken stock (see page 22)

¼ teaspoon freshly cracked black pepper

18 clams, cleaned of sand

18 shrimp, shelled and deveined

¼ cup torn fresh basil leaves

¼ cup chopped fresh flat-leaf parsley leaves

1 lemon: 1 half juiced and 1 half thinly sliced

Half a baguette, thinly sliced and toasted

1 tablespoon olive oil

2 tablespoons chopped fresh fennel fronds (optional)

1 Preheat the oven to 300°F.

2 To prepare the octopus, season it all over with kosher salt and place it in a 4-quart ovenproof saucepan. Fill the pan with cold water until it covers about half of the octopus. Put the lid on the pan, place it in the oven, and bake for 1 hour, or until the octopus is easily pierced with a knife. Cooking time can range from 1 to 4 hours, depending on the octopus, so check it every hour or so. Once the octopus is tender, remove it from the liquid and let it cool until you can handle it. Then remove the outer, darker skin and discard it. Remove the head of the octopus with a knife, and cut it into ½-inch-thick slices. Cut the octopus tentacles in half lengthwise and then into 1-inch chunks. Set aside.

3 Pour 4 cups of cold water into a medium saucepan and bring to a boil over high heat. Season the water with kosher salt, as you would pasta water, whisk in the farro, and turn the heat down to a simmer. Cook until al dente, 20 to 25 minutes. Drain the farro and rinse it under cool water. Set aside.

4 Melt the butter in a large sauté pan over low heat. Add the onions and cook, stirring frequently, for about 15 minutes. The onions should develop a nice golden brown color. Add the minced garlic, red pepper flakes, fennel, leeks, squash, and celery and cook for an additional 3 minutes. Add the white wine and continue to cook until the liquid is reduced by half, about 5 minutes.

5 Now add the farro, tomatoes and their juice, stock, cracked black pepper, and kosher salt to taste (keeping in mind that the clams will add more salt). Bring to a simmer and add the clams. After 5 to 7 minutes, the clams will begin to open. Then add the reserved octopus and the shrimp. Simmer for another 2 to 3 minutes, and discard any unopened clams. Finish the stew with the basil, parsley, and the lemon juice. Remove from the heat.

6 Rub the baguette toasts with the halved garlic and the olive oil. Serve the stew in bowls, garnished with the baguette slices, the sliced lemon, and the chopped fennel fronds, if using.

GREEN GARLIC

In Athens we have some ambitious farmers who grow up to twenty varieties of garlic, and the spring is an exciting time to compare and contrast their subtle differences in taste and structure.

Green garlic is young garlic that hasn't had a chance to fully expand and grow its bulb into cloves. Unlike its older brother, it is not hung and cured before use; rather it is chopped in its green form to give us a bright, redolent yet mild expression of garlic that to me is yet another waft of spring. You will also find scapes, which are the young garlic flower shoots from hard-neck varieties of garlic. They can be used much like green garlic.

PICKLED GREEN GARLIC

This is a great finish to a rich pasta or risotto, or just a nice addition to a roast beef sandwich. Harness the short season that green garlic has and get pickling. *Makes 1 quart or 2 pints*

4 cups chopped green garlic

1 teaspoon pickling salt

½ cup raw sugar

½ teaspoon yellow mustard seeds

½ teaspoon crushed red pepper flakes

½ cup cider vinegar

1 Pack the green garlic into a clean quart jar (or 2 pint jars), leaving 1 inch of headspace at the top, and set aside.

2 Combine the pickling salt, raw sugar, mustard seeds, red pepper flakes, vinegar, and 1 cup of water in a small nonreactive pot and bring to a boil. Reduce the heat to low and simmer for 5 minutes. Then carefully ladle the hot pickling mixture into the jar, leaving ½ inch of headspace. Cap with the lid and band, and let cool for 2 hours. The jar can be stored in the refrigerator for a month, or processed according to the jar manufacturer's directions and stored on the shelf for 9 months.

STEAMED NEW POTATOES WITH GREEN GARLIC

When working with the wonders of green garlic, realize that there is a lot there to work with—you just need to slice it really thin and against the grain. I would treat it generally like a leek: revere the white bottom, love the pale green middle, and relegate the top, darker green to the stockpot. *Serves 4 as a side*

¼ cup (½ stick) unsalted butter

1 cup finely sliced green garlic

1½ pounds small new potatoes, cut in half if they are larger than 1 inch in diameter

¾ cup chicken stock (see page 22), or water in a pinch

Kosher salt

Melt the butter in a medium saucepan over medium-high heat, and when it bubbles and froths, add half of the green garlic. Cook for 1 minute, until aromatic, and then add the potatoes, stock, and a few pinches of kosher salt. Reduce the heat to medium-low and cover with a tight-fitting lid. Cook for 15 to 20 minutes, until the potatoes are tender when prodded with a knife; if the pan becomes dry, add water and continue to cook until the potatoes are tender. Add the remaining green garlic and cook for 2 more minutes. Serve immediately.

SPAGHETTI WITH GREEN GARLIC, SPECK, AND BASIL

Simple pastas are the most revelatory to me, but they are also the ones that require the closest attention. Simplicity is the hardest thing to accomplish with aplomb in food. It's like looking fashionable in a flour sack; you can do it—you just have to really *do* it.

This recipe, like a stunning *cacio e pepe*, should holler from the hilltops about the beauty of a single ingredient. *Serves 4*

Sea salt

1 cup thinly sliced green garlic

3 tablespoons olive oil

1 teaspoon crushed red pepper flakes

1 pound spaghetti

¼ pound speck, thinly shaved and then cut into strips

3 tablespoons torn fresh basil leaves

1 In a large soup pot, bring 4 quarts of water to a boil and season it heavily with sea salt.

2 Meanwhile, place the sliced green garlic in a large saucepan (big enough to hold the cooked spaghetti), add the olive oil, and heat over medium-low heat for about 5 minutes. Make sure not to allow any color to develop on the garlic. Season the garlic with sea salt to taste and the red pepper flakes. Remove from the heat and set aside.

3 Once the water reaches a boil, add the spaghetti and immediately stir to ensure the pasta isn't sticking to itself. Cook the pasta for 8 to 10 minutes, until al dente. Drain the pasta, keeping some of the cooking water, and add it to the saucepan containing the green garlic and oil. Add a little of the cooking water if the pasta seems dry. Adjust the seasoning with more sea salt if needed, fold in the speck and the basil, and serve immediately.

STEAMED NEW
POTATOES WITH
GREEN GARLIC

GREEN GARLIC SOUP WITH POACHED EGG AND CRISP CROUTONS

I love creating an ode to food from faraway continents using the ingredients that grow in our backyards. This dish makes me think of the brothy soups of Spain, redolent with garlic and asparagus and finished with a beautifully poached egg. I can eat this every day.

Serves 4

2 tablespoons olive oil	¼ cup finely diced asparagus
½ cup finely chopped green garlic	½ cup sliced young hakurei turnips with greens
½ pound small potatoes	4 eggs
1 quart chicken or beet stock (see page 22)	¼ cup chopped arugula
Kosher salt	2 tablespoons Salsa Verde (page 240)
¼ cup finely diced celery	8 baguette slices, toasted
¼ cup finely diced carrot	

1 In your favorite soup pot, warm the olive oil over medium heat. Add the green garlic and cook for 5 minutes, not to char it but to really sweat it down. Cut the potatoes into ½-inch dice and add them to the pot. Cook for 2 minutes, and then add the stock with a few pinches of kosher salt. Bring the stock to a boil over medium-high heat, reduce it to a simmer, and cook for 10 minutes, until the potatoes are nearly tender. Add the celery, carrot, asparagus, and turnips and greens. Season with kosher salt to taste and cook for 5 more minutes. Keep the soup warm on the back of the stove while you poach the eggs (see page 184).

2 Ladle the soup into 4 warmed bowls, garnish each bowl with some chopped arugula, and then place a poached egg in the center of each. Garnish each portion with half a tablespoon of the salsa verde, and then gently lay croutons on top. Serve immediately.

MORELS

Morel mushrooms are the crown jewel of our local foraging world. Finding them is a difficult, bramble-laden task, which results in lots of scrapes and sore calves from meandering in the woods, but when you find a plot that yields results after every spring rain, it is a trek worth taking.

You do not have to forage for these deep-flavored beauties—you can just buy them from a reputable source. The key is to make sure they are sand- and grit-free. If they are gritty, soak them in repeated changes of cold water, stirring the mushrooms about to loosen the silt and sand, which will sink to the bottom of the bowl. Then make sure you get them as dry as you can before working with them.

MOREL COMPOUND
BUTTER

STEWED MORELS,
ASPARAGUS, RAMPS,
AND CRÈME FRAÎCHE
OVER GRITS

STEWED MORELS, ASPARAGUS, RAMPS, AND CRÈME FRAÎCHE OVER GRITS

A trio of spring harbingers with grits. It's a good mix and an easy vegetarian dinner for a nice spring evening. *Serves 4*

1 cup white corn grits

Kosher salt

2 tablespoons unsalted butter

¼ cup minced shallots

2 cups fresh morel mushrooms, washed and cut into ⅓-inch-thick rounds

¼ cup chopped ramps (see page 243)

8 asparagus spears, cut into 1-inch pieces

1 tablespoon sherry vinegar

¼ cup chicken stock (see page 22)

¼ teaspoon finely chopped fresh thyme leaves

¼ teaspoon finely chopped fresh flat-leaf parsley leaves

½ cup crème fraîche

Freshly ground black pepper

1 In a medium saucepan, combine the grits and 4 cups of water and bring to a boil over medium-high heat, stirring occasionally. Add kosher salt to taste, reduce the heat to medium-low, and continue cooking, stirring occasionally, for 30 minutes. You will be moving forward with the rest of the recipe but what you are looking for in the grits is a velvety-soft polenta texture, a bit thinner than you would envision on a plate. (The grits will set up as soon as you put them on the plate.) If you think the grits are too thick, add a touch of water or stock to bring them to the desired consistency.

2 While the grits are cooking, melt the butter in a large sauté pan over medium-high heat. When it bubbles and froths, add the shallots and sweat them for 1 minute. Then add the morels and cook for 10 minutes, until the mushrooms smell wonderful, look a little limp, and are browning slightly at the edges. Add the ramps and the asparagus, deglaze the pan with the vinegar, and cook down for 2 minutes. Then add the chicken stock, season to taste with kosher salt, and cook for 3 minutes longer, until the asparagus is crisp-tender. Stir in the thyme, parsley, and crème fraîche. Season with kosher salt and black pepper to taste, and serve over the cooked grits.

MOREL COMPOUND BUTTER

This makes a fair bit of compound butter, but it's so tasty and really versatile. It likes to be melted on grilled steaks, fish, grilled toast, fiddleheads, and asparagus and has many, many more friends. It is a spring building block that you will find many uses for. Mark it down on your list of things that shouldn't be forgotten about in the back of your fridge. *Makes ½ pound*

2 tablespoons unsalted butter, plus ¼ pound (1 stick) at room temperature

1 shallot, minced

¼ pound morel mushrooms, washed and chopped

Sea salt

1 tablespoon fresh thyme leaves, chopped

¼ teaspoon minced lemon zest

1 In a medium saucepan, melt the 2 tablespoons butter over medium heat. When it begins to bubble and froth, add the shallot and cook for 1 minute. Add the chopped morels and season with ¼ teaspoon sea salt. Cook the morels for 10 minutes, stirring constantly, until they are lightly golden on the cut sides and a little limp. Take the pan off the heat and stir in the thyme and lemon zest. Set the mixture aside to cool to room temperature.

2 In a food processor, whip the stick of butter for 2 minutes. Add the cooked mushrooms and pulse just to incorporate. Adjust the seasoning with more sea salt if needed, and pack the morel butter into a small mason jar or roll it into a log, using parchment paper. Place in the fridge and let chill until set before using. Tightly wrapped or covered, the butter will keep fresh in the fridge for up to 2 weeks.

STUFFED AND FRIED MORELS WITH LEEKS, RAISINS, RICOTTA, AND BASIL

Morels are ideal candidates for stuffing and frying or baking—that perfect core is just meant to be filled with something oozy and lovely. In this recipe the ricotta has a nice foil in the raisins and lemon.

Serves 4 as an appetizer or a side

1 tablespoon unsalted butter

1 cup sliced leeks (¼-inch-thick rings)

Fine sea salt

1 quart canola oil

2 tablespoons raisins, chopped

½ cup ricotta

1 tablespoon torn fresh basil leaves

Grated zest and juice of 1 lemon

1 teaspoon freshly cracked black pepper

2 tablespoons finely grated Parmigiano-Reggiano cheese

20 large morel mushrooms, washed

1 cup all-purpose flour

1 egg, beaten with a touch of water

1 cup fresh bread crumbs

1 In a medium saucepan, melt the butter over medium heat. When it begins to bubble and froth, add the leeks and season with fine sea salt to taste. Cook for about 10 minutes, stirring constantly to prevent any color from developing. When the leeks are very soft, almost jammy, remove them from the pan and set aside to cool.

2 Heat the canola oil in a large saucepan over medium heat to 350°F; use a deep-frying thermometer.

3 Meanwhile, in a medium mixing bowl, combine the leeks, raisins, ricotta, basil, lemon zest and juice, black pepper, and Parmigiano-Reggiano, and season with fine sea salt to taste. Put the filling into a clear resealable plastic bag and cut the corner so it can be used as a piping bag. Pipe the filling into each morel.

4 Set up a station of 4 pans: the first is the flour; the second is the egg wash; the third is the bread crumbs; and the last is for the finished breaded mushrooms. Coat each morel in the flour and shake off any excess. Place the floured morel in the egg wash, turning it to fully coat. Place it in the bread crumbs, turning to fully coat. Set the breaded morels aside on the last pan.

5 Add the morels, in small batches, to the hot oil, and fry for roughly 2 minutes, or until they are golden brown. Transfer them to a plate lined with a paper towel to drain, and then season with fine sea salt to taste. Serve immediately.

CHICKEN PAILLARD WITH MORELS, MOREL COMPOUND BUTTER, LEMON, AND PARSLEY

This dish has a strong kinship with chicken piccata, with its lemony finish and herbal beauty. Here the morels give it an earthy beauty. It's a great dish that takes little time to prepare, especially if you have the compound butter already made. *Serves 2 to 4*

2 boneless, skinless chicken breasts (about 1 pound)

Olive oil

Fine sea salt

½ cup all-purpose flour

2 tablespoons canola oil

1 tablespoon unsalted butter

½ pound morel mushrooms, washed and sliced

¼ cup chicken stock (see page 22)

2 tablespoons Morel Compound Butter (page 229)

½ teaspoon minced lemon zest

1 tablespoon freshly squeezed lemon juice

2 tablespoons chopped fresh flat-leaf parsley leaves

1 Take each breast, and using a sharp knife, slice it laterally to get 2 thin pieces. You now have 4 pieces. Place each piece loosely between 2 pieces of plastic wrap with a touch of olive oil so they don't stick. Using a mallet or a small, heavy pan, gently but firmly pound the breasts until they are an even ½ inch thick. Season with fine sea salt and dredge them in the flour. Shake off any excess flour.

2 In a large skillet, heat the canola oil over high heat. Given that the chicken pieces are thin but large in size, you may have to do the cooking in batches. If you are working them in batches, just hold the cooked chicken on a sheet pan in a warm oven as you cook the other pieces. So back to our pan: When the oil comes to a slight smoke, add the chicken breasts and reduce the heat to medium-high. Sear the chicken for 3 minutes, turn it over, lower the heat to medium, and add the butter. Cook for 2 more minutes and then remove the chicken from the pan.

3 Add the morels to the same pan, and season with fine sea salt. Cook the mushrooms for 10 minutes, stirring occasionally. Reduce the heat to low, deglaze the pan with the chicken stock, and add the morel butter, stirring well to create an emulsification. Add the lemon zest, lemon juice, and parsley.

4 Place the chicken breasts on individual plates, and pour the morel mixture over them.

CHICKEN PAILLARD
WITH MORELS, MOREL
COMPOUND BUTTER,
LEMON, AND PARSLEY

POTATOES

Potatoes are such a staple and so easy to cook, but there's a huge difference between cooking a potato and cooking it really well. Let's change that, because a truly perfect potato is a momentous achievement in food. Grab those spuds and let's get cooking.

POTATO PUREE

I can't overemphasize the importance of finding seminal, timeless recipes and learning their concepts in order to perfect and toy with them. Joël Robuchon's potato puree is one of those recipes. Chef Joël's nuance is a 2 to 1 ratio of potato to butter. This is a very French nuance. I have reduced that amount of butter by half and increased the milk to compensate. It's still a decadent puree, but your cardiologist will not get that angry with us. Here are some other things to keep in mind while making awesome mashed potatoes:

1. Do not use new, red, or other waxy potatoes. Whipping them is a gluey experience.

2. Never use an electric mixer for the potatoes, as it pulls out the starch too aggressively from the cooked potatoes, resulting in an elastic texture.

3. Keep the butter cold, and work it into the potatoes over low heat; high heat will break the emulsion of the butter into the potatoes.

4. If the finished mashed potatoes are lumpy, it's because you undercooked the potatoes. If they are watery, it's because you overcooked the potatoes. You want the potatoes to be very tender when poked with a knife but not falling apart. *Serves 4 to 6 as a side*

2 pounds Yukon Gold potatoes, peeled

Sea salt

1 cup whole milk

½ pound (2 sticks) cold unsalted butter, cut into tablespoon-size chunks

1 Place the potatoes in a large pot, add water to cover by at least 1 inch, and add 1 teaspoon sea salt. Bring to a simmer and cook, uncovered, over moderate heat until a knife easily pierces the potatoes, 20 to 30 minutes. When they are ready, drain the potatoes immediately.

2 Meanwhile, in a large saucepan, bring the milk just to a boil over high heat. Immediately remove the pan from the heat and set it aside.

3 Pass the potatoes through a ricer or a food mill into a large, heavy-bottomed saucepan. (The ricer or food mill is pretty important to get the texture right.) Set the saucepan over low heat. Stir the potatoes vigorously for 4 to 5 minutes, to steam off and dry them, and then begin adding the butter, a tablespoon at a time, stirring vigorously until each chunk of butter is fully incorporated; the mixture should be fluffy and light. Then slowly add the hot milk, stirring vigorously until it is fully incorporated.

4 Using a wooden spoon, press the potatoes through a mesh sieve or food mill into another heavy-bottomed saucepan set over low heat, and stir. This second step of pureeing is the true secret behind Chef Robuchon's recipe, and we're keeping the puree over heat to keep it warm up until serving. Season the puree with sea salt to your liking and serve immediately.

POTAYTO, POTAHTO

Here's a glimpse at the amazing breadth of potatoes that you can look for. At Woodland Gardens in 2013, our friends grew thirteen varieties, and that's just scratching the surface. Each has a different flavor, texture; it's a whole cast of spudly characters. Find a new potato variety and cook it up.

Yukon Gold

Rose Gold

Prairie Blush

King Harry

Kerr's Pink

Sangre

German Butterball

Russian Banana fingerling

Austrian Crescent fingerling

French fingerling

La Ratte fingerling

Swedish Peanut fingerling

Purple Peruvian fingerling

ROASTED POTATOES WITH YOGURT, DILL, LEMON, AND GARLIC

When do you know that a small roasted potato is done? It should be easy to pierce with a paring knife. It should be easy to squeeze it with two fingers and form an indentation. It should be tender and taste great, with no hard core. This dish is as good cold as it is warm, so don't be afraid to make too much. *Serves 2 to 4 as a side*

1 pound baby Yukon Gold potatoes

1 tablespoon olive oil

Sea salt

4 garlic cloves, shaved

1 bay leaf

1 sprig fresh thyme

2 tablespoons plain yogurt

½ teaspoon zest and the juice of 1 lemon

½ teaspoon freshly cracked black pepper

1 teaspoon cider vinegar

1 tablespoon small sprigs fresh dill

ROASTED
POTATOES WITH
YOGURT, DILL,
LEMON, AND
GARLIC
(PAGE 233)

1 Preheat the oven to 350°F.

2 Place the potatoes and the olive oil in a large cast-iron pan, and season them lightly with sea salt. Roast the potatoes in the oven for 30 minutes, or until they are tender. Remove the pan from the oven and add the shaved garlic. Return the pan to the oven and cook for an additional 2 to 3 minutes, until the garlic is aromatic and softened. Then remove the pan from the oven and add the bay leaf and the thyme sprig. Stir, and allow to rest.

3 Meanwhile, in a mixing bowl combine the yogurt, lemon zest and juice, pepper, vinegar, and sea salt to taste.

4 Discard the thyme sprig and bay leaf, and place the warm potatoes in a mixing bowl. Add the yogurt dressing and mix well. Place the potatoes in a serving dish and garnish with the dill sprigs.

MISO DASHI BRAISED POTATOES WITH BONITO, ORANGE, AND NORI

Earthy tastes like potatoes and miso match really well together. In this case we are finishing the potatoes with bonito flakes, orange segments, and nori seaweed, which will make the flavors shine with a lot of umami.
Serves 4 as a side

1 pound fingerling potatoes	1 sheet dried nori seaweed
Miso Dashi (recipe follows)	¼ cup dried bonito flakes
2 navel oranges	

1 Place the fingerlings in a wide saucepan and cover with the miso dashi. Place the pan over medium-high heat, and bring the dashi to a boil. Reduce the heat to a slight simmer and cook the potatoes for 15 to 20 minutes, until they are just fork-tender.

2 While the potatoes are cooking, prepare the remaining ingredients: Remove a few strips of orange zest with a vegetable peeler, and mince the zest to make 1 tablespoon. Using a paring knife, cut the top and bottom from the oranges and stand them up on one end. Use the same knife to cut off the rind of the fruit, making sure to get all of the white pith off as well. Cut the segments out individually by slicing along the white membranes. Make sure that you have removed any seeds, and reserve the segments.

3 Cut the nori into fine julienne strips.

4 To finish, put the potatoes and their broth in a large serving bowl and top with the orange zest and segments, followed by the nori, and then the bonito flakes.

MISO DASHI

Dashi, the mother stock of Japan, should be in your arsenal. It's easy to make and opens the doors to a lot of culinary possibilities. This is my embellished version of the timeless foundational stock. The basic recipe for dashi is on page 37 and should become a staple stock for much of your cooking.
Makes 1 quart

1 tablespoon light sesame oil	1 cup dried shiitake mushrooms
1 cup coarsely chopped yellow onion	One 8 × 8-inch piece dried kombu seaweed, cut in half
1 garlic clove	2 tablespoons white miso, or to taste
1 tablespoon minced fresh ginger	1 cup dried bonito flakes
1 quart chicken stock (see page 22)	

Place a large saucepan over medium-low heat, add the sesame oil, and then add the onion, garlic, and ginger. Slowly sweat for roughly 10 minutes, stirring to make sure you're not coloring the vegetables but are developing their sweetness. Add the chicken stock and bring to a boil over high heat. Immediately turn the heat down to low and add the dried mushrooms; cook them for 10 minutes. Add the kombu and cook for an additional 5 minutes. Remove the pan from the heat and whisk in the miso. Stir in the bonito flakes. Once everything is fully incorporated, strain the mixture through a fine-mesh strainer set over a container, and discard the solids. This miso dashi will keep in the fridge for 5 days. Stir well when you reheat.

WHY ARE YOU A FARMER?

I think it is important to understand the people behind the food, lest we all begin to really think that real food emanates from packaging machines in factories. Truly great food is a very personal item produced by real people.

Nicolas Donck is an amazing farmer who plows, plants, harvests, and just generally does what farmers do: he works harder than you and me. He is also my friend, as these relationships coalesce after many heartfelt transactions. There is a softer side of capitalism that comes from the proud purchase of meaningful products that someone has toiled over with their heart and soul.

Nicolas's family farm is Crystal Organic Farm, about a fifty-minute drive east of Atlanta—just west of the old Monticello Highway, for those of you who like bucolic back roads. When he comes in to Empire State South to deliver turnips and endives, beets and greens, he always has a smile on his face and wants to talk the week through. Those moments, talking with the growers, even about the weather, always make me happy. To them I am the end of the line for their hard work. I have a social contract, too: to use that produce, never forgetting where it has come from, the work that went into it, and the passion that the product exudes.

HA: When and how did you get into farming?

ND: Crystal Organic Farm was established in 1993. It is family land that my mother bought in 1982, after emigrating from Belgium. After a short stint in the export-import business, I started to farm a quarter-acre in 1993 and that grew to almost thirty acres today.

HA: Why do you do this? You could be a success in many things—why this?

ND: I have a real passion for everything in nature and I love the outdoors. Market farming is not an easy job but the rewards make it worth it . . . although they may not be financial rewards. My customers are real appreciative for the clean food we provide. We have become part of their family.

HA: How do you know you've succeeded as a farmer?

ND: When the soil has a consistent high organic matter count. Healthy soil means healthy plants that are strong enough to resist the bugs and disease, natural defenses that mean less need for things such as fertilizers and pesticides. It also means less work for the farmer, but still gets high yields.

HA: What do you need to be more successful?

ND: Many things would make us more successful, but this a slow money business, so nothing beats good soil, which takes time.

HA: What is the thing that most drives you nuts about farming?

ND: The weather has been so crazy lately and is always frustrating as it is out of our control. Also some folks do not understand the work that goes into vegetable production as they are used to getting it from the store any time they want.

HA: But do you think the future of the small farm is in better shape than it was ten years ago?

ND: Small farmers and their products are in higher demand than ten years ago. And more and more people and chefs do want to know where their food comes from, which is perfect for the small farmer.

RADISHES

I have a radish tattooed on my arm, not out of hope for some hipster credibility, but to remind me of the thing I grew first, in my little plot of a garden on East Broad Street in Athens, Georgia, in 1996. The radish is a vegetable that most people think of as a fiery thing, but good ones have a balanced flavor, a hint of heat with an icy crispness. I love 'em.

PICKLED RADISH PODS

POACHED SHRIMP OVER RADISHES WITH SALSA VERDE

PICKLED RADISH PODS

If you forget to harvest the radishes, the plant goes to seed, but with radishes the seeds are in a pod and each plant produces dozens of them. They taste like crunchy radish fresh peas, if that makes any sense. They are a treat and a natural for the pickling treatment, resulting in a briny crisp radish snack. *Makes 1 quart*

4 cups radish pods, washed, stem end removed

½ cup distilled white vinegar

2 tablespoons sea salt

1 teaspoon sugar

1 teaspoon black peppercorns

1 Pack the clean radish pods into a clean 1-quart mason jar, leaving 1 inch of headspace, and set it aside.

2 In a small nonreactive saucepan, combine 1 cup of water with the vinegar, sea salt, sugar, and peppercorns, and bring to a boil. Reduce the heat to low and simmer for 5 minutes. Carefully ladle the hot pickling mixture into the jar, leaving ½ inch of headspace. Cap the jar with the lid and band. The jar can be stored in the refrigerator for up to a month, or processed according to the jar manufacturer's directions for shelf storage of up to a year.

RADISH AND CUCUMBER SANDWICHES

My grandparents, Katherine and Hugh Stevens, showed me their love for radishes on Saturdays in the spring. At their house in Forest Hill in Toronto, lunch was served in the library, from a cart that Katherine, Kitto to us, had stocked in the kitchen. It was usually liverwurst and bread, radishes and butter, sliced cucumber, some old cheddar, and possibly a tomato. They would watch golf on television and eat well, but not too much, for later would come teatime and then drinks and then dinner. It was a very orderly day indeed.

This is such a simple plate of food but it has always been a staple in our family. Toast the bread very lightly, slice those radishes, and get the butter just barely to a spreadable temperature—one where you can still feel the refreshingly rich chill of the butter. *Serves 4*

4 diagonal slices of baguette, 7 inches long and ½ inch thick

¼ cup (½ stick) unsalted butter, a little chillier than room temperature

½ English cucumber, unpeeled, thinly sliced lengthwise into toast-length segments

12 small radishes, thinly sliced

½ teaspoon sea salt (Hawaiian is great for this)

1 teaspoon olive oil

1 Preheat the oven to 400°F.

2 Toast the bread on a baking sheet in the oven just until it turns a little golden. Remove the bread from the oven, and let cool.

3 Spread the butter evenly on the toasted bread, and then evenly distribute a layer of cucumbers and then a layer of radishes. Season with the sea salt, drizzle with the olive oil, and serve on a platter.

POACHED SHRIMP OVER RADISHES WITH SALSA VERDE

Poached shrimp take about three minutes. Salsa verde can be made ahead. Radishes take a minute to cut up, if that. The broth assembles in a minute and is cooked for fifteen before the shrimp go in. I guess what I am saying is that I realize you're busy but this is so easy, so fast, and so impressive that you need to go and make it.

When buying shrimp, hopefully you find them fresh. But if not, shrimp are one of the few things that freeze well, so find fishmongers whom you trust and buy from them. They'll know which ones are going to put a smile on your face. *Serves 4 as an appetizer*

1 pound shrimp (16 to 20 count)

1 teaspoon olive oil

¼ cup dry vermouth

3 cups chicken stock (see page 22)

¼ cup (½ stick) unsalted butter

1 sprig fresh thyme

1 leek, white and light green parts well washed and cut into 1-inch lengths

Kosher salt

12 small radishes, quartered

½ cup minced celery with leaves

¼ cup Salsa Verde (recipe follows)

1 Peel and devein the shrimp, leaving the tails on and reserving the shells. (Even better if you have the heads, but if you're buying head-on, buy about 1½ pounds.) Set aside.

2 In a 4-quart saucepan, heat the olive oil over medium-high heat. When the oil shimmers, add the shrimp shells (and heads if you have them) and cook for 3 minutes, until bright pink and aromatic. Add the vermouth and

deglaze the pan. Add the chicken stock, butter, thyme sprig, leek, and kosher salt to taste. Bring to a boil and then simmer over low heat for 15 minutes. Strain the mixture and return the liquid to the pan over medium heat. Discard the strained solids.

3 Season the shrimp with kosher salt, and immerse them in the poaching liquid. Cover and cook for 3 minutes, or until the shrimp are just cooked through.

4 Arrange the radishes and the celery in individual bowls for serving. Divide the shrimp among the bowls, and then ladle some of the poaching liquid over them. Finish each bowl with salsa verde and serve.

SALSA VERDE
Makes about 2 cups

½ cup packed fresh flat-leaf parsley leaves, finely chopped

1 tablespoon finely chopped fresh basil leaves

1 tablespoon finely chopped fresh mint leaves

1 tablespoon finely chopped fresh marjoram leaves

¾ cup olive oil, plus more to taste

2 garlic cloves, minced

Pinch of crushed red pepper flakes

1 tablespoon salt-packed capers, rinsed well and chopped

1 tablespoon salt-packed anchovy fillets, rinsed and minced

1 teaspoon Dijon mustard

1 tablespoon cider or white wine vinegar

Kosher salt

Freshly ground black pepper

Place the parsley, basil, mint, and marjoram in a bowl and pour in the olive oil. Add the garlic, red pepper flakes, capers, and anchovies. Stir well. Add the mustard and the vinegar. Season with kosher salt and black pepper to taste, and thin with more olive oil if necessary. It will keep fresh in the fridge for up to 5 days.

RED SNAPPER WITH SAUTÉED RADISH AND LEMON BROWN BUTTER

Try to find a stunning snapper that has an American passport. It makes a difference when we support our own fisheries.

I love the simplicity of a beautiful snapper with such redolent accompaniments: its meaty flesh and crisp skin balanced with the crunch of radishes and the acid of lemon and the nuttiness of brown butter.
Serves 4

8 Cherry Belle radishes or other classic small red radishes

4 red snapper fillets (5 to 6 ounces each), skin on

Peanut oil

Sea salt

4 tablespoons (½ stick) unsalted butter

1 teaspoon grated lemon zest

1 tablespoon freshly squeezed lemon juice

2 tablespoons coarsely chopped fresh flat-leaf parsley leaves

1 Wash the radishes and cut them into quarters, keeping a bit of the tops intact. Set them aside.

2 Pat the snapper fillets very dry with paper towels. Generously coat a large sauté pan with peanut oil and set it over high heat. Season the snapper fillets on both sides with sea salt. Once the oil has come to a light smoke, add the fillets, one at a time, skin side down. When you add each fillet, make sure to place it away from your body so the oil doesn't splash back at you. (Cook only as many fillets as will fit in the pan comfortably; work in batches otherwise, making sure the pan is very hot before each addition.) Immediately press the flesh side of the fish with a spatula so that it doesn't curl up. Gently but firmly press the fillets for roughly 30 seconds. Once the fillets are all added, reduce the heat to medium and continue to cook. When you see a golden crust starting to creep up the side of the fillets, add 1 tablespoon of the butter and baste the flesh side for 1 minute. Flip the fillets, cook for just a few seconds, and then place them on a plate lined with a paper towel. Allow the fish to rest.

3 In the same pan, cook the radishes over medium-high heat for 1 or 2 minutes, just until they get a little bit of caramelization but are still crisp and juicy. Transfer the radishes to a plate, season them with a few pinches of sea salt, and set aside.

4 Place the pan back over medium-high heat, and add the remaining 3 tablespoons butter. Cook the butter until it begins to brown, 2 to 3 minutes. Remove the pan from the heat and add the lemon zest, lemon juice, and parsley. Season with a few pinches of sea salt.

5 Place each snapper fillet on a plate and divide the radishes among the plates. Pour the butter sauce around the fish.

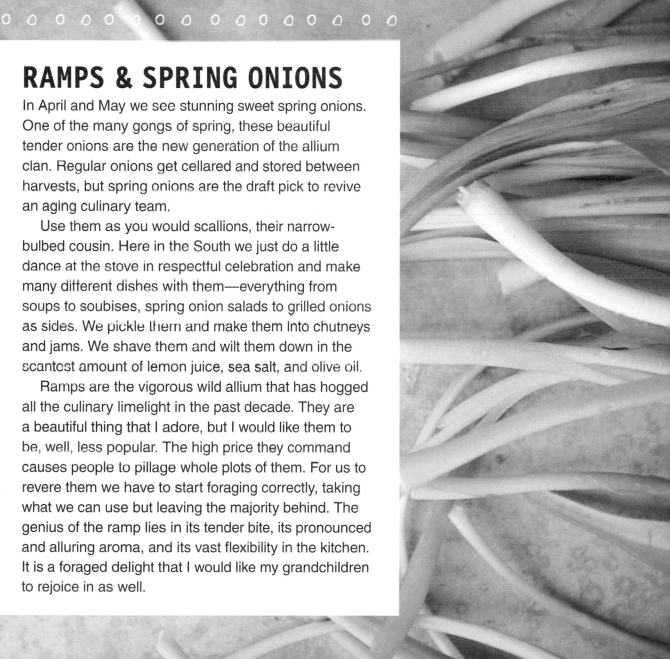

RAMPS & SPRING ONIONS

In April and May we see stunning sweet spring onions. One of the many gongs of spring, these beautiful tender onions are the new generation of the allium clan. Regular onions get cellared and stored between harvests, but spring onions are the draft pick to revive an aging culinary team.

Use them as you would scallions, their narrow-bulbed cousin. Here in the South we just do a little dance at the stove in respectful celebration and make many different dishes with them—everything from soups to soubises, spring onion salads to grilled onions as sides. We pickle them and make them into chutneys and jams. We shave them and wilt them down in the scantest amount of lemon juice, sea salt, and olive oil.

Ramps are the vigorous wild allium that has hogged all the culinary limelight in the past decade. They are a beautiful thing that I adore, but I would like them to be, well, less popular. The high price they command causes people to pillage whole plots of them. For us to revere them we have to start foraging correctly, taking what we can use but leaving the majority behind. The genius of the ramp lies in its tender bite, its pronounced and alluring aroma, and its vast flexibility in the kitchen. It is a foraged delight that I would like my grandchildren to rejoice in as well.

**GRILLED SPRING
ONIONS WITH
ROMESCO**

**RAMP
SCRAMBLED
EGGS**

RAMP JAM

I love savory jams and this one is a winner. The pectin will gel up the jam faster than just cooking it down to a paste, preserving the fresh flavor of the ramps. This is a go-to for a shaved pork loin or with steak and eggs on a Sunday morning. The recipe makes a lot, but it's worth canning and keeping through the year. *Makes 2 pints*

1 teaspoon olive oil	½ cup sugar
2 pounds ramps, bulbs cut into thin rings, leaves cut into small squares	1 cup white balsamic vinegar
	2 bay leaves
1 tablespoon sea salt	1 teaspoon powdered pectin

1 In a medium saucepan, warm the olive oil over medium heat. Add the ramps and sea salt and cook for 10 minutes, stirring often to prevent any color from developing, but really cooking down the ramps to a softer consistency. Then raise the heat to high and add the sugar, vinegar, and bay leaves. Bring to a boil and reduce the liquid by about half, about 5 minutes. Remove the pan from the heat, whisk in the pectin, and return it to the heat. Continue whisking for a minute or so; the mixture will thicken.

2 Spoon the jam into 2 clean pint jars, and cap them with the lids and bands. The jars can be stored in the refrigerator for up to a month, or processed according to the jar manufacturer's directions to store on the shelf for up to 9 months.

RAMP SCRAMBLED EGGS

Ramps and eggs are made for each other. I am not sure what their parents think of this spirited affair, but I am giving their relationship a big thumbs-up. In cooking any scrambled eggs, you need to have plates ready for the eggs so they don't sit in the pan and overcook. *Serves 4*

2 tablespoons unsalted butter	8 eggs
½ cup coarsely chopped ramps (1-inch pieces)	¼ cup whole milk
Sea salt	Finely grated Parmigiano-Reggiano cheese (optional)

1 In a large nonstick skillet, melt the butter over medium heat. When it begins to bubble and froth, add the ramps and a few pinches of sea salt. Sauté the ramps until they become slightly translucent, roughly 3 minutes.

2 While the ramps are cooking, whip the eggs in a bowl with sea salt to taste. Add the milk to the eggs and combine well.

3 Add the egg mixture to the pan of sautéed ramps and stir slowly with a heat-resistant spatula. Continue stirring while the eggs are cooking. Once the eggs are just cooked to your liking, divide them among 4 plates, top with Parmigiano-Reggiano, if desired, and serve immediately.

GRILLED SPRING ONIONS WITH ROMESCO

Charred spring onions are a beloved tradition across continents. My local taco stand in the nearby *supermercado* chars them slowly on the grill, resulting in a caramelized flavor that makes their *tacos al pastor* shine. In Spain they have festivals slathering a similar onion relative with garlicky, peppery romesco sauce after intense grilling. This is my take on that Spanish superhero. *Serves 4*

4 spring onions (bulbs about the size of a golf ball), green tops on	½ cup pimento peppers, roasted (jarred are fine)
3 tablespoons olive oil, plus a splash to finish the dish	1 roma tomato, seeded and diced
Kosher salt	Tiny pinch of cayenne pepper
2 garlic cloves, finely minced	½ teaspoon smoked sweet paprika (pimentón)
¼ cup pecan halves, toasted	1 tablespoon sherry vinegar
	2 tablespoons plain yogurt

1 Prepare an ice water bath and set it near the stove. Bring a small pot of water to a vigorous boil and immerse just the bulbs of the onions in the boiling water, taking care to keep the greens from drooping over onto the burner. Cook the bulbs for 3 minutes, then plunge them into the ice water to stop the cooking. Pat the onions dry and cut them in half lengthwise, from the tops of the greens through the bulbs. In a bowl, toss the onions with 1 tablespoon of the olive oil and season with kosher salt to taste.

2 Get a grill lit and let it warm up, or let the coals cook down, while you make the romesco sauce: In a blender, combine the garlic, pecans, peppers, tomato, cayenne, paprika, and vinegar and pulse until just beginning to get smooth. Turn the blender on low speed and drizzle in the remaining 2 tablespoons olive oil, and then finish

SPRING ONION
RISOTTO

by adding the yogurt and seasoning with kosher salt to taste. Blend well and set aside.

3 Place the onions on the hot grill and cook for about 3 minutes a side, until they are well charred and look scrumptious. Spread a dollop of romesco on a platter with an offset spatula, arrange the onions over the romesco, and drizzle with a splash of really good olive oil. If you have extra romesco it will keep for a week in the fridge.

SPRING ONION RISOTTO

This should be in your repertoire as a stand-alone dish, a course in a big meal, or a side to pair with something like spring lamb or wild salmon. There are three components using the onions: a bright green puree with the tops, caramelized bites with half of the bulbs, and the risotto base with the rest of the bulbs. It's an onion party. ***Serves 4 as a light supper, 6 as a side***

6 spring onions (bulbs about the size of a golf ball), green tops on	1 cup Arborio rice
Kosher salt	½ cup finely grated Parmigiano-Reggiano cheese, plus more for garnish
4 tablespoons olive oil	2 tablespoons unsalted butter
4 cups chicken stock (see page 22), plus more for finishing	1 tablespoon red wine vinegar

1 First let us prep the onions: Cut the tops away from the bulbs, and cut the tops into thin rounds, about ¼ inch thick. Take 1 tablespoon of these and set it aside for a garnish. Reserve the remaining sliced tops. Cut the roots away from the onion bulbs and discard. Cut the bulbs into quarters from top to bottom, so the root end is still holding each wedge together. Mince as many of the bulb wedges as you need to give you ½ cup of minced onion.

2 Make the onion-top puree: Prepare an ice water bath and place it near the stove. Bring a small pot of water to a rolling boil, salt it so that it's pleasantly salty, and then blanch the onion tops in the boiling water for 1 minute. Drain, and plunge the tops into the ice water to stop the cooking. Strain the cooled onion tops and place in a blender. Add just enough water to allow the onions to move in the blender. Puree until smooth, and set aside.

3 Place a medium sauté pan over medium heat and add 2 tablespoons of the olive oil. Arrange the onion wedges in the pan and caramelize until deeply browned but not burnt, about 15 minutes, flipping them over halfway through. If the onions are browning too quickly, turn the heat down. Season them with kosher salt.

4 While the onion wedges are cooking, start the risotto: Warm your chicken stock in a small saucepan over medium-low heat. Keep this on low heat on the back of the stove. Place a large, heavy saucepan or sauté pan over medium heat and add the remaining 2 tablespoons olive oil. Add the minced onion and cook, stirring with a wooden spoon, until the onion is translucent and aromatic but not browned, about 5 minutes. Add the rice and lightly glaze the rice in the oil.

5 Start adding the stock, about 1 cup at a time, stirring and cooking after each addition until the stock is absorbed. Repeat until all the stock is used. After a while you will see a luxurious starchy liquid surrounding those little rice kernels. This is good. After about 15 minutes of cooking, taste your rice. It should have a very slight crunchiness to it, but you have to soothsay what it will taste like after 3 more minutes, while it sits in the bowl. Let's finish this up: Add the Parmigiano-Reggiano and 1 tablespoon of the butter, and stir well to fold those beautiful finishes into the risotto. Then add the green onion puree and season with kosher salt to taste. The risotto should look looser than you would expect. When it gets into that bowl, it will set up well.

6 Quickly finish the onion wedges with the splash of red wine vinegar, a dash of chicken stock, and the remaining 1 tablespoon butter.

7 Spoon the risotto into shallow bowls and garnish with the caramelized onions, the reserved raw onion tops, and some more Parmigiano-Reggiano.

SALMON WITH RAMPS AND PEAS

Wild Pacific salmon season opens up, and ramps and peas are waiting for their friend. They meet in this American classic that just feels right. *Serves 4*

2 tablespoons canola oil

4 salmon fillets (6 ounces each), skin off

Sea salt

2 tablespoons unsalted butter

½ pound ramps, cut into 2-inch lengths

2 cups fresh English peas, blanched in boiling water for 1 minute

¼ cup chicken stock (see page 22)

1 tablespoon freshly squeezed lemon juice

1 In a sauté pan that is large enough to hold all the salmon fillets with space around each piece, heat the canola oil over high heat. Pat the fillets dry with a paper towel and season with sea salt on both sides. When the oil comes up to a slight smoke, add the fillets and sear them for 4 minutes. The bottom of the fillets should develop a good brown color. Add 1 tablespoon of the butter, flip the fillets over, and cook for 1 minute. Transfer the fish to a plate lined with paper towels.

2 Remove any excess oil from the pan and return it to medium heat. Add the remaining 1 tablespoon butter, and when it begins to bubble and froth, add the ramps and season with sea salt to taste. Cook the ramps for 2 minutes, stirring as they start to wilt. Add the blanched English peas and the chicken stock. Add the lemon juice and adjust the seasoning with more sea salt if needed.

3 Place a salmon fillet on each plate, and spoon the ramp and pea mixture over the top.

OTHER ODDITIES: YACON, BAMBOO & FIDDLEHEADS

Yacon is kind of like a white sweet potato crossed with jicama. Bamboo is like heart of palm but more beautiful. Fiddleheads are an edible fern that is the symbol of an unfurling spring. These are the oddities that dot our menu in springtime.

PICKLED BAMBOO

Sometimes people bring us things that I have never heard of or even thought of. I mean I guess I have eaten bamboo in Chinese restaurants and never really noticed, and there are plots of bamboo dotted around Athens—most notably at Michael Stipe's house, which is hidden by a huge planting of bamboo—but it was a culinarily surprising day when our friends Mandy and Steve brought us about twenty pounds of young foot-long shoots.

Peeling back the firm outer leaves revealed a tender core that is like the freshest heart of palm ever. Local bamboo is a rarity at the market, but if you find it, don't be shy. *Makes 1 quart*

¾ pound fresh, edible bamboo (find the species *Phyllostachys aureosculata* 'Spectabilis', *Phyllostachys elegans,* or *Phyllostachys nigra*)

2 cups rice vinegar

1½ tablespoons pickling salt

½ cup sugar

½ ounce dried kombu seaweed

1 To clean the bamboo, peel away the outer fibrous layers of leaves with your fingers. It is like a tightly clenched flower, and you are removing petals to get to the tender core, revealing the tender heart; it really does at this point look like heart of palm.

2 Combine 1½ cups of water with the vinegar, pickling salt, sugar, and kombu in a small nonreactive pot and bring to a boil. Turn the heat down and simmer for 5 minutes.

3 Meanwhile, cut off the tip of the cleaned bamboo, and then cut each heart in half lengthwise (and marvel at the fractal beauty). Chop each half into 4-inch lengths. Pack the bamboo pieces into a clean 1-quart mason jar, leaving 1 inch of headspace.

4 Using a funnel, pour the hot brine over the bamboo, taking care to include the seaweed, and leaving ½ inch of headspace. Cap with the lid and band, and let cool for 2 hours. The jar can be stored in the refrigerator for 2 months, or processed according to the jar manufacturer's directions and stored for up to 9 months on the shelf.

ROASTED YACON

Yacon grows like a weed around here. It looks like a small sweet potato with pale white to yellow flesh and has a fresh, clean taste that kind of says, "Jicama!" Also known as the "Peruvian ground apple," it is being nurtured by some awesome local farms. It is pretty cool stuff. The ones we get vary in size but are generally around two to three ounces each. In South America, the leaves are cooked like spinach or sweet potato leaves.

If you happen to find some yacon, enjoy. If not, buy some jicama instead. *Serves 4 as a side*

1 pound yacon

1 teaspoon freshly squeezed lime juice

1 tablespoon olive oil

1 teaspoon sweet smoked paprika (pimentón)

Kosher salt

½ teaspoon chopped fresh thyme leaves

1 tablespoon unsalted butter

1 teaspoon cider vinegar

1 Preheat the oven to 450°F.

2 Peel the yacon, slice it into ½-inch-thick rounds, and place them in a medium bowl. Add the lime juice, olive oil, paprika, a few good pinches of kosher salt, and the thyme leaves and toss well. Place the seasoned yacon into a large ovenproof skillet and roast in the oven for 15 minutes, until it is crisp and golden.

3 Remove the skillet from the oven and add the butter and the cider vinegar. Swirl around to incorporate the butter and vinegar, and then place the yacon on a serving platter. Eat.

YACON AND APPLE SALAD WITH PLUMPED RAISINS

I eat like a rabbit, so salads play an important part in my life. This one gets great crunch from the apple and yacon, sweet bits from the raisins, balanced acidity by way of the vinaigrette, and green goodness from the spinach. If you can't find yacon, you can use jicama. *Serves 4*

¼ cup golden raisins

¼ cup freshly squeezed orange juice

½ pound yacon

2 crisp apples

1 tablespoon freshly squeezed lemon juice

4 cups fresh spinach leaves

¼ cup shaved Parmigiano-Reggiano

Kosher salt

¼ cup Champagne Vinaigrette (recipe follows)

PICKLED BAMBOO

YACON AND APPLE
SALAD WITH PLUMPED
RAISINS

1 In a small saucepan, combine the raisins, orange juice, and ¼ cup of water. Bring to a boil and then reduce to a low simmer. Cook for 10 minutes, until the liquid is nearly evaporated and the raisins are plump and tender. Set aside.

2 Peel the yacon and cut it into ¼-inch-thick slices. Cut the apples into slices as well, avoiding the core and the stem. Combine the yacon and apple in a large bowl, and add the lemon juice. Toss well and then add the spinach, the plumped raisins, the shaved Parmigiano-Reggiano, and kosher salt to taste. Add the vinaigrette, toss well, and serve.

CHAMPAGNE VINAIGRETTE
Makes 1½ cups

1 teaspoon honey	Kosher salt
1 teaspoon Dijon mustard	Freshly ground black pepper
1 cup grapeseed or canola oil	2 tablespoons finely cut fresh chives
⅓ cup champagne vinegar	

Place the honey and mustard in a bowl. Blend lightly with a whisk, and then slowly start pouring in the oil, alternating once in a while with the vinegar. Once all is well incorporated, season with kosher salt and black pepper to taste, and finish with the chives. Stir to combine, and store in a pint jar. The vinaigrette will stay fresh in the fridge for up to 5 days.

FIDDLEHEAD FERNS AND MORELS ON GARLIC TOAST

I adore the simplicity of mushrooms on toast, but the addition of fiddleheads makes this a spring winner and brings me back to my younger days. The area of Canada that I am from is a fiddlehead trove, and the ferns are a hot topic in midspring when they pop up in the woods. *Serves 4 as an appetizer*

Kosher salt	Freshly ground black pepper
1 cup fresh fiddlehead ferns	¼ teaspoon minced fresh thyme leaves
2 tablespoons unsalted butter	
¼ cup minced shallots	¼ teaspoon minced fresh flat-leaf parsley leaves
2 cups fresh morels, washed and cut into ⅓-inch-thick rounds	¼ cup chicken stock (see page 22)
1 tablespoon sherry vinegar	Garlic Toast (recipe follows)

1 Prepare an ice water bath and set it near the stove. Fill a saucepan with a quart of water, season it well with salt, and bring to a boil. Blanch the fiddleheads in the boiling water for 2 minutes, then drain and shock in the ice water. Drain and set aside.

2 Melt the butter in a large sauté pan over medium-high heat. When it bubbles and froths, add the shallots and cook them for about 3 minutes, until aromatic and translucent. Then add the morels. (Morels, like any mushroom, will give off liquid, and you want that to happen. The key is to have the pan hot enough so the morels are browning while that's happening, so they don't just steam in their own juice.) Cook for 5 to 7 minutes, until the morels are tender and a little browned.

3 When the mushrooms are nicely cooked, deglaze the pan with the vinegar, add salt and black pepper to taste, sprinkle in the thyme and parsley, and cook for 4 minutes. Add the chicken stock and the fiddleheads, and stew for 2 minutes. Adjust the seasoning as needed. You can finish with a touch more butter if you want the richness to be more intense.

4 Serve over the garlic toast.

GARLIC TOAST
Makes 4 slices of garlic toast

¼ cup (½ stick) unsalted butter   1 garlic clove
4 slices of sourdough boule

1 Preheat the oven to 450°F.

2 Melt the butter in a small pan and then brush the melted butter over the slices of bread.

3 Place the bread on a baking sheet and toast in the oven for 3 to 5 minutes, until nicely toasted but still pliable in the middle. Remove from the oven, and rub the garlic clove over each piece of toast to impart its flavor.

SUMMER

The Cadence of Summer Eating

My way of eating in the summer is usually just a simple reaction to what's already in my kitchen. If I have slices of ripe tomatoes, I sprinkle on some salt and line them up on a mayo-swathed slice of fresh bread. It is a reaction to the heat and humidity. Tomatoes just taste better when you are all sweaty and tuckered out on a humid day. And it's the way I most prefer to eat.

It probably started at the summer cottage when I was a kid, with my mother having one too many afternoon beers or early evening cocktails, a common hobby—or ailment—in our family. We kids—all four of us—had to eat after conquering forests, lakes, and creeks all day. We'd empty the contents of the fridge and pantry onto the dining table: potato salad, pickles, cheeses, ham, sliced cucumbers, shaved lamb leg from the night before, corn cut from the cob and dressed with lemon and olive oil. Condiments would appear to garnish the speedy feast: black olive tapenade, strong mustards, chutney, and savory jam. A stack of plates, and there you have it: Summer Supper.

It taught me two things: Don't drink too much early in the day, and good food really doesn't need to be difficult at all.

The CSA box and the farmers' market abound for us in June, July, and August. They are plumb full of tomatoes, beans, herbs, corn, squash, okra, blueberries, blackberries, cucumbers, eggplant, and so much more. It makes the long Southern summer days bearable. It is a time to preserve early in the morning, when it's still cool enough in the kitchen without the AC running full-throttle. It is a time to can those tomatoes for a winter's feast, to pickle the okra for a future Bloody Mary, to jam those berries for the perfect toast in September. It is also a time to make that feast of many vegetable-rich dishes strewn along a long table, celebrating the family you love and the friends you adore. So get cooking, because the summer bounty lasts only so long.

BASIL

Basil evokes so much in my mind: the first time I made pesto; the time I learned to make ratatouille; thick slices of tomatoes, gently dabbed with sea salt and olive oil. It reminds me of a chef taking the time to show me how to delicately tear basil, a wonderful culinary oxymoron, to avoid the harsh discoloration that a knife can bring to something so fragile.

Basil is more than the leaf floating in the tomato sauce; it caresses with its herbal kick and sweet hint of heat, and it deserves a constant place at the summer table.

CRISP TOASTED BAGEL,
FROMAGE BLANC, TOMATO,
SEA SALT, AND BASIL

CRISP TOASTED BAGEL, FROMAGE BLANC, TOMATO, SEA SALT, AND BASIL

When I go out to breakfast, my continental disposition usually leads me to a fruit plate with some toast, or the ubiquitous toasted bagel plate. Four out of five times, the bagel is undertoasted, the smoked salmon just *meh*, the cream cheese rock-solid cold, and the onion sliced about ½ inch thick so it's virtually inedible. My nonconfrontational style means I eat it all, but I ain't happy about it.

In my kitchen I have control. I can toast the bagel how I like it, so that it's crispy with every bite. The fromage blanc is room temperature, the way the dairy gods intended. In the smoked salmon's place, I usually prefer a seasonal delight, in this case a perfectly ripe heirloom tomato, dotted with the crunch of coarse salt and adorned with little basil leaves, because they were meant to be together. And they were meant to be in my belly.

As for the flavor of the bagel, I like sesame, but we can still be friends if you go poppy. You are banished from the island if you go blueberry-flavored. *Serves 2*

2 bagels	Sea salt
2 tablespoons unsalted butter, at room temperature	Freshly ground black pepper
¼ cup fromage blanc, at room temperature	8 small fresh basil leaves (or torn large ones if you can't find small ones)
1 large ripe heirloom tomato, cut into 8 slices	Olive oil

1 Slice the bagels in half. Toast them in the oven or in a toaster until golden brown.

2 Remove and butter them while they are still piping hot. Then slather them with the fromage blanc. Place 2 slices of tomato on each bagel half, and season with sea salt and black pepper to your liking. Dot the bagels with the basil leaves and a drizzle of olive oil, and serve.

BUTTERED, ROASTED SUMMER SQUASH WITH BASIL

If you grow your own vegetables, you have waded into the squash patch. You know that you need new ideas to deal with the voluminous harvest, and a recipe for a quick dish like this can work you through a couple of pounds of squash in a jiffy. *Serves 4 as a side*

2 pounds small to medium mixed summer squashes (zucchini and yellow)	2 tablespoons unsalted butter
1 tablespoon canola oil	1 teaspoon freshly squeezed lime juice
Sea salt	¼ cup fresh basil leaves, torn into postage-stamp-size pieces

1 Preheat the oven to 450°F. Heat a large cast-iron skillet in the oven for 20 minutes.

2 Trim the root ends off the squashes. Dress the whole squashes with the canola oil and sea salt to taste. When the skillet is blazing hot, add the squashes directly to the skillet in the oven; they should sizzle immediately. Roast the squashes for a total of 8 minutes, turning them every 2 minutes to ensure even browning. (If you find your pan is crowded, do this in two batches.)

3 Carefully remove the skillet from the oven and place it over medium heat on the stove. Add the butter and cook for 1 minute to coat the squashes. Place the squashes on a cutting board and cut into large bite-size pieces. In a bowl, toss the squash pieces and their juices with the lime juice, torn basil, and more sea salt to taste. Serve.

BASIL AND PECAN PISTOU WITH PARISIAN GNOCCHI

Pistou is "pesto" in French. Simple and straight-forward. But the real difference here is the Parisian gnocchi, which differ from Italian gnocchi in that they are dumplings made with a choux paste base, the same classic dough that is used to make gougères and éclairs. It is a wonderful technique to have in your arsenal. *Serves 4*

1 cup whole milk

¼ pound (1 stick) unsalted butter

Sea salt

1 cup bread flour

1 tablespoon Creole mustard

1 cup finely grated Parmigiano-Reggiano cheese

5 eggs

½ pound fresh basil leaves

¼ cup pecan halves, toasted, plus more for garnish, coarsely chopped

3 garlic cloves, blanched in boiling water for 2 minutes

¼ cup olive oil

1 In a medium saucepan, bring the milk, butter, and 1 teaspoon sea salt to a boil over high heat. Then reduce the heat to medium-low and slowly add the flour, whisking to fully incorporate it, forming a paste. Cook for 4 minutes, stirring constantly to prevent sticking. When it starts pulling away from the sides of the pan, you're ready for the next step. Add the mustard and the Parmigiano-Reggiano, mix well, and remove from the heat.

2 Place the paste in a stand mixer fitted with the paddle attachment, and mix on low speed for 3 minutes to let it cool slightly. Then add the eggs one at a time, making sure each one is fully incorporated before adding the next. Place the dough in a piping bag, or in a self-seal plastic bag with the corner trimmed to form a ½-inch hole, and set aside.

3 Prepare an ice water bath and place it near the stove. In a medium saucepan, bring 4 quarts of water to a boil, and season the water with sea salt as you would pasta water.

4 Squeeze the dough from the piping bag, cutting it in ½-inch intervals with a paring knife or kitchen scissors, dropping the pieces directly into the boiling water. (It's easier if you have someone help you with this. You should cut about 20 pieces.) Then carefully stir the gnocchi. Once they have floated to the top of the water, remove them with a slotted spoon and place them directly in the ice bath. Repeat these steps until you have cooked all the gnocchi dough. Remove the gnocchi from the ice water, place them on a plate lined with paper towels, and reserve.

5 Prepare another ice water bath near the stove. In a large saucepan, bring 2 quarts of water to a boil and season with enough sea salt to make it pleasantly salty. Blanch all but 3 leaves of the basil in the boiling water for just a moment; you want it to still be bright green. Strain and immediately place it in the ice water to shock it. Remove the basil and squeeze out the excess water.

6 In a blender or food processor, combine the blanched basil, pecans, blanched garlic, and a few pinches of sea salt. Blend on high speed, and then, with the motor running, drizzle in the olive oil. Continue to puree until the pistou is smooth; and add more sea salt to taste.

7 Combine the pistou and the gnocchi in a medium saucepan and warm them through over medium heat. Remove from the heat, arrange the gnocchi on a serving dish, and garnish with the reserved basil leaves and chopped pecans.

BEANS

Bean terminology has some logic to it. Bush beans grow, well, like bushes. Pole beans will reach for the sky if given something to grab hold of. String beans have a string that you need to strip off. Snap beans audibly snap when you remove the stem end. It is a pretty basic family tree of names, but it works. In the summer season we get all types, including Provider, Royal Burgundy, Red Noodle, Northeaster, and Pension. With them we make salads, pickles, gratins, soups, and tempuras. I find the most basic preparation is sometimes the best: Take 2 tablespoons of butter, ½ cup of water, ½ teaspoon of sea salt, and 1 pound of cleaned beans and place them in a heavy pot with a lid. Bring the liquid to a boil, put the lid on the pot, and let the beans steam for 3 minutes. Remove from the heat and let them sit for another 2 minutes. Eat 'em up.

DILLY BEANS

This is a staple pickle of the South that belongs on your refrigerator door. Pop open the jar and use them in Bloody Marys, or chopped up in a salad, or just as part of the pickle plate that appears on our family table at least once a week. *Makes 1 quart or 2 pints*

1 pound green snap beans, stemmed

½ cup chopped fresh dill fronds

1 cup distilled white vinegar

½ tablespoon sugar

2 teaspoons pickling salt

½ teaspoon dill seeds

½ teaspoon coriander seeds

1 garlic clove, smashed

1 Pack the beans and the dill into a clean quart jar (or 2 pint jars), leaving 1 inch of headspace at the top. Set aside.

2 In a small nonreactive saucepan, combine 1 cup of water with the vinegar, sugar, pickling salt, dill seeds, coriander seeds, and garlic. Bring to a boil and then reduce the heat to a simmer; cook for 5 minutes. Pour the hot pickling mixture over the beans, covering them but leaving ½ inch of headspace. Cap the jar with the lid and band, and let cool for 2 hours.

3 These pickles like to mature for a little bit before eating, so put them in the fridge and they'll be ready in a week; they'll stay fresh for about a month after that if they are in the fridge. Otherwise you can process them according to the jar manufacturer's directions and store them for up to 9 months on the shelf.

HOW TO SHOP IN GOOD CONSCIENCE WITH GOOD SENSE

Buying groceries in a small town in the South is challenging. The age of convenience items has made it difficult to find the good stuff out there. I have some systems in place that make it a little bit better, though, and I encourage you to create your own map of your community to find the food you want to cook.

- Sure, shop at your supermarket or big-box store—just buy the right things. Buy the organically raised chicken, buy dried beans, and buy stuff in season. I am the father of two young kids and realize that I can't rely just on the stuff that has a complete local pedigree. Just be smart with your spending and try to make it have impact.

- Subscribe to a CSA box from a local farm. Duh. That's what this book is all about.

- Go to the farmers' market. They exist in almost all communities and if you don't encourage your local farmers to grow good food, we will lose a generation of local produce. We encourage by spending money.

- Find the local honey. Most communities have a producer and they know someone else who produces another cool food item. It's a network that you need to get in on.

- Find a farm that raises local meats and poultry. Support them, even though it seems really expensive. It doesn't have to be everything you buy, but at least invest some of your food budget in helping increase their volume. The higher the volume, the more likely the price will go down.

- Support the little guy. We belong to a local store that is a co-op. It has the basics of what we need, from good locally roasted coffee to milk and eggs. It is the place I go to when I have simple needs. They support our community in really direct ways and deserve my money.

- Eat in season. It helps your wallet and logically helps your local farmers.

- Try not to buy stuff with more than twenty ingredients, or with more than four ingredients that you have trouble pronouncing.

- Think before you buy. Impulse buying makes my wife buy Pop-Tarts.

- Little steps win this race. Change your patterns for the better every week.

FRIED GREEN BEANS WITH YOGURT SAUCE

I remember fried zucchini being a staple at the Bank Street Café, in Ottawa, Canada, the first restaurant I ever worked in. I was a fourteen-year-old dishwasher, watching the guys slug food around with the tenderness and attention to detail of a drunken sailor, but boy, that fried zucchini was good. These beans are my homage to those days, lightened up a bit with a refreshing yogurt sauce. *Serves 4 as a side*

2 quarts canola oil

1 cup plain yogurt

2 shallots, minced

Grated zest and juice of 1 lemon

2 tablespoons cider vinegar

2 tablespoons chopped fresh flat-leaf parsley leaves

Sea salt

1 cup plus 1 tablespoon all-purpose flour

¾ cup cornstarch

1 teaspoon baking soda

1 teaspoon sugar

1 cup ice water

1 pound fresh green beans, trimmed

1 In a large stockpot, heat the canola oil over medium heat to 350°F.

2 Meanwhile, in a medium mixing bowl, combine the yogurt, minced shallots, lemon zest and juice, cider vinegar, and chopped parsley. Adjust the seasoning with sea salt to taste, cover with plastic wrap, and chill in the refrigerator.

3 Combine the 1 cup flour, 1 teaspoon sea salt, the cornstarch, baking soda, and sugar in a medium mixing bowl and whisk in the ice water. The texture should be a little looser than pancake batter. Adjust the consistency with more water or flour as needed, and set aside.

4 In a large mixing bowl, toss the beans with the remaining 1 tablespoon flour to coat lightly. This will help the batter adhere to the bean. Then add the batter and toss to coat the beans. Working quickly, carefully place the beans, one at a time, into the oil. Fry the beans until they are golden brown, about 4 minutes. Remove the beans from the oil with a mesh strainer, and place them on a platter or baking sheet lined with paper towels. Season immediately with sea salt. Transfer the beans to a platter and serve with the yogurt sauce on the side.

GREEN BEANS WITH TARRAGON-LEMON SABAYON

Sabayon, or zabaglione, is a custard-like sauce usually found in the dessert area of a menu, but it can be applied in a savory way with very interesting results. I love it melting onto poached fish, paired with cold roasted chicken, or, as seen here, used as a dressing for beautiful, prime summer beans. This dish is a cold side, a genre of food that I love in summer as it evokes potlucks and picnics, docks and porches, some of my favorite eating places. *Serves 4 as a side*

Kosher salt

1 pound fresh green beans, trimmed

¼ cup heavy cream

2 egg yolks

½ teaspoon grated lemon zest

¼ cup sparkling wine

1 tablespoon champagne vinegar

1 tablespoon chopped fresh tarragon leaves

1 tablespoon chopped fresh flat-leaf parsley leaves

1 tablespoon chopped fresh chives

1 Prepare an ice water bath and place it near the stove. Bring 2 quarts of water to a vigorous boil in a pot, and add enough kosher salt to make it pleasantly salty.

2 Add the beans to the boiling water and cook for 5 minutes, or until just tender. Drain, plunge the beans into the ice bath to stop the cooking, and then transfer the cooled beans to a plate lined with a paper towel.

3 In a medium bowl, whip the cream to form soft peaks, and set aside.

4 Find a medium metal bowl that can nestle into a saucepan or a double boiler. Pour 2 inches of water into the saucepan and heat it over medium heat until it steams. Put the egg yolks, lemon zest, sparkling wine, vinegar, and a generous pinch of kosher salt in the metal bowl and place it on the saucepan, making sure the bowl doesn't directly touch the water. (The trick to a double-boiler is controlling the heat by being able to remove the bowl from the pot or keep it over the heat—primitive, yes, but functional.) Whisk vigorously until the liquid foams and then thickens, about 5 minutes. The egg yolks will cook into a luscious custard. Remove the bowl from the heat and continue whisking. Cool the custard in the fridge, lightly covered, and then remove from the fridge, and fold in the whipped cream and the tarragon.

5 Arrange the beans on a platter and top with the sabayon, parsley, and chives. Serve immediately.

FRIED GREEN BEANS WITH YOGURT SAUCE

GREEN BEANS WITH TARRAGON-LEMON SABAYON

STEWED POLE BEANS WITH FATBACK, TOMATO, AND GARLIC

When I first came to the South, I failed to understand the glory of long-cooked beans. But I turned a corner one day, eating beans from a local meat 'n' three. They were stewed and had developed their own potlikker, a very different likker than collards typically exude. It was like a bean consommé fortified by fatback, the salt-cured fat that is the simple Southern equivalent to *lardo*. I still love the blanched vegetables so ingrained in my French culinary training, but beans like this make me appreciate their versatility. Fatback adds a great richness to any stewed vegetable, but make sure you soak and rinse the fatback thoroughly in multiple changes of cold water and cut off the skin side. *Serves 4 as a side*

¼ pound salt-cured pork fatback, diced

1 cup diced yellow onion

2 garlic cloves, thinly sliced

Sea salt

1 pound pole beans, trimmed and cut into 1-inch pieces

1 bay leaf

2 cups peeled, seeded, and diced tomatoes

½ cup chicken stock (see page 22)

2 tablespoons red wine vinegar

2 tablespoons torn fresh basil leaves (optional)

STEWED POLE BEANS
WITH FATBACK,
TOMATO, AND GARLIC

1 In a medium soup pot, render the fatback over medium heat. Once it begins to crisp and brown, after about 8 minutes, add the onion. Reduce the heat to medium-low and cook for 5 minutes. Add the garlic and a few pinches of sea salt, and cook for 1 minute. Add the pole beans and the bay leaf; cook for 2 minutes. Then add the tomatoes and stock. Season with sea salt to taste and raise the heat to medium-high. Bring the liquid to a boil, turn the heat down to a simmer, and stew the beans for 10 minutes, or until they become tender, a tenderness that arrives just before limpness. Finish with the red wine vinegar and adjust the seasoning with more sea salt to taste.

2 Spoon the beans into a serving bowl and garnish with the torn basil, if using.

SUMMER BERRIES, CHERRIES & WILD GRAPES

The rhythm of my youth was this: blueberries to strawberries to blackberries to raspberries. After my move to the South, the beat went on, but now it ends with scuppernongs and muscadines, the beautiful rustic grapes of the South. Through grafting and years of growing, they are pretty much the same by either name, but I cling to the notion that the scuppernongs are the white/green ones and the muscadines are the red ones. A botanist I ain't.

In most cases, berries are quite interchangeable, so whatever the summer month, swap the berries in these recipes to match what's happening at the market.

blackberry vinegar

SCUPPERNONGS

PICKLED
BLUEBERRIES

BLACKBERRY VINEGAR

Most blackberry vinegar recipes are simple and to the point: you immerse blackberries in cider vinegar and wait. That's boring. In this technique we are creating an environment where acetobacter, the live culture in the vinegar, has a chance to transform real blackberry juice into its own awesome vinegar. *Makes 1 quart*

2 cups fresh blackberries

1½ cups filtered or spring water

⅓ cup sugar

⅓ cup Bragg cider vinegar

½ cup Everclear grain alcohol

¼ teaspoon sea salt

1 Combine the blackberries and the water in a blender and puree until smooth. Strain well through a fine-mesh strainer into a bowl. Discard the solids. Combine the pureed blackberries with the sugar, vinegar, grain alcohol, and sea salt. Puree the mixture again to aerate it, and then transfer it to a clean quart jar. Cover the top with a paper towel and secure it with a piece of kitchen twine or the O-ring of the jar. Leave the jar in a cool, dark place for 4 to 6 weeks.

2 When a good vinegar mother has formed—it will look like a layer of white mold, but don't worry—strain the vinegar into a clean jar and cover it with the lid. The vinegar will keep for many months on the shelf.

3 You can keep the mother going by putting it in a cup of wine . . . it just likes to eat and grow and make more vinegar. Good mother.

PICKLED CHERRIES

A little terrine, a sliced baguette, some whole-grain mustard, and pickled cherries . . . that could be a meal for me. *Makes 2 pints*

1¼ pounds pitted Bing cherries

½ teaspoon kosher salt

¼ cup sugar

2 star anise pieces

2 whole cloves

1½ cups white balsamic vinegar

1 Pack the cherries into clean mason jars, leaving ½ inch of headspace, and set them aside.

2 Combine the salt, sugar, star anise, cloves, vinegar, and 1 cup of water in a small nonreactive pot and bring to a boil. Reduce the heat to low and simmer for 5 minutes.

3 Carefully ladle the hot pickling mixture into the jars, leaving ½ inch of headspace in each. Cap with the lids and bands. Then store in the refrigerator for up to a month, or process according to the jar manufacturer's directions to store on the shelf for up to 10 months.

PICKLED BLUEBERRIES

Garnish duck or roasted turkey with these fun little sweet-and-tart blueberries. They are also great on vanilla ice cream with a drizzle of real maple syrup. *Makes 1 quart or 2 pints*

1¼ pounds fresh blueberries

½ teaspoon kosher salt

¼ cup sugar

2 star anise segments

1 whole clove

1½ cups white balsamic vinegar

1 Pack the blueberries into a clean quart jar (or 2 pint jars), leaving 1 inch of headspace at the top, and set aside.

2 Combine the kosher salt, sugar, star anise, clove, vinegar, and 1 cup of water in a nonreactive saucepan and bring to a boil. Reduce the heat to low and simmer for 5 minutes.

3 Carefully ladle the hot pickling mixture into the jar, leaving ½ inch of headspace. Cap with the lid and band, and then either refrigerate or process according to the jar manufacturer's directions. The berries can be stored in the fridge for 10 days; if processed according to the jar manufacturer's directions, they will keep for up to 10 months on the shelf.

SCUPPERNONG MARMALADE

The wild grapes known as scuppernongs and muscadines arrive late in Southern summers. In our backyard, two little bushes push up some gloriously sweet grape bundles, and if the harvest is enough to cover the incidental snacking as we pick, we make marmalade. The most difficult part of this recipe—tedious, in fact—is the peeling of the grapes, but you'll get the hang of it. *Makes ½ cup*

2 cups scuppernongs or muscadines

¼ cup sugar

2 teaspoons powdered pectin

1 teaspoon ascorbic or citric acid powder (or freshly squeezed lemon juice in a pinch)

Pinch of kosher salt

1 Peel the scuppernongs: Using a sharp paring knife, score the top of each grape with a shallow X. Then peel down each quarter of the skin, holding the skin between the blade and your thumb. Cut each peeled grape in half and pull out the seeds, using tweezers, pliers, or fingers if you are elfishly dexterous. Discard the seeds.

2 Place the halved peeled grapes in a small pot and add the sugar, pectin, ascorbic acid, and salt. Cook over medium heat for 15 to 20 minutes, until the fruit has cooked down and is thick like a jam. Chill and reserve. The marmalade will keep fresh in the fridge for up to 3 weeks, or process according to the jar manufacturer's directions to store on the shelf for up to 10 months.

RASPBERRY COBBLER WITH DROP BISCUIT TOPPING

I once cooked a guest-chef dinner at the great Atlanta restaurant Woodfire Grill, and the dessert course was made by chef Scott Peacock. Scott spent much of his professional life cooking and writing with Edna Lewis, one of my all-time favorite Southern culinary writers and one of the most important chefs in Southern food. Scott, who is himself a wildly talented man, clearly had learned some nuanced dessert skills from Edna because out of the kitchen emanated a truly scrumptious cobbler, wonderfully soupy with drop biscuits nestled into it, soaking up all of the fruit goodness from a mix of juicy berries. This recipe is an ode to both Scott and Edna, two of my favorite people ever to shape biscuits. *Serves 6*

3 pints fresh raspberries

¼ cup plus 1 tablespoon sugar

½ cup all-purpose flour

¼ cup cornmeal

1 teaspoon baking powder

1 teaspoon baking soda

¼ teaspoon sea salt

¼ pound (1 stick) cold unsalted butter, diced

¾ cup buttermilk

1 teaspoon grated lemon zest

1 teaspoon cornstarch

1 Preheat the oven to 350°F.

2 In a medium mixing bowl, combine the raspberries with the ¼ cup sugar and set aside to macerate at room temperature for 1 hour.

3 While the raspberries are macerating, assemble the biscuit dough: In a food processor, combine the flour, cornmeal, baking powder, baking soda, remaining 1 tablespoon sugar, and the sea salt. Pulse to combine, and then add the butter. Pulse until the butter has flaked into small pieces. Add the buttermilk and pulse until just combined. Remove the dough from the processor and set it aside.

4 Add the lemon zest and cornstarch to the raspberries, stir to combine, and place the mixture in a 6 × 8-inch baking dish. Dollop spoonfuls of the biscuit topping over the raspberries. Bake for 35 minutes, or until the topping is golden brown and the fruit is bubbly. Serve warm or at room temperature.

GRILLED VENISON WITH BLACKBERRY GASTRIQUE

In Georgia, camouflage outfits are not a fashion trend but a necessity. People take the hunt seriously down here, and the results are freezers full of venison.

Venison is a sustainable and lean alternative to many other red meats. If you don't hunt, you can still get great farmed venison, which is a little tamer, less gamey. Generally what you find in the market is farmed in New Zealand or Australia, and the animals are hormone- and steroid-free, truly pasture-raised, grass-fed, and ethically treated. If you can't find that venison at your local fine foods grocery, look online. Or learn how to hunt.

Blackberries are my favorite berry. At the height of their ripeness, they just ooze sweetness. They are a little more robust than raspberries, so they don't end up as a puddle after a day in your fridge the way raspberries often do. Celia and John, our fine farmer friends at Woodland Gardens, do a fantastic job with blackberries—so good that they don't usually last much longer than the walk home from picking up our CSA box. *Serves 4 to 6*

6 dried juniper berries, crushed with the side of a knife

1 teaspoon finely minced fresh thyme leaves

½ teaspoon finely minced fresh rosemary leaves

½ cup olive oil

½ cup dry red wine, something you would want to drink

1½ pounds venison strip loin (about 2 inches in diameter), silverskin removed

Kosher salt

1 tablespoon unsalted butter

1 shallot, minced

¼ cup minced celery

½ teaspoon coriander seeds

1 pint fresh blackberries

2 ounces white rum

¼ cup cider vinegar

2 tablespoons maple syrup

2 cups chicken stock (see page 22)

12 Pickled Pearl Onions (page 89)

12 medium fresh mint leaves

GRILLED VENISON
WITH BLACKBERRY
GASTRIQUE

1 Combine the juniper, thyme, rosemary, olive oil, and red wine in a bowl and stir to combine. Season the strip loin all over with kosher salt, and then place it in a large sealable plastic bag. Add the wine mixture, seal the bag, place in the fridge, and marinate for at least 3 hours and up to 8 hours.

2 About an hour before you are ready to grill the venison, make the sauce: Place a small saucepan over medium heat and add the butter. When the butter bubbles and froths, add the shallot, celery, and coriander seeds. Cook for 3 minutes, until aromatic, and then add half of the blackberries. Cook for 1 minute. Add the rum and cook for 2 more minutes. Add the vinegar and maple syrup and reduce the volume by half, about 10 minutes. Add the chicken stock, raise the heat to medium-high, and continue to cook the liquid down to make ¾ cup of sauce, which should take about 10 minutes. Strain the sauce into a small pot, discard the solids, and reserve the sauce in a warm spot on the stovetop, but not over direct heat.

3 Get the grill going. I prefer a charcoal or wood grill, but to each their own. The embers should be very cooked down and the heat should be pretty darned hot. Right

before using it, wipe the grill clean with a towel doused with a little vegetable oil. I do this with some long tongs, 'cause I like the hairs on my arms.

4 Remove the venison from the marinade, and pick out any juniper berries that may be stuck to the loin. Pat off any excess marinade, and place the loin on the grill. Without poking and prodding it too much, cook it for 2½ minutes; then make a quarter turn and cook it for another 2½ minutes. Now turn it over and repeat. The total cooking time is about 10 minutes, but check the internal temperature. You are looking for 120°F for rare, 125°F for medium-rare, or 145°F at the most; this is medium-well in most cases, but be careful because venison gets very dry if overcooked. Remove the venison from the heat, place it on a cutting board, loosely cover it with foil to retain some of the heat, and let it rest for 10 minutes before slicing.

5 Cut the loin into thin slices, against the grain, and place them on a warmed platter. Drizzle the sauce over and around the slices. Garnish with some pickled pearl onions, the remaining fresh blackberries, and the mint leaves.

CORN

Corn, when in its optimum state and just-picked-ness, is a revelatory thing and makes out-of-season, dry, starchy corn seem like a distant cousin who you hope never visits. Buy in season, buy as local as you can, and cook it shortly after you buy it. Corn does not like to sit for a week in your crisper drawer, just like it doesn't like to be shipped from half a country away and stowed on a supermarket shelf.

CORN
SPOONBREAD

SEARED
SCALLOPS WITH
CORN, SPINACH,
AND BACON

GRILLED CORN SALAD WITH CHILES, BASIL, AND LIME

The charred corn contrasts with the acid punch of lime, and the sweetness of the corn balances the fiery punch of the grilled chiles. This is a salad for every sunny night in July or August, using the best produce of the moment. *Serves 4 as a side*

4 ears fresh corn, shucked
2 red jalapeños
4 tablespoons olive oil
Sea salt

1 cup fresh basil leaves, torn to small pieces
2 tablespoons freshly squeezed lime juice

1 Light the grill and get it really hot. If you are using a charcoal grill, which I strongly recommend, make sure the coals are cooked down to a fiery-hot gray.

2 Place the corn and the jalapeños on a baking sheet, and brush with 2 tablespoons of the olive oil. Season the corn and chiles all over with sea salt, and place them directly on the grate of the grill. Cook for 4 to 5 minutes, turning halfway through, until well charred. Remove the corn and the chiles from the grill and set them aside to cool.

3 Using a knife or a corn shucker, cut the corn kernels from the cob and place them in a bowl. Finely chop the jalapeños, discarding the stem (I leave it up to you if you want the seeds in there). Add the jalapeños, basil leaves, and lime juice to the corn. Taste, and add more sea salt if needed. Toss well, then add the remaining 2 tablespoons olive oil and stir. Let the salad sit for 30 minutes at room temperature. Serve.

CORN SPOONBREAD

Spoonbread is essentially souffléd cornbread. Like any soufflé, it likes to be eaten right after it comes out of the oven, so timing is crucial in this recipe. *Serves 4 to 6 as a side*

2 tablespoons unsalted butter
½ cup all-purpose flour
1 cup fine yellow cornmeal
½ teaspoon kosher salt
1 teaspoon sorghum syrup or blackstrap molasses
3 eggs, separated

1 cup buttermilk
1 cup fresh white corn kernels
1 teaspoon baking soda
1 tablespoon chopped fresh flat-leaf parsley leaves

1 Preheat the oven to 375°F.

2 Butter a 6 × 8-inch baking dish with 1 tablespoon of the butter, and set it aside.

3 Bring 2 cups of water to a boil in a large saucepan over high heat. Combine the flour, cornmeal, and kosher salt in a bowl and then slowly whisk the mixture into the boiling water. Lower the heat to medium when all the dry mix has been incorporated. Add the sorghum and remaining tablespoon of butter, and stir well for about 2 minutes. The mixture will look like slightly lumpy gruel at this point but that's okay . . . everything is going to work out fine. Remove the pan from the heat and let the mixture cool for 2 minutes.

4 In a mixing bowl, whisk together the egg yolks, buttermilk, cut corn, baking soda, and parsley. Whisk this into the cornmeal mixture, stirring well to get the lumps broken down.

5 In a separate bowl, whisk the egg whites with a clean whisk to form stiff peaks, and then fold them into the corn mixture. Pour the batter into the prepared baking dish and bake for 40 to 45 minutes (do not use convection), until the top is browned but the interior is set but still moist.

6 Serve immediately. Use a spoon!

SEARED SCALLOPS WITH CORN, SPINACH, AND BACON

We don't put bacon in everything in the South, contrary to what some people think. But we do use it in this recipe because the kinship between corn, scallops, and bacon is undeniably great. You'll want to use really good scallops, and getting them is easiest if you have a good relationship with a fishmonger—a relationship that, when nurtured, will garner you the best seafood, always in season, that you could possibly get your hands on. *Serves 4 as an appetizer or a light meal*

½ pound bacon, diced
2 shallots, sliced into rings
4 ears corn, kernels removed from the cob
Sea salt
2 tablespoons unsalted butter
1 pound spinach

1 tablespoon freshly squeezed lemon juice
12 large (U10 size) dry-packed scallops (make sure they are preservative-free)
2 tablespoons canola oil

1 Place the bacon in a medium sauté pan over medium-high heat, and cook until the fat starts to foam and the bacon is crisp, about 4 minutes. Drain off most of the bacon fat and add the shallots to the pan. Cook the shallots for 2 minutes, and then add the corn kernels. Continue to cook for an additional 4 minutes, until the kernels are tender but still have some pop. Season with sea salt to taste, and add 1 tablespoon of the butter. Add the spinach and cook just to wilt it, about 1 minute. Then finish with the lemon juice and more sea salt to taste. Remove from the heat and keep warm on the stovetop, but not directly over the heat.

2 Pat the scallops dry with a paper towel and season them all over with sea salt. Heat the canola oil in a large sauté pan over high heat. Once the oil has come to a slight smoke, add the scallops and sear for 3 minutes on one side. They should caramelize and develop a good golden-brown color. Add the remaining tablespoon of butter to the scallops and allow it to melt. Flip the scallops over and quickly spoon the butter over them, cooking for 1 minute more. Remove the scallops from the sauté pan and place them on a plate lined with a paper towel.

3 Arrange the scallops on individual plates, and spoon the spinach-bacon-corn mixture on top. Eat.

PERFECT PAN-ROASTED CHICKEN BREASTS WITH CREAMED CORN, LEMONGRASS, AND CRISP SHALLOTS

So many people suffer from the terrible malaise of never really knowing creamed corn from scratch. It's wondrous stuff that is so easy to make. Also easy to make is a perfect chicken breast, which often gets botched by even the best home cooks, but pay attention and you'll make chicken you'll be proud of. An "airline" chicken breast just means that the skin is on and the wing drumette is still attached to the breast, but otherwise it is boneless. Why it has that weird name I do not know. You can Google that. As for the lemongrass, cut the tender root end after you have removed the woody exterior leaves. *Serves 4*

4 ears fresh corn, shucked
½ cup chicken stock (see page 22), chilled
1 tablespoon unsalted butter
½ cup minced sweet onion
1 teaspoon finely chopped lemongrass, from the tender interior
Kosher salt
1 tablespoon crème fraîche
4 "airline" chicken breasts (about 7 ounces each)
2 tablespoons olive oil
1 tablespoon fresh thyme leaves

1 Preheat the oven to 350°F.

2 Using a knife or a corn cutter, remove the kernels from the corn cobs, dropping them into a large bowl. Run the dull side of your knife down each cob to press out the corn milk, adding it to the bowl. Place half of the corn kernels and corn milk into a blender, add the cold chicken stock, and puree until very smooth. Set aside.

3 Place a large sauté pan over medium heat and add the butter. When it bubbles and froths, add the onion and cook for 4 minutes, until translucent. Then add the remaining whole corn kernels and corn milk, the lemongrass, and a pinch of kosher salt. Cook for 2 minutes, and then add the pureed corn. Cook for 5 minutes, until it thickens. Then stir in the crème fraîche and season with kosher salt to taste. Remove from the heat and keep warm on the back of the stove, away from direct heat, while the chicken cooks.

4 Pat the chicken dry with paper towels. Place a large cast-iron sauté pan over medium heat and heat it for about 5 minutes. Pour the olive oil into the hot pan, quickly season the chicken breasts all over with kosher salt, and place them, skin side down, in the pan. Press them down for a second with your hand so the skin doesn't buckle from the heat. You'll feel all cheffy.

5 Let the chicken breasts cook without fussing with them for 10 minutes. Then turn them over, place the pan in the oven, and bake for 8 to 10 minutes, until the internal temperature at the thickest point reads 150°F. The chicken will still cook a bit after it comes out of the oven, and by all means we are trying to avoid the heresy of overcooked chicken. Remove the breasts from the oven and let them rest on a cutting board for 5 minutes before slicing.

6 If needed, reheat the corn to warm it through while you slice the chicken. Serve the chicken with the corn and sprinkle on thyme leaves. Eat.

CUCUMBERS

I don't know that anything is quite as refreshing as a cucumber. Crisp and quenching with a smidgen of acidity, cucumbers get a lot of use in our kitchen: We make pickles in a large crock, we sauté them, we make finely chopped salads, and we slice them thinly for a simple sandwich. They are omnipresent in a bagged lunch for the kids and end up being a great snack for me many days. Cucumbers are also really inexpensive, and when in season, they grow like mad . . . getting good ones is not an issue. So go find that farmer who is growing General Lee, Olympian, Tasty Jade, or Striped Armenian, all great varieties.

CHILE-MINT SAUTÉED CUCUMBERS

A cucumber is not a thing we normally think to cook, but this simple recipe is a revelation that shows it has a world outside its raw form. They cook up beautifully—just don't cut them too thin or they will get all soft on you. *Serves 4 as a side*

1 pound cucumbers
1 tablespoon olive oil
1 tablespoon unsalted butter
1 shallot, minced
¼ teaspoon crushed red pepper flakes

1 tablespoon freshly squeezed lemon juice
2 tablespoons chopped fresh mint leaves
¼ teaspoon kosher salt

1 Peel the cucumbers, cut them in half lengthwise, and then remove the seeds by running a small spoon down the seed seam. Cut the cucumbers into ¼-inch-thick half-moons and set aside.

2 Heat the olive oil in a large skillet over medium-high heat. When the oil is hot, add the butter and the shallot and cook for 1 minute, until aromatic. Add the sliced cucumbers and toss to coat. Cook for 3 minutes, until the cucumbers are hot and just tender; then add the red pepper flakes, lemon juice, and fresh mint. Remove from the heat and season with the kosher salt. Toss, and place in a shallow bowl to serve.

CUCUMBER SUNOMONO

Sunomono is the quintessential quick-pickled cucumber of Japan; washing cucumbers in vinegar and dashi results in a very flexible staple. It has a synergy with tuna, octopus, shrimp, and really whatever is most beautiful from the sea. I like to finish a poached salmon with the sunomono over the top or to pack it as a simple side in the kids' lunch boxes. They eat it up. *Makes about 3 cups*

1 pound English or other thin-skinned cucumbers
1 teaspoon kosher salt
½ cup dashi (page 37)
½ cup rice vinegar

1 tablespoon soy sauce
1 teaspoon sugar
1 tablespoon toasted sesame seeds

1 Peel the cucumbers and then, using a mandoline or a very sharp knife, slice them into very thin rounds. Spread the slices in one layer on a baking sheet and sprinkle with the kosher salt. Set aside.

2 Combine the dashi, vinegar, soy sauce, and sugar in a small saucepan and bring to a boil. Remove from the heat and let cool completely.

3 Rinse the cucumbers well and squeeze out any excess liquid. Place them in a bowl, pour the dashi mixture over them, and let them sit at room temperature for an hour.

4 When you are ready to serve the cucumbers, top them with the sesame seeds. The cucumbers can keep, in the refrigerator, for up to 5 days.

FULL-SOUR DILL PICKLES

Come on, you can do this. It's fun. Impress yourself and your neighbors by making your own full sours.

Fermentation is the great unknown to the average American, but it surrounds us daily, from coffee to bread, miso to wine; it's what makes those delicious things delicious. The classic sour dill is a core concept in food that we need to continue to teach and practice. So grab that crock and get fermenting.
Makes 4 to 5 quarts

24 small Kirby cucumbers
¼ pound fresh dill fronds
3 garlic cloves (optional)
3 grape leaves (optional)

⅓ cup plus 1 tablespoon pickling salt
2 tablespoons pickling spice

1 Wash the cucumbers well and lay them in a crock (see page 199) or a couple of large mason jars, layering in the dill, garlic, and grape leaves, if using, as you go. Set aside.

2 Combine the pickling salt, 2 quarts of water, and the pickling spice in a large nonreactive saucepan and bring to a boil; then reduce the heat and simmer for 10 minutes. Let the pickling mixture cool completely.

3 Pour the cooled mixture over the cucumbers to fully cover. Cover the crock with the lid; or if you are using mason jars, cover with a paper towel and the metal band to let them breathe. Set the crock in a place that hovers around 70°F for about 5 days. Every day during that time, ladle off any impurities that rise to the top.

4 After 5 days, pack the pickles into clean jars, cover with the brine, and store in the fridge. They will stay good for weeks, and fermentation will cease at that temperature. (I like to store these in the fridge, as opposed to heat processing, because the heat just mauls that beautiful lactic goodness that you have created.) They will keep for 2 months. I mean, you have that jar of pickles that you've been eating from for 8 months and you look fine.

THE IMPORTANCE OF SEEDS

The variety of our seed stock has been abysmally watched over; we have let corporations take it over. While we used to have thousands of varieties of every fruit and vegetable, we have whittled that diversity down to a couple of lifeless varieties, robbed of their natural beauty, natural defense mechanisms, and most of all, flavor. We have lost all this in favor of what we are told is easiest and sellable.

I find our trail toward this limited seed store terrifying. Those few varieties that have legal counsel instead of agrarian lineage show no respect for the bounty that the earth once offered. Who would have thought a hundred years ago that you would one day be prohibited, by patent, from planting the seeds from a tomato that you bought at the store? Or that a plant would produce seed that is sterile due to a gene swap? Or that a farmer could be sued for cultivating seeds that grew on his land as a result of wind pollination from a neighboring farm? All of these things are true today, the result of a handful of corporations that have cornered the market on seeds. These hijinks are all about greed, and move us away from a connection with our foods and their historical importance. It makes food into more of a commodity than it has already become, when what we really need to do is to show people that food is something truly beautiful from the seed to the kitchen, not just something to be traded for money. We have lain down and let this happen.

Well, it is time to act and to encourage seed diversity once again.

And we have many leaders to show us the way. One educator, writer, environmental activist, community leader, and purely awesome voice is Janisse Ray. One of her many books is called *The Seed Underground: A Growing Revolution to Save Food.* In it Ray documents, through stunning stories, the amount of diversity we truly have lost in the agrarian land she and I both call home: the American South. My copy is all torn up, smudged and stained, evidence of a book that has been read and read again. You should pick up a copy and verse yourself on the laments of modern agrarianism. It is an important read.

Be conscious of where your seeds are coming from. If you garden at home, try to raise plants that have come down through your family or your community. Start saving your seeds, going to swaps, and buying from really great sources like the Southern Exposure Seed Exchange. I once had a dream of trying to help out by saving seeds in my retirement, but by then it may be too late. We have to start fighting now.

LIVERWURST AND CUCUMBER SANDWICHES

My family's summer cottage is in Canada, north of Toronto. It is a place with many food memories for me. We would eat tomatoes and corn and green beans. We would hunt blackberries and raspberries in the woods. Lunch was pretty much self-service, and I remember making myself sandwiches out of things that would perplex the average ten-year-old, like tongue, aged dry salami, and liverwurst. Still to this day, I love a liverwurst and cucumber sandwich. To me, it exemplifies summer simplicity. *Makes 4 sandwiches*

8 slices sourdough bread
2 tablespoons unsalted butter
1 tablespoon Dijon mustard

¼ pound liverwurst (recipe follows, if you want to make a great one)
½ English cucumber, thinly sliced, skin on
Salt

1 Toast the bread.

2 Butter the bread.

3 Dijon on one side.

4 Liverwurst on the other.

5 Cucumbers on liverwurst.

6 Season.

7 Eat.

LIVERWURST

Simple and wonderful, and a first step in learning about the vast art of charcuterie. This recipe is from the brain of Ryan Smith, my very talented friend who used to be the chef at Empire State South. It makes about 4 pints of finished product, enough to feed a good-size party some wonderful sandwiches. Life couldn't be better than watching U.S. Open tennis with a bunch of friends while eating liverwurst sandwiches. *Makes 4 pints*

⅔ pound chicken livers
⅔ pound 70% lean ground pork shoulder (also called sausage grade ground pork)
½ tablespoon sea salt
¼ teaspoon Instacure #1 (available at Sausagemaker .com)
1 teaspoon canola oil

1 cup diced yellow onion
¼ cup brandy
¼ teaspoon freshly ground black pepper
¼ teaspoon ground cardamom
¼ teaspoon ground ginger
¼ teaspoon ground mace
4 tablespoons unsalted butter, melted

1 Combine the livers and the ground pork in a mixing bowl. Season with the sea salt and the Instacure #1. Place the meat mixture, uncovered, in the refrigerator to cure for 1 hour.

2 While the meat is curing, heat the canola oil in a medium sauté pan over medium heat. When the oil begins to shimmer, add the onions and cook for 5 minutes, stirring often, until soft and just browning. Deglaze the pan with the brandy, and cook for about 1 minute to reduce the liquid by half its volume. Remove from the heat and chill in the refrigerator.

3 After the meat has cured for 1 hour, place the mixture in a food processor, add the chilled onions, and puree. Make the mixture as smooth as possible without the processor warming it too much. Transfer the mixture to a metal bowl, and stir in the pepper, cardamom, ginger, and mace. Cover with plastic wrap and return to the refrigerator to chill for 30 minutes.

4 Preheat the oven to 350°F. Bring 2 quarts of water to a boil in a tea kettle or saucepan.

5 Evenly distribute the liver mixture among 4 clean 1-pint mason jars. Cover each jar with foil and place all the jars in a baking pan. Fill the baking pan with enough boiling water to reach halfway up the height of the jars. Place the pan in the oven and bake the liverwurst for 30 minutes, or until it has reached an internal temperature of 150°F.

6 Remove the baking pan from the oven and carefully remove the jars to a cooling rack. Allow the jars to cool to room temperature and then pour 1 tablespoon of the melted butter on top of each potted liverwurst to preserve it. These will keep for 1 week, covered, in the fridge.

FIELD PEAS

To me, the use of local field peas is an angelic, luminous halo above the head of true Southern food. They are a seasonal gem that reminds us why this region is so important agriculturally. If someone goes out of their way to find beautiful, seasonal field peas like the crowder, the pink lady, or the zipper cream, it usually means that they have been cooking from scratch in a family kitchen that never *stopped* cooking from scratch. This is a really important distinction in the South: while much of the population succumbed to the ease of Jell-O and instant gravy, many others are hell-bent on keeping their culinary traditions alive. To me that is no more well represented than in cooking the simple field pea.

FIELD PEAS 101:
WITH FATBACK AND HERBS

Sometimes you have to throw away all the recipes and just work with what you have in your head. You work with logic and good ingredients and skills that will carry through to a great finish. This process doesn't have to be especially complex.

I was watching a documentary on "Popcorn" Sutton, a deity in the world of Appalachian moonshiners. At one point at his camp, he dumps some dried beans in a pot and soaks them a spell. He then puts in a big square of fatback from Virginia and lets it sit all day. And then he cooks the beans slowly over the heat generated by his still, deep in the woods. The beans are so good that he claims, "When you take a bite out of 'em, your tummy will slap your brains out." Well said.

So the thing with dried beans is to get good ones from the current year. Sort through them well, getting rid of the odd pebble or gnarly-looking bean, and then soak them a bit. The twenty-four-hour soak is more of an invitation to fermentation than a plumping up of dried legumes. I like soaking beans for five to six hours—current-year beans don't need a very long soak. If you want the best dried beans available in North America, order them from Rancho Gordo.

As for relishing in the glories of field peas, you need to do a couple of things: you need to find a source for peas so fresh they make you feel like you are eating summer, and then you need to concentrate on your potlikker. The pea potlikker is like a summer spa, all porky and buttery with specks of thyme, red pepper flakes, and a lucky bay leaf or two. That fatback, good-quality stuff, the *lardo* of America, has released its goodness into the likker, bolstering the basic liquid into an ethereal elixir. Do these things and you will win with field peas. Sourcing and cooking, that's really what this is all about.

The following recipe should get you in the right place when it comes to the simple preparation of dried peas and beans. Simple and proven, beans feed our Southern souls. ***Serves 4 to 8***

1 cup dried peas or beans (of recent harvest and of good pedigree, like Sea Island red peas)

¼ pound salted fatback

½ yellow onion, sliced

1 bay leaf

1 quart chicken stock (see page 22) or water in a pinch

¼ teaspoon crushed red pepper flakes

1 tablespoon chopped fresh flat-leaf parsley leaves

1 teaspoon chopped fresh thyme leaves

1½ teaspoons kosher salt

1 Put the peas in a bowl, add cold water to cover, and let sit at room temperature for 5 to 6 hours.

2 Rinse the fatback really well under cold running water, and then cut it into ½-inch-thick slices. Place a heavy pot over medium heat, add the sliced fatback, and cook for 5 minutes, until it starts to render. Then add the onion and the bay leaf to the pot. Cook for 10 more minutes, so the onion and fatback get to know each other really well. Pour the stock into the pot.

3 Drain the soaking peas and add them to the pot. Turn the heat to high, bring to a boil, and then reduce the heat to a simmer over low heat. Cook the peas for about 1 hour, but peas and beans vary a lot. They should be tender to the bite but the skins should not be bursting or broken. Remove from the heat when they are cooked, and finish with the red pepper flakes, parsley, thyme, and kosher salt. Stir well and serve. The lucky person gets the bay leaf.

GRATIN OF
FIELD PEAS
AND ROASTED
TOMATOES

FRIED
BLACK-EYED
PEAS

GRATIN OF FIELD PEAS AND ROASTED TOMATOES

This is a classic gratin that warms the soul on a chillier summer night. Pair it with a roast of some kind. Lamb leads the charge in my mind. Gratin, roast lamb leg, salsa verde, and a Pinot Noir? Invite me over. *Serves 4 as a side*

Sea salt

1 pound fresh field peas

6 roma tomatoes

1 garlic clove, thinly sliced

1 teaspoon chopped fresh thyme leaves

1 tablespoon olive oil

1 tablespoon unsalted butter

3 shallots, sliced

1 cup chicken stock (see page 22)

1 cup heavy cream

½ cup finely grated Parmigiano-Reggiano cheese

1 Preheat the oven to 300°F.

2 Bring a large pot of water to a boil and season it well with sea salt. Add the field peas and reduce the heat to a simmer. Slowly cook the peas for 30 minutes, or until they are completely tender. Once the peas are cooked, drain and set them aside.

3 While the peas are cooking, start the tomatoes: Bring a medium pot of water to a boil, and prepare an ice water bath. Score an X in the bottom of each tomato to make it easier to peel them after they're blanched. Individually blanch the tomatoes in the boiling water for 20 seconds, or until the skin begins to visibly peel away. Then immediately shock them in the ice water.

4 Peel the tomatoes and cut them in half lengthwise. Place them in a mixing bowl, and toss with the garlic and the thyme. Arrange the tomatoes on a rimmed baking sheet, cut side down, and drizzle with the olive oil. Roast the tomatoes in the oven for 30 to 40 minutes, until they have shriveled and given up some of their juices.

5 In a medium saucepan, melt the butter over medium heat. Once the butter foams, add the shallots and season with sea salt to taste. Cook the shallots over medium-low heat for 10 minutes, or until they become very soft. Add the chicken stock, raise the heat, and bring to a boil. Reduce the stock by half the volume, approximately 4 minutes. Add the heavy cream and bring to a boil. Add the field peas, stir, season with sea salt to taste, and remove from the heat.

6 When the tomatoes are done, remove them from the oven and raise the oven heat to 350°F.

7 Pour the field peas into a medium cast-iron sauté pan and arrange the roasted tomatoes over the top. Top the mixture with the grated Parmigiano-Reggiano, and bake in the oven for about 30 minutes, until the top is golden brown. Serve piping hot.

FRIED BLACK-EYED PEAS

Well-seasoned fried black-eyed peas will make you wonder why they aren't on every table across the land. They are completely addictive—crisp and light with a rich, nutty flavor. *Serves 8 as a snack*

1 pound dried black-eyed peas

Fine sea salt

2 quarts canola oil

½ cup chopped fresh flat-leaf parsley leaves

1 Put the peas in a bowl, add 2 quarts of water, and soak overnight in the fridge.

2 The next day, drain the peas and place them in a large pot. Cover with water that measures at least two times the volume of the peas. Heat to a simmer over medium-high heat. Lower the heat so that the water is just barely simmering. Skim off any foam that comes to the surface. Cook the peas for 30 minutes, or until they are very tender but not bursting. Add enough fine sea salt to the cooking water to make it pleasantly salty. Remove the pot from the heat and allow the peas to cool to room temperature in the pot. Then drain the peas well and pat very dry with paper towels.

3 Heat the canola oil to 350°F in a large pot over medium-high heat. Line a large bowl with paper towels as a landing pad for the fried peas.

4 Fry the peas in the hot oil, in several batches, until they are golden brown and crisp, about 3 minutes—if they are overfried they will burst open and if they are underfried they will just be hot and not crispy. The oil temperature should be maintained at 350°F for each batch. Remove the peas from the oil with a mesh strainer and place them in the waiting paper-towel-lined bowl. Immediately season with fine sea salt.

5 When all of the peas have been fried to a beautiful crispy snackiness, toss them with the chopped parsley and serve immediately.

CRISP FLOUNDER WITH FIELD PEA RAGOUT AND HERB SALAD

Flounder is a bountiful spring and summer fish in the South. The crisp fillets work so well here with the herbs and the fresh field peas. *Serves 4*

Fine sea salt

1 pound fresh field peas

4 skinless flounder fillets (5 ounces each)

2 tablespoons canola oil

¼ cup all-purpose flour

2 tablespoons unsalted butter

2 shallots, sliced into rings

¼ cup chicken stock (see page 22)

1 teaspoon grated lemon zest

1 tablespoon freshly squeezed lemon juice

1 tablespoon fresh flat-leaf parsley leaves

1 tablespoon cut fresh chives (1-inch pieces)

1 tablespoon fresh tarragon leaves, chopped

¼ cup chopped fresh pea shoots

1 teaspoon olive oil

1 Bring 4 quarts of water to a boil in a soup pot over high heat. Season the water well with fine sea salt and add the field peas. Reduce the heat to medium and simmer the field peas for 30 minutes, until they are tender. Skim off any foam that rises to the surface during cooking. When the peas are done, remove the pot from the stove and allow the peas, still in the cooking liquid, to cool to room temperature.

2 Season the flounder fillets with fine sea salt to taste. Heat the canola oil in a large sauté pan over medium-high heat. Dredge each flounder fillet in the flour and shake off any excess. Once the oil reaches a slight smoke, add the fillets, one at a time, and sauté for 4 minutes on one side, lightly pressing down on the fillets during the first 30 seconds to keep them from buckling. The fillets should develop an even, golden-brown color on the bottom. Add 1 tablespoon of the butter to the pan, turn the fish over, and just finish the cooking, about 1 minute. Remove the fillets from the pan and place them on a plate lined with paper towels. (Do this in batches if the fillets don't all fit at once.)

3 Add the remaining tablespoon of butter to the same pan, and cook the shallots over medium heat for 2 minutes, or until they become slightly translucent. While the shallots are cooking, drain the peas.

4 Add the drained peas and the chicken stock to the shallots. Season with sea salt to taste. Stir to fully incorporate, finish with the lemon zest and juice, and heat through.

5 Divide the peas among 4 plates and top each with a flounder fillet. Toss the parsley, chives, tarragon, and pea shoots in a small mixing bowl, and season with sea salt and the olive oil. Arrange the herb salad on top of the flounder.

LEEKS

Tim and Alice Mills are old friends who run the local gristmill. When we say "mill," it's not like a lumber mill or a woolen mill; rather it is a shack beside their house where they grind grains. Wonderful grits, oats, and flours emanato from that little shack. About fifty yards away Tim has his fields, and in those fields he nurtures the most beautiful slender, sweet leeks that I have ever found. They are a treat of summer.

LEEK FONDUTA

GRILLED
LEEKS

LEEK SOUP WITH
YOGURT AND CRISP
POTATOES

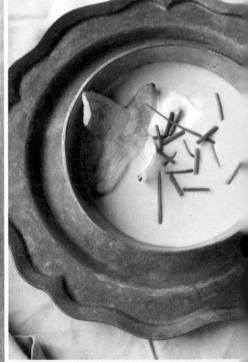

LEEK FONDUTA

Fonduta is the Italian version of fondue. Beautifully cooked leeks, with the natural sweetness that alliums exude, matched with melted cheese, butter, cream, and toast. It's all the things I love, but these are ingredients that my doctor gets all concerned about. So, the answer is moderation. Should you eat this every month in leek season? Oh hell yes. Should you eat it every day for breakfast and dinner? Nope. But I wish I could. *Serves 4 to 6*

2 pounds leeks, white and light green parts, washed and thinly sliced in half rounds	1 cup finely grated Parmigiano-Reggiano cheese
3 garlic cloves, thinly sliced	2 tablespoons chopped fresh flat-leaf parsley leaves
2 tablespoons unsalted butter	1 teaspoon grated lemon zest
1 teaspoon sea salt, plus more to taste	1 teaspoon freshly cracked black pepper
1 cup heavy cream	1 baguette, cut into 1-inch-thick slices and toasted
½ cup crème fraîche	

In a large saucepan, combine the leeks, garlic, butter, and the 1 teaspoon sea salt. Place the pot over medium heat and cook until the leeks are tender and translucent, about 20 minutes. You are trying to really pull the sugar out of the leeks without browning them much at all. Add the cream and crème fraîche, bring the liquid to a boil, and then reduce the heat and simmer for 5 minutes. Add the Parmigiano-Reggiano, parsley, lemon zest, black pepper, and more sea salt to taste, and stir to incorporate. Transfer the fonduta to a serving bowl and serve alongside the baguette slices. Encourage your eaters to dip the bread into the fonduta.

GRILLED LEEKS

Leeks come in all sizes, but this recipe will work well with medium leeks, 1 to 1½ inches in diameter and 10 to 12 inches long, with half of the leek being a pearly white. By all means use smaller ones if you find them in your CSA box or at the farmers' market, but cut down the cooking time accordingly. *Serves 4 to 6 as a side*

2 pounds young leeks, white and light green parts	1 tablespoon unsalted butter, at room temperature
1 tablespoon olive oil	1 tablespoon freshly squeezed lemon juice
Sea salt	

1 Preheat a grill to medium heat.

2 Cut the leeks in half lengthwise and wash them thoroughly, being sure to rinse out the dirt between the leaves. Pat them dry with a paper towel. Place them in a mixing bowl with the olive oil and a few generous pinches of sea salt, and toss.

3 Place the leeks on the hottest part of the grill, cut side down, perpendicular to the grate. Grill them for 3 minutes. Flip them and cook for 3 more minutes. Now place the leeks on a cooler section of the grill, away from direct heat (if you have an upper level, this is a good place). Cook for another 10 minutes, or until the leeks are tender.

4 Place the leeks in a mixing bowl, and add the butter and lemon juice. Toss, and serve immediately.

LEEK SOUP WITH YOGURT AND CRISP POTATOES

One of my jobs growing up in a French kitchen in Canada was to make vichyssoise, the classic potato and leek soup. I would make it every day and you get pretty good at figuring out the nuances of a dish when you make it every day for a year or two. This is a warm soup that has a lot of kinship with the classic vichyssoise but is amped up with yogurt and a crunchy finish of crisp potatoes. *Serves 8*

3 tablespoons unsalted butter	2 bay leaves
8 medium leeks, white and light green parts, well washed and cut into ¼-inch-thick rings	1 cup heavy cream
	4 fingerling potatoes
Sea salt	1 quart canola oil
2 quarts chicken stock (see page 22)	¼ cup plain yogurt
	Snipped chives (optional)

1 In a soup pot, melt the butter over medium heat. Once the butter bubbles and froths, add the leeks and 1 teaspoon sea salt. Cook the leeks for 20 minutes, stirring quite often to make sure no color develops. Add the chicken stock and bay leaves, raise the heat to high, and bring the liquid to a boil. Turn the heat down to a simmer and cook for 15 minutes. Then add the cream and cook for 5 minutes more. Remove the bay leaves, and puree the soup in a blender until completely smooth. Strain the pureed soup through a fine-mesh strainer into a saucepan. Taste, adjust with more sea salt if needed, and keep the soup warm on the stove over low heat until ready to serve.

2 Shave the fingerling potatoes lengthwise as thin as possible, using a peeler or a mandoline. Soak the sliced potatoes in cold water for 10 minutes to rinse off the starch.

3 Meanwhile, heat the canola oil to 325°F in a large saucepan over medium heat.

4 Remove the potatoes from the water and thoroughly pat them dry with paper towels. Carefully add the potatoes to the hot oil and stir with a metal spoon. Once they are golden brown, 2 to 3 minutes, remove them from the oil with a slotted spoon and place them on a plate lined with paper towels. Season with sea salt.

5 Divide the soup among 8 bowls and top each one with a dollop of yogurt, chives, if using, and a pile of potato chips.

CHICKEN BREASTS OVER RAGOUT OF LEEKS AND SEA ISLAND RED PEAS

Sea Island is a community along the coast of South Georgia, a land of luxury golf courses and beautiful hotels and condos. But back in the day, it was a coastal agrarian hub, and one of the crops raised there was a tasty little red pea that has come back into the culinary landscape thanks to the unstoppable wonders of Mr. Glenn Roberts of Anson Mills, in Columbia, South Carolina. Go online to AnsonMills.com and order some up, and while you're there, take a look at the many grain treasures Glenn is responsible for.

Serves 4

1 cup dried Sea Island red peas or other high-quality dried pea

Sea salt

1 tablespoon unsalted butter

1 pound leeks, white and light green parts, well washed and cut into ¼-inch-thick rings

2 tablespoons sherry vinegar

¼ cup chicken stock (see page 22)

1 tablespoon chopped fresh flat-leaf parsley leaves

4 chicken breasts, bone in and skin on

2 tablespoons canola oil

2 tablespoons Pickled Peppers (page 310)

Pea shoots (optional)

1 Place the peas in a bowl, cover with triple their volume of water, and soak overnight in the refrigerator.

2 Drain the peas, put them in a soup pot, and cover them with fresh water. Bring the water to a boil over high heat, skim off any foam that floats to the top, and then reduce the heat to a slow simmer. Cook the peas for 50 minutes, or until they are tender but not yet bursting. Remove the pot from the heat and add enough sea salt to make the water taste like the ocean but not the Dead Sea. Allow the peas to rest for 10 minutes and absorb the seasoning.

3 In a medium saucepan, melt the butter over medium heat. When it begins to bubble and froth, add the leeks and cook, stirring often, until they are limp and sweet tasting but not very caramelized, 10 minutes. Drain the peas and add them to the leeks. Add the vinegar, stock, and parsley, and cook for 5 minutes to combine the flavors. Then remove the pot from the heat and set it on the back of the stovetop to keep warm.

4 Meanwhile, preheat the oven to 350°F.

5 We are going to cook the chicken breasts much the way they are cooked in Perfect Pan-Roasted Chicken Breasts on page 276, except this time the breastbone is still intact. Season the chicken breasts generously with sea salt. In a large ovenproof sauté pan, heat the canola oil over medium heat. When the oil is hot, add the chicken breasts, skin side down. Cook the breasts for 10 minutes, then turn them over and place the pan in the oven. Bake for 8 to 10 minutes, until the internal temperature in the thickest part reads 150°F. Remove the chicken from the oven and allow it to rest on a cutting board.

6 Spoon the pea and leek mixture onto a platter. Place the chicken breasts on top, and garnish with the pickled peppers and pea shoots, if desired.

MELONS

South of Athens by about a hundred miles, you start getting into melon country, and in the season, you see the pickups loaded down with the fragrant fruits. Locally, Woodland Gardens grows some Charentais melons that exude sweetness and good mustiness. We also see Canary, Crenshaw, Sun Jewel, Honey White, and Athena melons. Any of these will work well in all of the following recipes.

The wonder about melons is that many parts of the country have them, but you may have to find that lonesome highway with the pickup truck by the side of the road selling them. Part of the fun of great food is finding such places.

HONEYDEW AGUA FRESCA

Agua frescas are the fruit waters of Spain, Portugal, South and Central America, and the Caribbean. They are very popular in my house because they are a drink that we can all imbibe, regardless of age. Simple, refreshing, and utterly seasonal, these straightforward beverages make everybody happy.
Makes 4 quarts

1 honeydew melon
1 cup sugar
1 tablespoon grated lime zest

1 cup freshly squeezed lime juice
2 tablespoons honey

Cut a small disc from the top and bottom of the melon, at the poles. Place the melon, with one of the cut sides down, on a cutting board and, using a sharp knife, cut away the skin by following the shape of the melon. When all the skin has been removed, cut the melon in half, scoop out the seeds and discard them, and cut the melon into 1-inch chunks. Combine the melon, sugar, lime zest and juice, honey, and 2 cups of water in a blender and puree on high speed until smooth. (Work in batches if it all doesn't fit in the blender comfortably.) Pour the *agua fresca* into a pitcher and fill it with ice.

CANTALOUPE WITH PROSCIUTTO, PURSLANE, AND VIDALIA VINAIGRETTE

This is a classic, done a little differently from the usual. It takes the bright sweetness of the melon and the rich saltiness of prosciutto, and matches them with earthy caramelized Vidalia onions and the sour punch of purslane. Purslane is a succulent. It grows like wildfire, so it's one of those things that we should probably enjoy eating. I love it. It's refreshingly sour and chewy without being tough.
Serves 4 as an appetizer

1 Vidalia onion
1 tablespoon unsalted butter
Kosher salt
1 teaspoon Dijon mustard
2 tablespoons cider vinegar

½ cup olive oil
1 cantaloupe
½ pound very thinly sliced prosciutto
¼ pound purslane leaves and stems

1 Slice the onion in half lengthwise, and then cut each half into ½-inch-wide wedges. Melt the butter in a large sauté pan over medium heat, and add the onions. Cook for 10 minutes on each side, until a rich brown. Season the onions with salt to taste and transfer half of the onions to a blender; reserve the other half.

2 Add the mustard and vinegar to the blender and puree. With the blender running, slowly add the olive oil to emulsify the vinaigrette. Season with a pinch of salt.

3 Cut a small disc from the top and bottom of the melon, at the poles. Place the melon, with one of the cut sides down, on a cutting board and, using a sharp knife, cut away the skin by following the shape of the melon. When all the skin has been removed, cut the melon in half, save one half for another use, and scoop out the seeds from the other half and discard them. Place the seeded melon scooped side down on a cutting board and slice it into very thin half-moons.

4 Arrange the prosciutto on a platter and lay out the melon slices as well. Find your inner food stylist and make it pretty, but don't turn it into some meticulous exercise.

5 Place the purslane and the reserved caramelized onion wedges in a bowl, and add 1 tablespoon of the vinaigrette. Toss well. Arrange the purslane and onions with the prosciutto, and then spoon vinaigrette to your liking around the platter. (If you have leftover vinaigrette, no biggie. Use it in a salad.)

CANTALOUPE AND MINT SOUP WITH CRAB AND CURRY OIL

Sweet crab, sweet melon, the punch of mint, and the spice overtones of curry oil make this a great chilled summer soup. *Serves 6*

1 cantaloupe

1 tablespoon curry powder

¼ cup olive oil

½ cup plain yogurt

2 tablespoons champagne vinegar

Sea salt

2 teaspoons fresh mint leaves

1 pound jumbo lump crabmeat, picked over for cartilage and shells

1 Cut a small disc from the top and bottom of the melon, at the poles. Place the melon, with one of the cut sides down, on a cutting board and, using a sharp knife, cut away the skin by following the shape of the melon. When all the skin has been removed, cut the melon in half, scoop out the seeds and discard them, and cut the melon into 1-inch chunks. Set aside.

2 In a small saucepan, warm the curry powder with the olive oil over medium heat for 5 minutes, whisking to thoroughly combine. Remove the pan from the heat and allow the mixture to cool to room temperature.

3 In a blender, combine the cantaloupe, yogurt, champagne vinegar, sea salt to taste, half the mint leaves, and ½ cup of water. Puree until the soup is smooth. (Work in batches if it all doesn't fit in the blender comfortably.) Adjust the seasoning with sea salt if needed, and the consistency with more water if needed.

4 Pour the soup into 6 bowls and divide the crab among the bowls, placing it in the middle of each. Garnish with the remaining mint leaves and a drizzle of the curry oil.

SAUTÉED CATFISH WITH CANTALOUPE, LIME, AND CILANTRO SALSA

Catfish is one of those things: buy it American. I know that I sound like a broken record imploring you to support your community, but this one is important. The amount of catfish flooding into our markets from Asia is having a devastating impact on U.S. producers. And I will also go on record with this: our catfish is a lot better.

The trick to cooking fish on the stove is that it must be pretty dry and your pan has to be really hot when you add it; this way, the fish will not be prone to sticking. And give it time to crisp up properly. *Serves 4*

½ cup finely minced cantaloupe

1 fresh red Fresno chile, thinly sliced on the bias

½ cup minced fresh cilantro leaves

3 tablespoons olive oil

1 tablespoon freshly squeezed lime juice

Kosher salt

4 catfish fillets (5 to 6 ounces each), trimmed of any connective tissue

3 tablespoons all-purpose flour

1 tablespoon unsalted butter

4 sprigs fresh cilantro

1 Place the cantaloupe, chile, minced cilantro, 1 tablespoon of the olive oil, the lime juice, and kosher salt to taste in a small bowl. Mix well and set aside.

2 Pat the catfish dry with paper towels and season all over with kosher salt. Dredge the catfish fillets in the flour, shaking off any excess. Place a large skillet over medium-high heat, and add the remaining 2 tablespoons olive oil. When the oil is shimmery-hot, place the catfish in the pan and cook for 5 minutes on one side. Then add the butter, let it foam, and baste the fillets with it, using a spoon. Turn the fillets over and continue cooking the catfish until just done, about 3 minutes, depending on how thick the fillets are. Catfish should be cooked through but still be very moist.

3 Transfer the fish to individual plates, and top them with the cantaloupe salsa. Garnish with the cilantro sprigs, and serve.

CANTALOUPE WITH
PROSCIUTTO,
PURSLANE,
AND VIDALIA
VINAIGRETTE
(PAGE 295)

SAUTÉED CATFISH
WITH CANTALOUPE,
LIME, AND CILANTRO
SALSA

CANTALOUPE AND
MINT SOUP WITH
CRAB AND CURRY OIL

OKRA

If there was a contest called "Make them love this vegetable," I would show up with okra in my pockets. If people hate okra, it's because they haven't ever had great okra, cooked correctly. I can convince people to love okra. It should not be the slimy thing that your mama made you eat. It should be a treat of summer, and in these recipes it is.

GRILLED OKRA

The robust, dry, yet flavorful heat of a grill leaves the slimy factor of okra behind. The result is a lightly charred offering that really shows off what okra should be: tender, full of flavor, not woody, not slimy. This is a recipe that will convert the masses to loving their okra. *Serves 4 as a side*

2 pounds okra, cut in half lengthwise

Sea salt

1 tablespoon olive oil

1 teaspoon grated lemon zest

1 tablespoon freshly squeezed lemon juice

1 tablespoon coarsely chopped fresh flat-leaf parsley leaves

1 Get your grill lit and hot. If you use charcoal, make sure you burn it down to nice hot embers.

2 Place the cut okra in a mixing bowl and season it well with sea salt. Add the olive oil and toss to combine. Place the okra on the grill, cut side down, perpendicular to the direction of the grates. Grill for 3 minutes, or until slightly charred. Turn the okra over and cook for 3 more minutes, until it is nicely charred and a little softer, but not really soft.

3 Return the okra to the mixing bowl and add the lemon zest, lemon juice, and parsley. Toss to combine, and serve.

FRIED OKRA WITH REMOULADE

The Southern classic of fried okra is a classic for a good reason: it is addictively great, because that's what happens when you fry good food. People love crispy, mostly with okra. So get a fryer set up and make the family a fried treat. *Serves 4 as a side or a snack*

2 quarts canola oil

2 pounds okra, cut in half lengthwise

Sea salt

2 cups buttermilk

1 cup mayonnaise

¼ cup Creole mustard

1 tablespoon Worcestershire sauce

1 teaspoon Louisiana-style hot sauce

1 teaspoon grated lemon zest

1 tablespoon freshly squeezed lemon juice

1 shallot, minced

6 scallions, thinly sliced, white and light green parts

2 teaspoons cayenne pepper

1 cup all-purpose flour

2 cups cornmeal

1 teaspoon freshly ground black pepper

GRILLED OKRA

STEWED OKRA WITH
TOMATOES, GARLIC,
CUMIN, AND PEPPERS

CURRIED OKRA
OVER CAROLINA
GOLD RICE

FRIED OKRA WITH
REMOULADE

1 Pour the canola oil into a large pot, and heat it to 350°F over medium heat.

2 While the oil is heating, place the cut okra in a mixing bowl, season it with 2 teaspoons sea salt, and let it sit for 10 minutes. Then add the buttermilk to the bowl and let it sit for an additional 5 minutes.

3 Meanwhile, make the remoulade: In a small mixing bowl, combine the mayo, mustard, Worcestershire, hot sauce, lemon zest and juice, minced shallot, scallions, and 1 teaspoon of the cayenne. Adjust the seasoning with sea salt and hot sauce if needed, and reserve.

4 In a large mixing bowl, combine the flour, cornmeal, 1 tablespoon sea salt, the remaining teaspoon of cayenne, and the black pepper. Drain the okra and toss it in the cornmeal mixture. Add the okra, quickly but one by one, to the hot oil and cook until it is golden brown, 3 to 4 minutes. Remove the okra from the fryer and place it on a platter or baking sheet lined with paper towels. Season the okra with sea salt and serve with the remoulade for dippin'.

STEWED OKRA WITH TOMATOES, GARLIC, CUMIN, AND PEPPERS

Simple stewed okra is a Louisiana thing, but like many things in Louisiana it just tastes right. When I say "stewed," I don't mean cooked into a mush; rather I mean laden with flavors, hugged by the peppers and the tomatoes, moist and flavorful. This is a side that loves to be pushed against some steamed rice, eaten with gusto, and washed down with a very cold beer.
Serves 4 as a side

1 tablespoon olive oil

1 pound okra, cut into ½-inch-wide rings

Sea salt

2 garlic cloves, thinly sliced

2 shallots, thinly sliced

1 cup julienned red bell pepper

1 bay leaf

1 teaspoon cumin seeds, toasted

2 cups peeled and diced roma tomatoes

1 teaspoon grated lemon zest

1 tablespoon freshly squeezed lemon juice

1 In a large saucepan, heat the olive oil over medium-high heat. Once the oil is shimmery-hot, add the okra and a pinch of sea salt and sauté, stirring occasionally, for 3 minutes, until the okra develops some color.

Reduce the heat to medium-low and add the garlic. Cook for 1 minute, until aromatic, and then add the shallots and bell peppers. Continue to cook for 5 minutes, or until the shallots become translucent. Season with a generous pinch of sea salt and add the bay leaf, toasted cumin seeds, and tomatoes. Cook for 15 minutes, until the tomatoes soften.

2 Remove the bay leaf, add the lemon zest and juice, and adjust the seasoning with more sea salt if needed. Serve warm.

CURRIED OKRA OVER CAROLINA GOLD RICE

Okra and curry match up really well together. This is a West Indies hug with Low Country overtones.

Here I cook the rice in a way that is a little different but historically very accurate. It results in fluffy rice that's buttery and nutty on the palate. It is a technique where you boil the rice, then simmer it, then drain it, fluff it, and put it in a very wide pan to warm it through in the oven. Comes out like a dream. Carolina Gold is a heritage-grain rice that has found an ecstatic proponent in Glenn Roberts at Anson Mills. Go and buy some online if you want what I consider the best rice in the world. That said, the cooking method will work with any long-grain rice.

First we make the rice, then we make the curry powder. Then we cook the curry, leaving the yogurt and okra out until we are just about ready to plate. Then we heat the rice. Then we eat. *Serves 4*

FOR THE RICE

2 teaspoons kosher salt

1 cup Carolina Gold rice

1 tablespoon olive oil

2 tablespoons cold unsalted butter, cut into small pieces

FOR THE CURRY POWDER

½ teaspoon chile powder

½ teaspoon ground turmeric

1 teaspoon cumin seeds

¼ teaspoon black cardamom seeds

1 teaspoon coriander seeds

1 teaspoon fennel seeds

FOR THE CURRIED OKRA

2 tablespoons unsalted butter

3 shallots, finely minced

1 tablespoon tomato paste

2 bay leaves

2 cups chicken stock (see page 22) or vegetable stock

Kosher salt

1 pound fresh okra

1 cup plain Greek yogurt

¼ cup crushed roasted peanuts

2 tablespoons chopped fresh mint leaves

2 tablespoons finely minced scallions, white and light green parts

2 tablespoons chopped peanuts

1 First, let's cook the rice: In a heavy pot set over high heat, bring 2 quarts of water to a boil, then add the kosher salt and the rice. Stir once, turn the heat down to medium-low and cook, uncovered, at a bubbling simmer until the rice is tender with still a tiny little firmness to its core, about 15 minutes. Drain the rice in a fine-mesh sieve.

2 Place the olive oil in a large, wide ovenproof pan (I use a 12-inch cast-iron sauté pan), and spread the rice in an even layer in the pan. Dot with the butter pieces and set aside.

3 Time to make some curry powder: Set a heavy sauté pan over medium heat. While it is heating, combine the chile powder and turmeric in a small bowl and set it aside. Place the cumin, cardamom, coriander, and fennel seeds in the hot pan and toast for 30 seconds, until aromatic and just starting to change color. Transfer the toasted seeds to a spice grinder and grind to a fine powder. Add the ground, toasted spices to the bowl containing the chile powder and turmeric. You should have about 1 heaping tablespoon of curry powder. Set it aside.

4 Now we make the curried okra: Set a shallow braising pan over medium heat, add the butter, and let it bubble and froth. Add the shallots to the pan and cook them for 2 minutes, until starting to get translucent. Add the tomato paste and the curry powder you made, stir, and continue cooking for 3 minutes. Add the bay leaves and the stock. Cook for 20 minutes, uncovered, still over medium heat. Season with the kosher salt to taste.

5 While the mixture is cooking, preheat the oven to 300°F. Place the rice in the oven to heat through.

6 Cut the okra into ½-inch-thick rings, discarding the tops. Add the okra to the curry, and cook for 5 minutes. Remove the pan from the heat, remove the bay leaves, and add the yogurt, peanuts, and mint. Stir well and adjust the seasoning to taste.

7 Remove the rice from the oven and divide it among 4 bowls. Top with the stewed okra and finish with the scallions and peanuts. Eat.

CURRIED
OKRA OVER
CAROLINA
GOLD RICE

PEACHES

Georgia was the Empire State of the South before it was the Peach State, but I kind of like both monikers. One points to our rebirth after the Civil War and the other points to our most storied crop, even if South Carolina now leads the way in peach production. We continue, undeterred by this eastern meddling, to grow some fantastic peaches. Think outside the sweets box when it comes to peaches; they lend a certain beauty to many savory dishes.

PEACH SALAD WITH PROSCIUTTO, ARUGULA, MINT, PICKLED PEPPERS, PINE NUTS, AND BALSAMIC VINEGAR

This is an ode to Italy. Find a balsamic vinegar you like and spend a good amount on it. The cheap ones are made from water and melted tires (unproven), while the good ones are beautiful, wafting the woodsy aromas of the barrels they were aged in. *Serves 4 as an appetizer*

8 freestone peaches

¼ pound very thinly sliced prosciutto

½ pound arugula

2 tablespoons fresh mint leaves

¼ cup Pickled Peppers (page 310), julienned

3 tablespoons pine nuts, toasted

2 tablespoons balsamic vinegar

1 tablespoon olive oil

½ teaspoon coarse sea salt

Cut the peaches in half and remove the pits. Slice each peach half into 4 wedges and arrange them on a platter. Artfully arrange the prosciutto, arugula, mint, pickled peppers, and pine nuts around the peaches. Drizzle the vinegar and olive oil over the top, and finish with the sea salt.

PICKLED PEACHES

I like these pickled peaches cut up and served over a roasted pork shoulder, or in a salad with crisp lettuces and a buttermilk dressing. They are a versatile preserve, but will work better with firmer peaches so you can still slice them when you open that jar. *Makes 2 quarts or 4 pints (use widemouthed jars)*

8 to 10 small peaches, ripe but on the firmer side

2 tablespoons pickling salt

1½ cups sugar

2 cinnamon sticks

4 whole cloves

¼ teaspoon crushed red pepper flakes

1 teaspoon yellow mustard seeds

1½ cups distilled white vinegar

1 Prepare a large ice water bath, and set it near the stove. Bring a pot of water to a vigorous boil.

2 Score a shallow X in the bottom of each peach, and then plunge them into the boiling water for 30 seconds. Remove and submerge the peaches in the ice water. When they are cool, drain the peaches, peel them, and discard the skins. Cut the peaches in half and remove the pits. Pack the peaches evenly into 2 clean wide-mouthed 1-quart mason jars (or 4 pint jars), leaving 1 inch of headspace at the top, and set aside.

3 Combine the pickling salt, sugar, cinnamon sticks, cloves, red pepper flakes, mustard seeds, vinegar, and 1½ cups of water in a nonreactive saucepan and bring to a boil. Reduce the heat to low and simmer for 5 minutes.

4 Carefully ladle the hot pickling mixture into the jars, leaving ½ inch of headspace in each. Cap with the lids and bands, and let cool for 2 hours. Store in the refrigerator for use within 2 weeks, or process according to the jar manufacturer's directions and store on the shelf for up to 10 months.

STEEL-CUT OATS WITH PEACHES AND SORGHUM CREAM

Steel-cut oats from Anson Mills are nothing like the instant gruel that absconded with the title "oatmeal." They are organic, nutty in flavor, redolent with a beautiful cinnamon overtone, and they cook up in about twenty minutes. Here the oats are finished with peaches sautéed in butter and a simple mix of heavy cream and sorghum. You could use maple syrup if sorghum is unavailable. If you can't get Anson Mills's beautiful oats, then use any steel-cut oats, just not instant or quick oats. *Serves 4*

1 cup steel-cut oats

½ teaspoon kosher salt

1 cup heavy cream

1 tablespoon sorghum molasses

1 tablespoon unsalted butter

1 peach, pitted and cut into 12 slices

1 Bring 2 cups of water to a boil in a saucepan over high heat, and then pour in the oats in a steady stream, whisking all the while. Add the salt, reduce the heat to medium-low, and cook, stirring every minute or so, for about 20 minutes, or until the oats are tender.

2 While the oats cook, whisk the cream and sorghum together in a small bowl until the mixture is a little thickened but by no means whipped cream. Set the cream aside.

PICKLED
PEACHES

STEEL-CUT OATS
WITH PEACHES AND
SORGHUM CREAM

3 Place a small sauté pan over medium heat and add the butter. When the butter bubbles and froths, add the peaches in one layer and cook for 5 minutes, until they are soft and have some caramelization. Then remove them from the heat and let them sit until the oats are done.

4 To serve, scoop the oats evenly into 4 bowls, top each with ¼ cup of the sorghum cream, and then evenly distribute the peaches among the bowls. Eat immediately.

VEAL LOIN WITH SAUTÉED PEACHES AND ARUGULA

Simple, beautiful, ethically raised veal from farms like Strauss, a wonderful outfit out of Wisconsin, is a game changer when we talk about animal husbandry. It is done right, which, when it comes to veal, is correcting a lot of past mistakes. The good modern veal farmer is raising grass-fed, free-roaming animals, the way real veal was once produced, stopping the strange penned-up system that was unethical and just plain weird. It is veal you can feel good about, and it also tastes amazing.

Here the veal is simply pan-roasted and served with peaches and arugula, a meal that will be at home on a picnic table outside on the lawn. This is a dinner that should be balanced with a slightly chilled bottle of Pinot Noir. *Serves 4 to 6*

1½ pounds boneless veal loin, trimmed

Sea salt and freshly cracked black pepper

2 tablespoons canola oil

2 freestone peaches

2 tablespoons unsalted butter

5 garlic cloves

8 sprigs fresh thyme

1 pound arugula

½ teaspoon grated lemon zest

1 tablespoon freshly squeezed lemon juice

1 Preheat the oven to 400°F.

2 Pat the veal dry with a paper towel, and season it all over with sea salt and cracked black pepper. Heat the canola oil in a large ovenproof sauté pan over high heat. When the oil comes to a slight smoke, add the veal loin. Sear the veal for 4 minutes per side, pretending that there are two sides. I know it's kind of got four, but I am just searing the large two. Each of the two sides should be a crisp dark golden brown. Place the sauté pan in

the oven and roast for 10 minutes, or until the internal temperature is 125°F for medium-rare.

3 While the veal is in the oven, cut the peaches in half, remove the pits, and slice the halves.

4 Remove the pan from the oven and place it over medium heat. Add the butter, garlic, and thyme sprigs, and baste the veal with the bubbling butter for 2 minutes. Remove the veal from the pan and let it rest, lightly covered in foil, on a cutting board for 10 minutes. Remove the garlic and thyme sprigs from the pan.

5 Return the pan to high heat and add the sliced peaches. Cook for 2 minutes to lightly caramelize them. Remove the pan from the heat and add the arugula, lemon zest, and lemon juice, and toss to wilt the arugula over the residual heat. Place the peaches and arugula on a platter, and then slice the veal. Serve.

PEPPERS

Sweet and hot and everything in between—that's what grows around here. You see the insanity of ghost peppers, the sweet beauty of Nardellos, the very popular Padrón, and the classic cayenne. And when I say we see them, I mean bushels and bushels of them. It's a good thing I love them. You should, too.

PICKLED PEPPERS

This recipe will work with just about any pepper, but I really love the horn-shaped Jimmy Nardello pepper. It's got a touch of heat but more than that, it has deep flavor. I use these pickled peppers in broths and salsas, on burgers and hot dogs, or even as an addition to pimento cheese. *Makes 1 quart or 2 pints*

1 pound small, mildly spicy sweet peppers

1 tablespoon pickling salt

1 tablespoon sugar

2 garlic cloves

2 bay leaves

1½ cups distilled white vinegar

1 If the peppers are smaller than an Anaheim chile, just leave them whole. If they are larger, then cut them in half or quarters. Pierce each pepper a few times with a knife. Pack the peppers into a clean 1-quart mason jar (or 2 pint jars), leaving 1 inch of headspace at the top, and set aside.

2 Combine the pickling salt, sugar, garlic, bay leaves, vinegar, and 1 cup of water in a small nonreactive pot and bring to a boil. Reduce the heat to low and simmer for 5 minutes.

3 Carefully ladle the hot pickling mixture into the jar, leaving ½ inch of headspace. Cap with the lid and band, and let cool for 2 hours. The jar can be stored in the refrigerator for 3 weeks, or processed according to the jar manufacturer's directions and stored on the shelf for up to a year.

PICKLED PEPPER AND FETA SALAD WITH CHICKPEAS, OLIVES, RAISINS, ORANGE, AND MINT

Hopefully, you have made my pickled peppers, 'cause now here's a simple salad that loves them as an ingredient. This dish is a celebration of Middle Eastern cuisine, where chiles are loved for flavor and texture as much as for heat. *Serves 4 as a side*

1 orange

1 teaspoon Dijon mustard

1 tablespoon champagne vinegar

1 shallot, minced

2 cups sliced Pickled Peppers (above)

3 tablespoons olive oil

2 cups arugula

1½ cups canned chickpeas, rinsed, skins removed

¼ cup Kalamata olives, pitted and sliced

¼ cup raisins

Sea salt

½ cup diced feta cheese (½-inch pieces)

1 tablespoon fresh mint leaves

1 Grate enough zest from the orange to make 1 teaspoon, and set it aside. Peel the orange and cut out the individual segments by slicing along the membranes, catching the juice and the membranes in a bowl.

2 In a medium mixing bowl, combine the mustard, champagne vinegar, shallot, juice from the orange, and 1 teaspoon of the pickling liquid from the pickled peppers. While whisking, slowly drizzle in the olive oil. The dressing should thicken slightly.

3 To the same bowl add the arugula, peppers, chickpeas, olives, raisins, and the 1 teaspoon orange zest, and toss. Season with sea salt to taste, and place the salad in a serving bowl. Top the salad with the feta, reserved orange segments, and mint.

PICKLED PEPPER AND FETA
SALAD WITH CHICKPEAS,
OLIVES, RAISINS,
ORANGE, AND MINT

FERMENTED
PEPPERS

FERMENTED PEPPERS

You remember back in 1998 when everyone told you to brine your turkey? Well, that little culinary trick seems to have really caught on, evidenced by the fact that we can now buy brining kits at most every grocery store nationwide. Well, the formula is the same for the brine we use to create fermented vegetables. The salt in the brine keeps out bad bacteria and lets your fermented-food friend, lactobacilli, convert the food's sugars to lactic acid and create terrific flavors in the process. *Makes 2 quarts*

2 tablespoons fine sea salt, or 3 tablespoons kosher salt

4 bay leaves

½ teaspoon allspice berries

Pinch of merkén or other smoked chile powder

½ teaspoon yellow mustard seeds

1½ pounds mixed mild sweet peppers, seeded and sliced

1 In a medium saucepan, combine 1 quart of water with the salt, bay leaves, allspice berries, merkén, and mustard seeds. Bring to a boil and then allow to cool.

2 While the salt solution is cooling, pack your peppers into 2 clean quart-size mason jars, leaving 1½ inches of headspace. Pack them tight by pushing them down with a wooden spoon. When the brine is cool, use a wide funnel to get the brine cleanly into the jars, leaving 1 inch of headspace. Cover each jar with a small piece of cheesecloth, and tighten the metal band over the cheesecloth to secure it in place. Put the jars in a cool, dark spot, somewhere around 65°F, and check on the peppers daily, skimming off any white silt or foam that accumulates on top. They take 5 to 8 days to ferment well. After that you can just cap the jars and store them in the fridge.

THE DELICIOUSNESS OF FERMENTED RED PEPPER BROTH

Ryan Smith, who was for years the executive chef at my restaurant Empire State South in Atlanta, came up with this idea for using the fermented peppers he had gone, well, overboard on producing. It is a really killer broth, showing your palate something totally new—fruity and complex and savory. You will have to start this about a week in advance, though, so get that ferment started.

How would I use the broth? Well, here's a little list:

- Seared scallops with okra, pickled tomatoes, and red pepper broth
- Leek risotto, finished with buttery red pepper broth
- Crisp pork belly with grits and red pepper broth
- Spanish chorizo, crisp potatoes, poached egg, kale, and red pepper broth
- Sweet carrot soup with fermented pepper broth, yogurt, and lobster

Makes about 1½ cups of broth

4 large red bell peppers, stemmed, cored, and seeded

1 teaspoon sea salt

1 Using a vegetable juicer, juice the peppers and strain the juice from the pulp through a large sieve or strainer into a bowl. Add the sea salt to the juice and whisk until the salt dissolves. Pour the mixture into a large mason jar, cover it with cheesecloth, and secure the cheesecloth with the metal ring or a rubber band. Place the jar in a cool cupboard for 5 to 7 days. Check daily and just skim off any white mold.

2 Strain the juice again through a fine-mesh strainer into a small saucepan, and bring the liquid to a boil over high heat. Reduce the heat to medium-low and reduce the pepper liquid by half its volume. Serve, or chill for storage. It will keep for a week in the fridge.

SUMMER SQUASH

Summer squash, and their pattypan ilk, are the never-ending crop of summer. I adore them, so it's easy for me to eat up their abundance, but most of America needs a little help to get through the prolific squash season. Here are three ways to do so.

BREAD-AND-BUTTER SQUASH PICKLES

Squash is one of those gremlin-like vegetables that just multiplies until you don't know what to do with the harvest. This recipe uses the little ones in the sweet-sour style of a classic b-and-b pickle. It's stellar. *Makes 2 quarts or 4 pints*

3 cups thinly sliced pattypan or other small summer squash (¼-inch-thick slices)

1 medium sweet onion, Vidalia if possible

1½ tablespoons pickling salt

¼ cup fresh celery leaves

¼ teaspoon crushed red pepper flakes

½ teaspoon curry powder

½ teaspoon fennel seeds

½ teaspoon celery seeds

1 teaspoon yellow mustard seeds

4 allspice berries

1½ cups cider vinegar

½ cup sugar

1 Place the sliced squash in a large bowl. Slice the onion lengthwise into ⅓-inch-wide strips. Add the onions to the squash, and sprinkle with half of the pickling salt. Toss well and let sit for 1 hour at room temperature.

2 Rinse the onions and squash well in a colander under cold running water to remove the salt. When thoroughly rinsed and drained, place them in a medium nonreactive bowl, and tear the celery leaves into the mixture. Pack the squash, onion, and celery leaves into 2 clean 1-quart mason jars (or 4 pint jars), leaving 1 inch of headspace, and set aside.

3 Combine the remaining pickling salt and the red pepper flakes, curry powder, fennel seeds, celery seeds, mustard seeds, allspice berries, vinegar, sugar, and 1 cup of water in a small nonreactive pot and bring to a boil. Reduce the heat to low and simmer for 5 minutes.

4 Carefully ladle the hot pickling mixture into the jars, leaving ½ inch of headspace. Cap with the lids and bands, and let cool for 2 hours. The jars can be stored in the refrigerator for use within 10 days, or processed according to the jar manufacturer's directions and stored for up to 9 months on the shelf.

SQUASH BLOSSOM TACOS WITH QUESO FRESCO AND SIMPLE SALSA

I love squash blossoms but usually they get stuffed and fried, and though that's a wonderful preparation, it does limit the squash experience. Here we look to the streets of Mexico for inspiration and discover that tacos are a great way to use a pile of squash blossoms. Make sure you cook the blossoms very soon after buying them (or better yet, after picking them), or you'll have some limp compostables. And always check the blossoms for bugs, 'cause bugs like to hang there, and who can blame them? *Serves 4*

½ red onion, finely minced

1 scallion, minced, white and light green parts

½ pound tomato, minced

1 fresh serrano chile, stemmed, seeded, and minced

1 tablespoon freshly squeezed lime juice

1 tablespoon red wine vinegar

1 tablespoon olive oil

Kosher salt and freshly ground black pepper

2 tablespoons grapeseed or canola oil

1 sweet onion, sliced into 16 slices

16 squash blossoms, checked for bugs

8 white corn tortillas

1 ripe avocado

3 tablespoons sour cream

1 lime

2 tablespoons chopped fresh cilantro

¼ cup queso fresco

1 Combine the red onion, scallion, tomato, chile, and lime juice in a bowl, and toss. Add the vinegar and olive oil, and stir well. Season with kosher salt and black pepper to taste, cover, and set aside at room temperature. You've got salsa!

2 In a large cast-iron skillet, warm the grapeseed oil over medium heat. When the oil is shimmering, add the sweet onion slices. Cook for 6 minutes, or until their edges begin to caramelize. Turn the heat to high, add the squash blossoms to the skillet, stir to incorporate, and cook for 4 minutes, until the blossoms have wilted a bit and browned a touch. Season the onions and blossoms with kosher salt to taste, stir lightly, and set aside in a warm spot.

3 Using a large, heavy pan set over medium-high heat, warm your tortillas, two at a time, flipping to heat both sides. As they get warm and pliable, pile them up and wrap them in a clean kitchen towel, like a cozy cowl. Pit, peel, and slice the avocado into 8 slices.

SQUASH BLOSSOM TACOS
WITH QUESO FRESCO
AND SIMPLE SALSA

4 Place 2 warm tortillas on each plate. Divide the squash and onion mixture evenly among the tortillas. Put about a tablespoon of the salsa, a teaspoon of sour cream, and a slice of avocado on each one. Cut the lime in half and spritz each taco with a hit of lime juice, chopped cilantro, and queso fresco. Eat.

TIAN OF SQUASH, ZUCCHINI, TOMATO, AND BASIL

This layered vegetable dish shows off the flavors of Provence in a stunning presentation, and that presentation is named after the dish that it is traditionally served in: a shallow earthenware baking dish called a *tian*. Depending on geography the tian is based on different ingredients, but the Provençal version is a response to summer in Aix, resplendent with squash, tomatoes, and basil. It is a great dish to bring to a potluck, or just a homey (but said with a French accent) way to plow through the bounty of the market. *Serves 4 as a side*

3 salt-packed anchovy fillets, rinsed and chopped

2 garlic cloves, minced

2 tablespoons chopped fresh flat-leaf parsley leaves

1 teaspoon chopped fresh thyme leaves

¼ cup plus 1 teaspoon olive oil

Kosher salt

Freshly ground black pepper

2 small yellow crookneck squash

1 zucchini

4 roma tomatoes

12 fresh basil leaves

2 tablespoons fresh bread crumbs

1 Preheat the oven to 375°F.

2 In a small bowl, combine the anchovies, garlic, parsley, thyme, the ¼ cup olive oil, and kosher salt and black pepper to your liking. Mix well and set aside.

3 Slice the squash and zucchini into ¼-inch-thick rounds, discarding the ends. Set aside. Slice the tomatoes into ¼-inch-thick slices and lay them flat on a cutting board. Sprinkle some kosher salt over the tomatoes and let them sit for 5 minutes. Then take a piece of paper towel and dab the moisture off of the tomatoes.

4 Lightly oil a shallow-sided 7- or 8-inch round earthenware or ceramic baking dish with the remaining 1 teaspoon olive oil. Arrange one layer of tomatoes in the dish, starting in the center and working outward in circles. Repeat the process with the zucchini, and then the squash, seasoning each layer with a little salt. When the vegetables are all arranged, tuck the basil in, one leaf at a time. Spoon the olive oil mixture over the vegetables. Bake in the oven for 30 minutes, or until the vegetables are tender.

5 Remove the dish from the oven and set the oven to broil. Scatter the bread crumbs on top of the tian and broil for 4 minutes, until the bread crumbs have browned nicely. Remove from the oven and serve hot or at room temperature.

TOMATOES

We have fought hard to get good tomatoes back in the market. To me, tomatoes are a fruit that reminds us of how much we lose when we ship them halfway around the world. There is nothing wrong with the occasional roma tomato purchased at the grocery store, but the beautiful heirloom tomato in all its sweet, juicy, umami glory is something you buy at the farmers' market from the person who grew it, or you grow it yourself. Find a farmer who has a particular affinity for great heirloom varieties and your tomato life will change forever.

PAPPA DI POMODORO WITH EDAMAME TOASTS

The world has become a better place thanks to the influence of Ruth Rogers and the late Rose Gray, the inspiring chefs of the River Café in London. This is a recipe based on their utterly simple *pappa di pomodoro,* an Italian bread-and-tomato soup that amazes. There is not a soul in the world who is unhappy with this soup. So simple and so good. *Serves 6*

1 cup shelled edamame

Kosher salt

3¼ cups chicken stock (see page 22)

¼ teaspoon crushed red pepper flakes

2 pounds heirloom tomatoes

8 tablespoons olive oil

1 small sweet onion, minced

4 garlic cloves

2 cups torn sourdough bread, with crusts

6 slices of baguette

1 cup torn fresh basil leaves

Freshly ground black pepper

1 Prepare an ice water bath and place it near the stove.

2 Pour 2 quarts of water into a pot and place it over high heat. When the water boils, add the edamame and blanch for 30 seconds. Remove them with a slotted spoon and shock them in the ice water. Drain the edamame and place them in a blender. Add a big pinch of kosher salt, ¼ cup of the chicken stock, and the red pepper flakes, and pulse until you have a coarse puree. Set it aside.

3 Score an X in the bottom of each tomato and blanch them in the same pot of boiling water, one at a time, for about 20 seconds, until the skin starts to curl at the X. Then plunge them in the ice water. When they are cool enough to handle, remove the tomatoes, peel them, and coarsely chop.

4 In a soup pot, warm 4 tablespoons of the olive oil over medium heat. Add the onion and cook, stirring once in a while with a wooden spoon, until very soft and showing some color but more golden than brown, about 10 minutes. Add the garlic and cook for 2 minutes. Add the tomatoes, bring to a boil, and then reduce the heat to a simmer and cook for 30 minutes, until they smell heavenly and are totally broken down. Add the remaining 3 cups chicken stock, bring to a simmer, and cook for another 20 minutes.

5 While that's going on, preheat the oven to 400°F.

6 Let's toast the bread: Put the torn sourdough in a bowl, add 2 tablespoons of the olive oil, and toss well. Place the bread on a baking sheet, and toast in the hot oven until golden brown, about 5 minutes—but keep an eye on it. After the bread is done, set it aside. Place the slices of baguette on the same baking sheet and brush them with 1 tablespoon of the olive oil. Toast in the oven for 3 to 4 minutes, until crisp, and then remove from the oven.

7 Add the toasted sourdough and the basil to the soup and stir gently, maybe only once, to soften and thicken the soup. Put the soup into a soup tureen, 'cause when was the last time you used that? Garnish the soup with a good drizzle of the remaining tablespoon of olive oil and a heavy-handed grind of black pepper. Dollop the edamame spread on the toasted baguette slices, and serve alongside the soup.

TOMATO CONFIT

Makes 4 cups

10 roma tomatoes

3 tablespoons olive oil

2 tablespoons sea salt

2 sprigs fresh thyme, leaves pulled from the stems

2 garlic cloves, finely minced

1 Preheat the oven to 200°F. Bring a large pot of water to a boil. Prepare an ice water bath.

2 Score an X in the bottom of each tomato, and blanch the tomatoes in the boiling water for just 10 seconds. Take them out of the pot and place them directly into the ice bath.

3 Once they've cooled, peel the tomatoes and cut them in half lengthwise. Place the tomato halves, cut side down, on a baking sheet. Drizzle the tomatoes with 2 tablespoons of the olive oil, the sea salt, thyme leaves, and garlic. Place the baking sheet in the oven and cook for 3 hours.

4 Let the tomatoes cool on the baking sheet, and then carefully transfer them to a clean mason jar. Pour all of the cooking juices into the jar and then top with the remaining tablespoon olive oil. Cap and seal. They will stay fresh in your fridge for up to 10 days, or you can really prolong their shelf life by processing them according to the jar manufacturer's directions.

SOUTHERN RATATOUILLE

I love ratatouille. It screams "summer" in all the right ways and is a great place to put pounds of your garden's bounty. When the tomato and squash harvests are getting a little out of control, this is the best way to use them up. *Serves 6 to 8 as a side or a light entrée with some bread and wine*

1 globe eggplant

½ teaspoon ascorbic acid or freshly squeezed lemon juice

8 tablespoons olive oil

1 large yellow summer squash, cut into ¼-inch-thick rounds

1 large zucchini, cut into ¼-inch-thick rounds

Fine sea salt

1 red bell pepper, diced

1 yellow bell pepper, diced

6 garlic cloves, minced

2 large tomatoes

1 cup chopped pickled green tomatoes or dill pickles (see page 280)

1 cup torn fresh basil leaves

Freshly ground black pepper

1 Preheat the oven to 450°F.

2 Cut the eggplant into ½-inch cubes and place them in a large bowl. Cover with cold water, add the ascorbic acid, and stir well. Let it sit for 10 minutes. Then drain the eggplant and pat it dry with paper towels to blot up as much of the water as possible.

3 Find the largest sauté pan in your arsenal and place it over medium-high heat. Add 4 tablespoons of the olive oil, and when the oil is shimmery-hot, fry the eggplant, in batches, being wary of overcrowding the pan. Cook for about 2 minutes a side, until the eggplant is golden and just about cooked through. As the batches finish, use a slotted spoon to transfer the eggplant to a plate lined with paper towels. When all the eggplant is cooked, discard the oil that you just worked with and clean out the pan because we'll be using it later.

4 In a mixing bowl, toss the sliced squash and zucchini with 1 tablespoon of the olive oil and fine sea salt to taste. Place them on a large baking sheet and roast in the hot oven for 5 minutes, until just tender. Remove from the oven and set aside, still on the baking sheet, to cool.

5 Take the cleaned sauté pan and place it over medium-high heat. Add the remaining 3 tablespoons olive oil, and when the oil is hot, add the peppers to the pan. Cook for 10 minutes or until tender. Then add the garlic and cook for 2 minutes, until aromatic. Add the eggplant, squash, and zucchini. Lower the heat to medium and simmer for 5 minutes to bring the flavors together.

6 Cut the tomatoes in half and grate them into a bowl using a box grater. Discard the tomato skins. Pour the grated tomato into the pan of vegetables and simmer for 5 minutes. Then add the chopped pickled green tomatoes and fine sea salt to taste. Stir to combine, and finish with the torn basil leaves and black pepper to taste. Serve warm or at room temperature.

TOMATO, OKRA, AND CORN MAQUE CHOUX

Maque choux is a simmered braise of peppers, tomatoes, and corn, and this time it gets a little okra. This is a perfect side to a summer roast chicken and some simple steamed rice. *Serves 6 to 8 as a side*

3 ears white corn, shucked

1 tablespoon bacon fat

2 shallots, minced

1 celery stalk, peeled and finely diced

1 fresh poblano chile, finely diced

2 large tomatoes, peeled, seeded, and finely diced

1 scallion, chopped

¼ pound okra, cut into ¼-inch-thick rounds

½ cup chicken stock (see page 22)

1 teaspoon chopped fresh oregano leaves

Pinch of cayenne pepper

½ teaspoon sweet smoked paprika (pimentón)

1 tablespoon freshly squeezed lime juice

1 tablespoon crème fraîche

Kosher salt

1 Using a sharp knife, carve away the kernels of the corn, letting them fall into a wide bowl. Then place the dull side of the knife perpendicular to the cob and scrape all of the corn milk and juices into the bowl on a second go-round. (You could also use an old-school corn cutter.) Set the bowl of corn aside and compost the cobs.

2 In a large cast-iron skillet, melt the bacon fat over medium heat and then add the shallots. Cook the shallots for 2 minutes, and then add the celery and the poblano. Turn the heat up to medium-high and cook for 5 minutes. Then add the corn, with its juices, and the tomatoes and bring to a simmer. Simmer for 5 minutes, and then add the scallion, okra, chicken stock, oregano, cayenne, and paprika. Bring back to a simmer and cook for yet another 5 minutes. Stir in the lime juice and the crème fraîche, and then season with kosher salt to taste. Serve.

SOUTHERN
RATATOUILLE

TOMATO SALAD WITH
CRISPED FARRO,
PURSLANE, ARUGULA,
AND ROASTED TOMATO—
MISO VINAIGRETTE

TOMATO SALAD WITH CRISPED FARRO, PURSLANE, ARUGULA, AND ROASTED TOMATO–MISO VINAIGRETTE

Great tomatoes sprinkled with kosher salt are enough to make me giddy, but when you add an awesome vinaigrette, some wonderfully fresh greens, and the crisp texture of fried farro, then I am over the moon. This is summer. Bring on the front-porch dinners. *Serves 4*

Kosher salt
½ cup farro
2 cups peanut oil
2 pounds heirloom tomatoes, cored, halved, and sliced into half-moons
⅓ cup Roasted Tomato–Miso Vinaigrette (recipe follows)
2 cups fresh purslane
2 cups arugula leaves
Freshly ground black pepper

1 Bring 2 cups of water to a boil in a saucepan, and add ½ teaspoon kosher salt and the farro. Lower the heat to a simmer and cook the farro until it is tender, 25 to 30 minutes. Strain the farro. Spread it out on a large platter lined with paper towels to steam off and drain off as much of the water as possible.

2 In a large saucepan, heat the peanut oil to 350°F. Add the farro, in batches, and fry until crisp, 1 to 1½ minutes. You want the grains to be crisp but not like little rocks. Remove from the oil and drain on the platter, lined with fresh paper towels. Season with kosher salt to taste.

3 Arrange the sliced tomatoes on a large platter and season them with kosher salt. Drizzle half of the vinaigrette over the tomatoes. In a large bowl, combine the purslane and the arugula. Dress the greens with the remaining vinaigrette. Place the greens in the center of the platter. Garnish with the crisp farro and season with freshly ground black pepper to taste. Eat, and eat well.

ROASTED TOMATO–MISO VINAIGRETTE
Makes about 1½ cups

1 large heirloom tomato
¼ teaspoon kosher salt
1 tablespoon fresh thyme leaves
1 tablespoon white miso
1 teaspoon Japanese soy sauce
2 tablespoons rice vinegar
⅓ cup olive oil

1 Preheat the oven to 400°F.

2 Core the tomato and cut it into thick rounds. Season the tomato slices with the kosher salt and arrange them on a parchment-lined baking sheet. Place in the oven and roast for 30 minutes, until the tomato slices are concentrated and very soft.

3 Remove the tomatoes from the oven and let them cool to room temperature. When they have cooled, place them in a blender and add the thyme, miso, soy sauce, and vinegar. Puree until smooth, and then, with the motor still running, slowly drizzle in the olive oil. The dressing will keep for a week in a jar in the fridge.

TOMATO PRODUCTION AT HOME, OR IN A PARKING LOT AT THE LOCAL HARDWARE STORE

We have one of those old-school hardware stores about four blocks away, the kind you hope never goes away but also have no idea how they make it through the week. I try to shop there when I need things like an odd fastener, a cast-iron pan, a case of Ball jars, or some tomato cages. One of the guys who works there, well, he's no spring chicken and has probably worked there pretty much his whole adult life. Come May you see him out back, tilling away at a tiny little stretch of green space for his tomato plot. It is urban farming at its best: a small space that nobody thought to farm on, elegantly gracing the edge of the parking lot. He has about twenty plants there, and through the summer they will grow to great heights, be nurtured and fretted over, checked for pests and plagues, brilliantly caged in to support their weighty limbs bearing increasingly abundant fruit. You see him in the morning before his shift begins, pruning and checking things out, watering and feeding the Early Girls and romas. It's not a fancy organic operation, probably not free of pesticides or planned with any biodynamic aspirations, but none of that really matters in this instance. What does matter is his pride in growing those tomatoes, year after year, on a 12 × 3-foot slice of land in a parking lot in Athens, Georgia.

ACKNOWLEDGMENTS

Writing a book takes a lot of help and I am lucky enough to have a team, a family, and a community who have my back at every turn of the page.

I would first like to thank my assistant, Ashley Malec, who makes everything happen in my world of work. Without her nothing would get done and my office would be a wreck. Ashley is assisted by the immensely talented Couper Cox, who helps me learn about coffee, home ec, selvedge denim, Tweet forums, and branding.

At Clarkson Potter/Publishers, hearty shout outs go to my editor, Francis Lam, a writer whose work is always cherished and whose soft-spoken direction is my food compass, and to the design team of Rae Ann Spitzenberger and Danielle Deschenes, who did a fantastic job. To Doris Cooper and Pam Krauss, thanks for making this happen and leading the best cooking imprint in the business.

Kyle, Peter, Josh, Jason, Mike, Chris, and Brooke are the chefs at my restaurants, chefs who lead our teams with professionalism, imagination, and unfathomable talent.

Ryan Smith, a chef who wears many hats, was indispensable to this book, coming up with recipes, figuring out systems and helping me get my ideas onto paper. He is a friend and ally that I am thankful for every day.

Many thanks for the design and camera talents of Rinne Allen, her sister Lucy, and assistants, Chrissy and Michelle. Working with all of them is one of the many beautiful things about living in Athens, Georgia.

To the farmers and the food of the South. Without you we can't do this. Celia and John, Lauren, Nicolas, Steve and Mandy, Ed J, and many more: you all are growing goodness.

To the town of Athens, Georgia: I love you.

To my wonderful family: Mary, my wife and unpaid editor; Beatrice and Clementine, my daughters who are food savvy beyond their years; and the cat, Fig, who would give me a glaring look if I didn't give her a shout-out.

INDEX